A Duel of Giants

A Duel of Giants

BISMARCK, NAPOLEON III, AND THE ORIGINS
OF THE FRANCO-PRUSSIAN WAR

David Wetzel

The University of Wisconsin Press

The University of Wisconsin Press
1930 Monroe Street
Madison, Wisconsin 53711

www.wisc.edu/wisconsinpress/

3 Henrietta Street
London WC2E 8LU, England

Library of Congress Cataloging-in-Publication Data
Wetzel, David.
A duel of giants : Bismarck, Napoleon III, and the origins
of the Franco-Prussian War / David Wetzel.
260 pp.   cm.
Includes bibliographical references and index.
ISBN 0-299-17490-5
1. Bismarck, Otto, Fèurst von, 1815–1898.
2. Napoleon III, Emperor of the French, 1808–1873.
3. Franco-Prussian War, 1870–1871.
4. France—Foreign relations—Germany.
5. Germany—Foreign relations—France. I. Title.
DC292.W48   2001
943.08′2—dc21   2001002003

To the memory of my godparents
Ruth and Burr Epstein

Contents

Illustrations

Preface

In late November 1870, the French statesman and politician Adolphe Thiers visited Vienna and urged Baron Friedrich von Beust, the Austro-Hungarian chancellor, that Europe should mediate in the Franco-Prussian War. Beust replied: "I do not see Europe anymore," and it is not difficult to see what he meant. By 1870 the Europe into which Beust had been born sixty-one years before had changed beyond recognition. Less than five years previously, Prussia, by force of arms, had smashed the German confederation; its oldest member, imperial Austria, had been thrown out, and some lesser members she had ruthlessly seized and made into Prussian provinces. Twenty-three northern states were gathered into a new federation led and controlled by Berlin. Now, with the aid of this geographically limited though much more closely knit and powerful Germany, Prussia was victoriously concluding another gigantic test of strength, this time with France. France—who had dominated European affairs since the days of Louis XIV and who, under the first Napoleon, had overrun the continent—was at last brought low, single-handedly, by the new German Empire. In the past, France had been able to exploit, in the interests of her own security, the differences *among* the various German states. She was now faced, if she was to work her way out of the isolation in which the unhappy ending of the Franco-Prussian War had left her, with the necessity of looking for support *outside* Germany—support against the united Germany, with whom, alone, she felt unable to cope.

The Franco-Prussian War has long attracted the interest of historians. As Sir Michael Howard has pointed out, it is unlikely that any war (the First World War not excepted) has been the focus of such concentrated attention in proportion to its duration. A bibliography compiled as early as 1898 could list 7,000 titles, and the flood was to continue unabated for at least another generation. The last forty years have, however, been another matter. No book on a subject that seemed for so long to preoccupy historians and that was to form the foundation upon which not a few of their careers were built—those, for instance, of Albert Sorel and Barthélemy Edmond Palat in France; Federico Chabod in Italy; Heinrich von Sybel, Richard Fester, and Jochen Dittrich in Germany; and Robert H. Lord in the United States, to name only the most outstanding—has appeared in English since *Bismarck, the Hohenzollern Candidacy, and the Origins of the Franco-German War* by Lawrence D. Steefel appeared in 1962. What started as a flood became, in the years after 1940 or thereabouts, first a current, then a stream, then a rivulet, and finally a dry creek.

The present work is an attempt to break the clouds. Its aim is to tell a story and to tell it in chronological order, to provide a detailed view of the diplomacy that culminated in the outbreak of the Franco-Prussian War in July 1870, and to do so with a sense for the essential drama that this process involved.

Like the history of the last spasm of anarchy before the foundation of the Roman republic, the period dealt with here would be of commanding interest simply because of the personalities of the actors on the political stage—even if the tale of their action had, to all intents and purposes, signified nothing. Each of the outstanding figures on the opposing sides, Napoleon III and Otto von Bismarck, is a fascinating subject of psychological study in his own right, each of them piquantly different from his enemies both abroad and at home, and the encounter between the two was the epitome of epic confrontation, at close quarters, of striking personalities. A single volume discussing the events recounted here may fill the gap in the literature addressed to this subject, and it is in this spirit that I have the temerity to offer the present work.

The book brings together the fruits of various researches in order to address a series of questions to which, in the recent literature, no fully satisfactory answers have been found. To what extent was the outbreak of the Franco-Prussian War the product of the civilian chauvinists in France and the nationalists in Prussia or of the military hotheads on both sides? What value is to be attached to the extravagant claims of such flamboyant figures as Émile Ollivier and Antoine Agénor, duc de Gramont, to have been the defenders of French pride and honor? How did the French ambassador to Prussia, Vincent Benedetti, come to believe that his superiors at home were secretly undermining every effort he was making to reach agreement with the king of Prussia? What was the role of public opinion on each side? What were the circumstances in which the Prussian minister president, Bismarck, received word of the success of the French efforts to secure the renunciation of the Spanish throne by Leopold of Hohenzollern-Sigmaringen? To what extent, in other words, were the various responses of the actors in the French and Prussian capitals to the pressures that they faced the product of well-considered and compelling national interests and to what extent the product of self-interest, prejudice, and intrigue?

I have felt obliged to satisfy myself as best I could about the answers to these and other such questions, and the reader, it seems to me, has the right to see the evidence upon which such conclusions are based. It is these considerations that have dictated in large measure the scholarly character of the book. But it is also my hope that the work will serve, in addition to this severely academic purpose, to illuminate something of the diplomatic customs of the time—for the more I saw of the evidence, the more it was borne in upon me that a genuine image of the diplomatic process is hardly to be recaptured in a historical narrative unless the lens through which it is viewed is a sharp one and the human texture of which it consists becomes visible in considerable detail. The acts and the decisions of statesmanship will seldom be entirely intelligible if viewed apart from the immediate context of time and circumstance—information, pressures, impulses, and momentary necessities—in which they occur.

More important still, it is my hope that the reader who has the patience to follow this account from beginning to end (if such there be) will, by dint of repeated example, be brought to share its fundamental assumption—namely, that the circumstances in which the Franco-Prussian War unfolded contradict, wholly and emphatically, the determinist view of history, the conviction that the fate of humankind is beyond the influence of the accidental and the personal; that it is shaped by forces beyond the play of human personality. On the contrary, these circumstances encourage the view that things happen because individual and discoverable people decide things and do them; that greatness in politics can exist; that there are overwhelming personalities in history; and that the activities of a few have been disproportionately important for all. Should this story illumine these larger themes for the reader, the effort embodied in these pages will prove doubly rewarding.

Acknowledgments

The number of those from whom I have received assistance and support in the preparation of this volume is so great that I despair of trying to mention them all in a note of this nature.

First of all, most important, most lastingly, and most deeply, I must acknowledge once more a special debt to Gordon A. Craig, whose books on the period of time with which this volume deals were among the first works I ever read on European history. Without this counsel and support, my efforts would have been much longer, much harder, and, as we both know, surely much less adequately performed.

I must also acknowledge my indebtedness to my colleague and dear friend, Theodore S. Hamerow, for his generosity in reading the entire manuscript and giving me the great benefit of his experience and knowledge. For their kindness in evaluating and commenting on various portions of the work, I have also to thank Paul W. Schroeder, Gaines Post, Jr., and Diethelm Prowe.

This study required recourse to the governmental archives in the great European capitals: the Archives du ministère des affaires étrangères at the Quai d'Orsay in Paris; the Geheimes Staatsarchiv and Bildarchiv in Berlin; the Haus-, Hof- und Staatsarchiv in Vienna; the Public Record Office in London; and the Ministero degli affari esteri, Archivo storico, in Rome. In all these places I was treated with unfailing courtesy and helpfulness, and I regret only that the limitations of space prevent me from acknowledging the names of those in whose debt I find myself.

Among the many other individuals who have contributed to this study, I must mention Uwe Rupp for the help she extended me in sharpening my proficiency in spoken German. As well, I am grateful to my editors at the

University of Wisconsin Press, especially Raphael Kadushin and Sheila McMahon, for the patience with which they endured the inquires of an anxious and often importunate author. Finally, I want to express my thanks to the staff of the library and administration of the University of California, Berkeley, and particularly to my supervisor, Eric P. Anglim, who extended to me a work schedule flexible enough for me to organize and arrange my time in such a way that this effort, begun six years before, could at last bear fruit and who patiently (though I hope not too frequently) suffered lack of attention to his concerns because my mind was wandering away to July 1870.

A Duel of Giants

1

A Bit about Personalities

Before turning to the events to be recounted, let us briefly consider the situations that prevailed respectively in the two capitals at the beginning of the year 1870 as well as the personalities who occupied positions of preeminence at them.

In France uncertainty had turned into confidence. A plebiscite on 8 May, asking the population whether they approved of a new constitution that had been drawn up by the government of Emperor Napoleon III, went overwhelmingly in imperial favor. The voters who wrote "Oui" numbered 7,300,000; those who wrote "Non," only some 1,570,000. Even allowing for the fact that the big towns voted once again with the opposition and that there were nearly 1,900,000 abstentions, the vote was a massive verdict in favor of the regime. However, if the result was overwhelming, its meaning was still open to question. Although the opposition to the policies of the emperor had now disappeared, the flood tide of feeling on which that opposition had been carried had not disappeared at all; not only was this tide still running stronger than ever beneath the surface, it was also serving as a rallying point for French political forces that had hitherto been kept apart by deep ideological divisions.

The decade of the 1860s had seen unmitigated reversals for French policy. The dominant position that Prussia had acquired in Germany divided French opinion. It was the persistent and appallingly successful development of the Prussian armed forces in the victories over Denmark in 1864 and over Austria in 1866 that created a sensation. Even Napoleon III's most intimate advisers were insistent that French opinion resented the aggrandizement of Prussia, and this attitude seemed to be confirmed by the attacks made upon the government in the organs of the press and from the tribune of parliament—so much so that by 1870 opinion had come to regard Königgrätz (the great, decisive battle of the war of 1866) as much a defeat for France as for Austria, indeed as a second Waterloo. The British ambassador, Lord Cowley, observed: "There is no doubt that the emperor is seriously alarmed by the information he has received from the country. The empress told Goltz [the Prussian minister] that she looked upon the present state of things as *le commencement de la fin de la dynastie.*"[1]

He spoke truly. Not only had Austria ceased to be the dominant power in Germany, France had ceased to be the dominant power in Europe, and the speed of her decline in the decade after 1860 only intensified this embitterment. For those deep currents of French feeling in which the accumulated frustrations of the four years that had passed since Königgrätz were struggling to find their release, there was no focal point that held higher emotional value than the dream of a reformed French army. For years, however, this dream had proved a will o' the wisp, a delusion. France had given birth to the Nation in Arms, but in the nineteenth century she continually refused, for reasons political and economic, to base her military organization on the pattern of her revolutionary armies. Napoleon III had been a critic of this practice, and once in power it might have been expected that he would throw himself into the task of reform. French opinion was too strong for him. There was great activity upon the surface of what was fundamentally an unsound system. The result for which the ruler and ruled were equally to blame was that by the spring of 1870, the country as a whole, quite unable to follow the prolonged discussions of military reform, fondly believed that France now had the trained army of 1,200,000 men that Napoleon III had proclaimed as his objective. The French were soon to make the bitter discovery that they had been living in a paradise of fools.

In the first weeks of May this seemed not to matter. Napoleon III had a new grant of authority; for him the plebiscite met a deeply felt want. Here was a recovery of lost identity for a France whose confidence in her very greatness had been shaken by the events of 1866 and by a series of reversals of policy in the four years that had followed. To be sure, the opposition clung to the crumb of comfort that over 50,000 soldiers had voted "Non." Other Frenchmen were puzzled that only 300,000 soldiers had taken the trouble to vote at all.

Where were the remaining 150,000 of what had been assumed to be the most formidable fighting machine in the world? But these critics and wondering statisticians could not hide from themselves the fact that the Second Empire had, to all intents and purposes, won a triumphant vindication. Here was reassurance. Here was irrefutable proof that the "liberal empire" was what the people really wanted. Ollivier, the prime minister, was so elated by the news that he declared: "The strength given to the government by this vote is such that the emperor can with impunity commit every possible mistake and remain unshaken on his throne." He went further and announced that the vote was an indication that the French government had realized that peace had her victories no less renowned than war, a belief whose sincerity had been shown by the government's decision to reduce the annual contingent of conscripts for the army by ten thousand. This last was a gesture toward an era of disarmament of which Napoleon III himself had dreamed.[2]

This, then, was the political soil out of which the most important elements in French statesmanship over the ensuing weeks would grow. None of the manifestations of French policy are fully intelligible unless this background of feeling is taken into account.

In Prussia the situation was quite different. Flush with success from her victory over Austria in 1866, Prussia had become the indisputable power in north and central Germany. As a result of her annexations in that war, she comprised four-fifths or the bulk of the population north of the river Main. The decisiveness with which her victory had been achieved opened up the possibility of greatly expanding her power base by absorbing the southern states—Bavaria, Württemberg, Baden, and Hesse-Darmstadt—themselves magnets that had for centuries attracted the attentions of hostile powers. If Austria sought to turn the tables and to avenge her defeat—and it was not obvious at first that she would not seek to do so—these states might prove useful allies, and for France they served as a shield against further Prussian expansion.

As to internal politics, too, matters here were less complex. Prussia had a king and a minister president, neither of whom was responsible to parliament.

There were also, of course, ministries of the king: of finance, of the interior, of war. In the personal incumbencies of these offices there reigned (again in contrast with the situation in France) a great stability. Of the two preeminent figures, one, King William I, had ruled since 1858, first as regent and then (after 1861) as king; the second, Otto von Bismarck, the minister president, had been in office since 1862. William would reign until his death in 1888; Bismarck, until he was dismissed from office in 1890. Each of these men needed the other. Each was fundamentally a Prussian rather than a German figure.

William was a staunch conservative by nature and by conviction, and he was a professional soldier to his fingertips. He had served with the Prussian army in the campaign against Napoleon, and he had commanded the Prussian forces that had put down the revolt in Baden in 1848. His interest in German unity was stronger and deeper than that of his predecessor, and in May 1849 he had written: "Whoever wishes to rule Germany must conquer it. . . . Our whole history shows that Prussia is destined to lead Germany but the question is how and when."[3] Gracious, retiring, given to burying himself in his various palaces, William I was not really so dependent upon Bismarck as is commonly supposed. His political instincts were of a high order; he wished, he wrote upon taking the throne, to end the intrigues of obscurantist and reactionary cliques and the dark years of suppression that had character-ized the rule of his brother, Frederick William IV. He announced that he would accept the constitution of 1850 because it had been granted by the former king, but he interpreted it strictly; he would rule constitutionally, but according to the "rigid limits set by me."[4] By this, he meant that ministers could debate and advise, but that the king of Prussia was above party and ultimately responsible to God. William was not one to shrink from action, and he punished ruthlessly what he saw as attempts to overthrow the social order or to undermine the royal system. He took—particularly at the time with which this account deals—a keen interest in foreign affairs, and when-ever his personal sensitivities were not too extensively involved, his judg-ments on such matters were not devoid of perception and of good sense. His sensitivities, on the other hand—his likes, his dislikes, his reactions to what he saw as slights to his person or to his authority—could be lively in the extreme. Once aroused, they were not easily assuaged.

William I was a devout Protestant, a man of his word. A rather stiff soldier,

William I, king of Prussia (From Dietrich Schäfer, *Bismarck: Ein Bild seines Lebens und Wirkens,* 2 vols. [Berlin: Verlag von Reimar Hobbing, 1917], 1:facing p. 224)

he disliked public appearances. Though by no means the most outgoing of personalities, he had the advantage of being married to a princess, Augusta, daughter of Charles Augustus, the grand duke of Saxe Weimar—the enlightened ruler who had persuaded Goethe to enter his service as minister of state. Augusta's mother had been a close friend of Goethe, respected and admired by him as a patroness of the arts; a woman of sharp, restless intellect, she was a wholly pleasant personality, widely liked at court. Augusta inherited her mother's spirit. Not only that, she was a granddaughter of Catherine the Great of Russia and niece of two tsars, the brothers Alexander I and Nicholas I. Augusta was an altogether admirable personality. Measured and prudent in judgment, her eye registered with passionate sincerity and intensity whatever lay before it. She took in the development of events and could be counted upon to be a voice of caution and of conciliation in the most adverse of circumstances—a contrast, to say the least, with her fierce counterpart across the Rhine in Paris. Until her death in January 1890 she remained one of Bismarck's fiercest opponents, causing him, he once said, "more problems than all the foreign powers and opposition parties at home."[5]

William had spent much of his life in the shadow of his predecessor, Frederick William IV, but in the 1850s he came into his own. During 1858 Frederick William's health broke down, and when he became totally incapacitated, William succeeded him as regent. Three years later, upon Frederick William's death, he became King William I. Frederick William had once said: "If we had been born as sons of a petty official, I should have become an architect, William, an NCO."[6] Though a reputed reactionary during the great disorders from 1848 to 1850, William had none of his brother's high-flown mysticism. During the Crimean War he had wished to go to war with Russia on the side of the western powers; now he thought it his duty as a good German to cooperate with Austria and, indeed, as late as the summer of 1866, when the mobilization arrangements against her were being brought into operation, hesitated to authorize them at all, in order to avoid any appearance of aggression against an empire with which he felt such a profound sympathy. At home he planned a policy of "moral conquests," intending to give Prussia a more liberal government and so to make her more popular in Germany. Dismissing the clique of ministers to which Frederick William had clung, he opened "a new era" by appointing a liberal ministry.

When he came to the throne at the age of sixty-three, William was set in his ways, and his mind was dominated by one overriding obsession: the army. The liberal politician, Ludwig Bamberger, put it rather succinctly when he observed that for William "the state consisted of soldiers and the soldiers were the kings."[7] No words were ever truer. William loved the army with a passion for which, save perhaps for his ancestor Frederick William I, it is impossible to find a parallel in the entire history of modern Germany. For both, military efficiency came before everything else; everything else had to be crossed off the agenda until that had been taken care of. William never envisaged the army as the agent through which Prussia would achieve the mastery of Germany, but the plans for the army that he had in mind could never be launched (let alone accomplished) without a political crisis as wrenching as that through which England had passed in the 1640s and whose outcome was every bit as decisive for the future character of the state. To do its job the army had to be reformed from head to toe, and for a long time, first as prince of Prussia and then as regent, William had been thinking of little else.

To understand the position of the army in William's thought in the period of time with which this book is concerned, it might be well to go back a bit and to note the early experiences of the king with regard to the reform of this institution and the conflict with the Prussian parliament into which these experiences brought him. The population of Prussia had more than doubled in the forty years before he became regent, but the annual intake of 40,000 recruits had remained the same. By 1859, 23,000 young men were escaping military service each year. William I and Roon, his minister of war, proposed to increase the number of regiments and the barracks provided for them so that every Prussian would receive his three years of military training. Contrary to what has often been supposed, there was no conflict with the Prussian parliament about this; the Prussian liberals admired the tradition of Scharnhorst and Gneisenau and regarded universal military service as an enlightened measure.[8] The dispute between William I and parliament centered on quite other concerns. It had been an essential part of the Scharnhorst system that after three years' active service and two in the reserve, every Prussian citizen should pass into the Landwehr, a sort of territorial army with its own units and its own officers, most of them not drawn from the nobility.

The Landwehr was a symbol of pernicious nationalism. Roon despised it. It was, he said, "politically a false institution because it no longer impressed the foreigner."[9] There was a deeper consideration. Now that Prussia was a constitutional country, the members of the Landwehr—especially the officers—were also voters. This did not trouble Roon. He had made his way to the top of Prussian politics when, as Erich Marcks observed long ago, "the philosopher was retreating and the king was coming forward."[10] He proposed to increase the years spent in the regular reserve and to whittle the Landwehr to almost nothing. With these proposals William wholeheartedly agreed. The liberals, on the other hand, wished to reduce the period of service to two years and to make the Landwehr the core of the Prussian army. A rousing constitutional crisis thus ensued.

By September 1862 parliamentary opposition had reached the point where the assembly refused all further grants for the army, and William, on Roon's advice, summoned as minister president the ruthlessly unorthodox Otto von Bismarck. Within fifteen months of taking office, Bismarck had involved Prussia in a war with Denmark; two years after that, he entered her into a struggle with Austria for the mastery of Germany. With these two wars all the unity and fervor of the opposition began to melt, and the constitutional conflict was decisively resolved in favor of the king at the battle of Königgrätz on 3 July 1866. On 20 October 1867 Roon could write jubilantly to William that the struggle was over at last.[11] And so it was: not only had the Prussian army been remodeled along the lines he had fashioned, the forces of the North German Confederation (whose creation the victories of the armies had made possible) were put under Prussian control as well. By July 1870 the entire Prussian government, from the king on down, could take comfort in knowing that they had under their hands one of the greatest engines of war the world had ever known.

William I, of course, was not responsible for this alone. Quite the contrary, the achievement belonged to his minister president, Otto von Bismarck. The personality of Bismarck and his role in Prussian life during this period are so well known that one hesitates to expand on them, but certain aspects of his personality are particularly relevant to the subject at hand and deserve special mention.

Bismarck was born on 1 April 1815 at Schönhausen, in the Old Mark of Brandenburg, just east of the Elbe—in appearance a typical Junker estate, in a district inhabited largely by Protestants. Bismarck himself was unmistakably north German in appearance and in outlook. Compared to his contemporaries—to Napoleon III, with his appreciation of the modern forces of Europe and his understanding of the career of his great uncle, Napoleon I, and even to Emperor Francis Joseph of Austria-Hungary, who despite being a wooden-headed character had in him all of the traditions of the Habsburgs—Bismarck was pretty small beer. In physique he was a big man, but he belonged to what we would call the modest gentry. He had a humble upbringing, living on a farm, doing plenty of the farm work himself; he did not have a particularly distinguished career at the university. There was another extraordinary thing about him: until he became prime minister, almost dictator of Prussia, he had never held political office. He held important diplomatic offices, and from these he seems to have got his vision of the world.

A few years before becoming minister president, during the revolutions of 1848, he was a violent reactionary; he thought that the masses should be shot down, that one should return to extreme conservatism—or so he said. No great statesman has ever been more solitary. He lived to be eighty-three, and in all this long life he had hardly a friend, and the friends he had were outsiders like himself—none from his own class of Prussian gentry, or, later on, of German nobility; among other German statesmen, no friends at all. He never visited other great houses. In fact he hated these; they did not give him enough to eat or drink, for one thing. It was only at his own house that he could get those enormous whole hams on the sideboard, and bottles of champagne before dinner just because he was thirsty, and the bottle or two of brandy afterwards, and the eight or ten Havana cigars that he smoked in the course of an afternoon or evening.[12]

Bismarck seems to have grasped what was going on in the world by solitary meditation—plodding along in those plains of north Germany, observing the birds and the trees, brooding a great deal—he was a tremendous brooder. His great strokes of policy came after long, solitary brooding, not after dis-

Otto von Bismarck, minister president of Prussia, at Putbus in 1866 (From Fürst Herbert von Bismarck, ed., *Fürst Bismarcks Briefe an seine Braut und Gattin* [Stuttgart: J. G. Cotta'sche Buchhandlung Nachfolger GmbH, 1900], 481)

cussion with others, and in a long life of conflict, he fought himself most of all. Yet he also possessed certain qualities of mind and of personality that bewitched his contemporaries and that undoubtedly contributed to the success of his statecraft. His cutting wit delighted dinner companions for decades. Once turned to his voice—thin and reedy, by the way, almost a falsetto, the voice of an academic, not of a man of action—they learned to watch him as if he were a trapeze artist, soaring through every imaginable subject, spinning, flipping, hanging by his heels—the quintessential showman. Though he had a good opinion of himself, he was free of the kind of personal vanity that made some of his contemporaries ludicrous and that ruined others. Though clever in dealing with subordinates, Bismarck as a rule observed the core of the diplomatic code: diplomats do not lie to one another. For all of these reasons, foreign diplomats enjoyed doing business with him and frequently came to the point of giving him their full faith and trust.

Bismarck grew up at a time when Prussia was the least of the Great Powers of Europe. When brought to power on the heels of the constitutional crisis just recounted, he was forty-seven years of age. He had never been a minister and had spent much of his rebellious youth in the government twenty years before. His diplomatic experience had been shaped by his years as the Prussian delegate to the Frankfurt assembly (from 1851 to 1859) and by two ambassadorships, the first at St. Petersburg from 1859 to 1862, the second at Paris from May to September 1862. It was at Frankfurt that Bismarck first set foot on the ladder of power; his years there were decisive for his future policies, and for this reason, they will stand a word or two of comment here.

With the restoration of the German confederation in 1851, Prussia needed a delegate to the federal diet. A new diplomacy, new principles of action, a new attitude of mind, and a new interpretation of Prussia's interests were urgently required to rescue her from the blunders of the past and from the menaces of the future—surrender to liberalism or, worse still, surrender to Austria. Who better than Bismarck, the one Prussian distinguished from the liberals in 1850 by preaching cooperation with Austria? Bismarck, perhaps, went to Frankfurt with the sincere intention of cooperating with Austria; for him, at any rate, the dangers and the memories of the revolutionary year

13

were not far from his mind. More probably, he had not thought about his future policy, and in fact it seems to have sprung from immediate concerns. In the Prussian parliament, the liberals had been his mortal foe, and he defied them by urging cooperation with Austria. Now, at Frankfurt, his opponent was the Austrian delegate, who put on airs, scheduled business, decided questions without consulting anyone. Bismarck would have none of this. Two trivial gestures announced the coming struggle for mastery in Germany. Only the Austrian delegate smoked at meetings. Bismarck pulled out a cigar and asked the Austrian for a match. Received some days later by the Austrian delegate in his shirt sleeves, Bismarck pulled off his coat; "I agree," he said, "it is a hot day."[13] These were trifles, but precious trifles. Each gesture showed that Bismarck was a man of a new sort, and Prussia a new sort of state. Prussia now vied openly with Austria for control of Germany, but the conflict on which Bismarck set out could not be settled by votes at the Frankfurt diet. It would not be resolved for fifteen years—when Bismarck, as prime minister of Prussia, turned European politics upside down by destroying Austria as a German power at Königgrätz.

In his first weeks as delegate at Frankfurt, Bismarck had written: "In the art of saying absolutely nothing with a lot of words, I am making raging progress; I write reports of many pages that read just as plain and as blunt as any leading article, and if Manteuffel [the Prussian minister president] can say what's in them after he has read them, then he can do more than I."[14] Like many of the brilliant but willful passages with which Bismarck's writings are replete, this comment need not be taken at face value; the noteworthy feature is rather the thoroughness with which Bismarck mastered the mechanics of his craft and the thirst with which he drank in the atmosphere of the Frankfurt of his day. He studied everything—men, women, machinery. His dispatches are filled with vivid vignettes—penetrating miniatures and character sketches of the diplomats who made up the Frankfurt world—and Manteuffel certainly could have no difficulty understanding what they were about. Like the instructions that he was to write to his ambassadors later on, Bismarck's reports were models of their kind; sometimes his words, preserved for posterity by the written page, stand out on his lips like the little balloons of speech that emerge from characters in a cartoon strip. And these words are famous not only for their forceful characterizations, the incisiveness of their analysis, and the compelling clarity of their language, but also because they are studded with judgments that continually compel one to stop and to reflect not only upon their content but also upon the breathtaking beauty with which they are expressed. The famous Splendid Dispatch (*Prachtbericht*) of May 1856—in which he diagnosed the general state of European politics with masterly precision and depicted Prussia and Austria as two mortal antagonists "plowing the same disputed acre" and "waiting for war to set the clock of evolution at the right hour"[15]—illustrates these qualities to perfection, as do his letters to the Prussian generals in the period leading up to the outbreak of war with France in 1870.[16] Bismarck despised writers and literary men, but only Luther and Goethe rank with him as masters of German prose.

Ludwig Bamberger once jeered that "Prince Bismarck believes in a God who always has the unique capability of agreeing with him,"[17] and his comment has sometimes been cited as evidence that faith was something in which Bismarck had no serious interest and which he brought in only to justify what he had decided already. This is certainly unfair. True, Bismarck was not outwardly devout; his religion, acquired with not inconsiderable misgivings when he was young, was far removed from the humanitarianism of the twentieth century, and there was little love in it except perhaps for his own family. But that is only one side of the medal. The truth was that Bismarck embraced faith because it sustained him and helped him to shoulder the duties that came with the authority of his position, not the least of which was power over life and death. He said once: "Peoples and men, folly and wisdom, war and peace come and go like waves but the sea remains. Our states and their power are nothing to God but ant-heaps which are trampled on by an ox's hoof or snatched by fate in the shape of a honey gatherer."[18] And again: "I am God's soldier and wherever He sends me I must go, and I believe that He does send me and that He shapes my life as He needs to."[19] The plain fact was that dreadful work had to be done, and the person who did it had constantly to fall back upon God's grace and to hope that it would be extended to him. He once wrote: "Had it not been for me there would not have been three great wars; 80,000 men would not have perished, and

15

parents, brothers, sisters wuold not be in mourning. But that is something I have to settle with God."[20]

There is a deeper point. Faith strengthened Bismarck's ambition in what was surely a gigantic struggle for self-control. In July 1851, after a few lonely weeks away from his wife, Bismarck described to his friend Hans von Kleist-Retzow (in a letter that was suppressed by the editors of his collected works) the temptations by which he was constantly assailed: "The greatest weapon with which evil assaults me is not the desire for external glory, but a brutal sensuality that leads me so close to the greatest sins that I doubt at times that I will gain access to God's mercy. At any rate, I am certain that the seed of God's word has not found fertile ground in a heart laid waste as it was from youth. Otherwise I could not be so much of the plaything of temptation which even invades my moments of prayer. . . . I am often in hopeless anxiety over the fruitlessness of my prayer. Comfort me, Hans, but burn this without speaking of it to anyone."[21] In the end, he formed the opinion that the "usefulness of prayer" lay in its implied "submission to a stronger power," not in the beneficence of God's intercession: "I am conscious of that Power which is neither arbitrary nor capricious."[22]

The faith on which Bismarck often drew when faced by questions of life and death also gave his not infrequently turbulent life a sense of purpose and stability and a comfort with which he could console himself when he reflected on the triviality of human affairs. He wrote to his wife Johanna: "I cannot conceive how a man who reflects and yet knows nothing of God, and will know nothing, can endure his life for contempt and boredom. I do not know how I formerly endured. If I lived now as I once did without God, without you, without children, I cannot think why I should not put life aside like a dirty shirt."[23] And in 1870: "I know not whence I should derive my sense of duty, if not from God: orders and titles have no charm for me; I firmly believe in a life after death, and that is why I am a royalist; by nature I am disposed to be a republican. . . . Were I not a staunch Christian, did I not stand upon the miraculous basis of religion, you would never have possessed a Federal Chancellor."[24]

Had Bismarck been asked to appraise his own qualities, he would, as Gordon A. Craig has pointed out, almost certainly have stressed caution and patience.[25] He always shrank from action until the time was perfect, and he was convinced that true wisdom was to recognize that "we can set our watches, but the time passes no more quickly because of that, and the ability to wait while conditions develop is a requisite of practical policy."[26] And again: "We all carry national union in our hearts, but for the calculating statesman the necessary comes first and then the ideally desirable . . . if Germany attains her desired goal in the nineteenth century, I should regard that as a great achievement, if it were reached in ten or fifteen years it would be something extraordinary, an unexpected crowning gift from God. . . . No one can assume the responsibility for the outbreak of a war that would perhaps only be the first in a series of *Rassenkriege* [wars between nationalities]."[27]

These words have often been quoted and deservedly so, for they reflect a fundamental element of his personality and character. War should, in his view, be fought only for essential interests, not for reasons of sentiment or of prestige. Bismarck's writings show quite conclusively that he understood the anguish that war could inflict upon a society—breaking the rhythms of generations, loosening social bonds, sowing sadness, bewilderment, and skepticism where once the opposites of those qualities had prevailed. This made rashness and precipitous action anathema to him, and he warned against these all the more in view of his belief that these were temptations to which his countrymen all too easily fell prey. He said late in life: "It was always a failing of the Germans to attain all or nothing in their impetuous way, to place too much emphasis on one particular policy."[28] This was a weakness against which he set his face while he was prime minister; it was only after he had left the scene that it resumed its unchecked sway in the key departments of German policy.

All this is not to suggest that the baser emotions never overcame Bismarck, for they did. The personal spite, the raucous evocation of power, the infuriation at opposition—these were the qualities that Bismarck shared with his countrymen and that once led him to confess that he had often lain awake whole nights, hating. To this heritage, however, Bismarck himself added markedly different qualities: restraint, moderation, an ability to peer into the minds of others, a readiness to risk his prestige for the sake of peace and moderation. Whoever concerns himself with the diplomatic documents of the period will not be able to escape the conclusion that the record of European diplomacy in the second half of the nineteenth century contains the

17

name of no more competent professional diplomat, and none who has set so indelible a mark upon his time.

William I and Bismarck were not the only permanent figures of the Franco-Prussian relationship. There were three others whose roles in the designing and in the bringing about of the war were so dominant and whose names will appear so frequently in this account that they may as well be identified at the outset. These were Napoleon III, the emperor of the French, and two principal members of his government: Émile Ollivier, the prime minister, and Antoine Agénor, duc de Gramont, the minister of foreign affairs.

Napoleon III is worth writing about. Seldom has so controversial a character held the scepter of such power in Europe. Napoleon III ruled France for twenty-two years, longer than anyone else in her modern history, yet few men are more unknowable. The more we strip off his disguises, the more new disguises appear. Conspirator and statesman; dreamer and realist; despot and democrat; maker of wars and man of peace; creator and muddler—one could go on indefinitely. All the greatest political observers of his time tried to penetrate his secret—Tocqueville, Marx, Thiers, Victor Hugo—all failed to make sense of him. Bismarck called him a sphinx without a riddle; rather he was a man of too many riddles, and riddles to which he himself did not know the answer. Everything about him baffles inquiry. Was he the son of his father? If not, then of whom? He was a master of concealment. The correspondence of his uncle, Napoleon I, in whose shadow he was to live out his life, runs to sixty-one volumes; that of Napoleon III, even if it could be brought together, would not fill one. Walewski, illegitimate son of Napoleon I and later foreign minister to Napoleon III, once complained: "The ambassadors see my door open, but they walk right by it; they prefer, in matters of great sensitivity, to deal with the emperor alone."[29] Napoleon III talked endlessly to a great variety of witnesses, but the talk, like the smoke of the cigarettes that he was one of the first to favor, was vague and intangible; it vanished into the air, leaving only a faint romantic odor, a thin cloud of mystery.[30]

Napoleon III, emperor of France (From Dietrich Schäfer, *Bismarck: Ein Bild seines Lebens und Wirkens,* 2 vols. [Berlin: Verlag von Reimar Hobbing, 1917], 1:facing p. 144)

All the same, Napoleon III was remarkable man. His mind teemed with original, often dangerous ideas that were years ahead of his time. His intellect was enriched by great personal charm. He was vain, maybe moody, but—as Queen Victoria once said—"a prince among men."[31] He was a beautiful speaker, with a ravishing voice and a fine turn of phrase. There were political gifts behind the cloud of phrases. He was a skilled and successful negotiator. His reading during long years of prison in his early life had made him better educated than the average ruler of the day; taking up chemistry, he had written a treatise on beet sugar competent enough to be accepted seriously by the industry. Though he appealed to the fears of the middle class, he was also a socialist, and a pamphlet on unemployment gained him considerable (though short-lived) popularity among workers. He did more for the poor than any other French statesman before or since, and (like Benjamin Franklin) he was working on an economical stove to improve their lot when he died. First and foremost his inventiveness took a military bent. An excellent horseman, as early as 1835 his *Manuel d'artillerie* impressed the professionals, and a few years later he was busy improving the French army musket. Ironically, in 1843 he was recommending something similar to the Prussian system of conscription that would eventually be his ruin, and even as Bismarck's captive at Wilhelmshöhe, after his defeat in the Franco-Prussian War, he soon busied himself collecting material on Prussian military organization.

Napoleon III stood—in competence, in intelligence, and indeed in all the qualities that make for a successful political career—among the leading French figures of the century. Among his many ideas there was one that was truly overpowering, and that was his belief in the power of self-determined nationalism. Here was the cure for every ill. Antagonism among nationalities was a canker at Europe's heart; remove this antagonism and peace would follow. It was for France to take up the cause of nationalism and discharge her mission in Europe. But how? By promoting the United States of Europe. Everything in Europe called for unification. More uniform in climate than China; less diverse in religion than India; less diverse in race than the United States of America; a single culture and a common social structure. Self-determination ascertained through a plebiscite was Napoleon III's goal; then and only then could free nations live side by side as happy neighbors.

Championing nationalism had for Napoleon III a second advantage; it would open the door to a general revision of the territorial settlement that had been laid down through the treaties of Vienna of 1815. Here was another point from which he never deviated. He said in 1852: "Nations are not thrones and crowns but men; people have a right to assert themselves against masters not of their own choosing."[32] To those who created the Vienna system this sounded like the trumpet of doom. They had played out their lives in the shadow of the Napoleonic Wars. They saw in Napoleon III's program no mere revision of grievances and defects. Europe which existed on the basis that France had lost the wars was to be rearranged on the basis that she had won. And in this presumption itself there lay paradox, contradiction. Napoleon III liked to suppose that the congress of Vienna had brought France down from her high estate in Europe; on the contrary, this settlement had given her a position of preeminence in Europe and had made her secure. If it were changed France was bound to suffer. Hence Napoleon III was constantly driven forward, yet shrank from the results.

There were still more contradictions. Napoleon III came to power proclaiming that *"L'Empire c'est la paix,"* but within three years Frenchmen were dying on the battlefields of the Crimea. In 1859 embroilment in the first of the national wars in Italy gave France Nice and Savoy but at the cost of Italian affections, as did his sending of French troops to Rome in 1849 and again in 1867 to protect the pope. At the same time, the principle of nationalities led him to support Polish aspirations of independence at the cost of friendship with Russia. Most dangerous of all, the example that he had set in siding with the unification of Italy morally forced him not to interfere with Bismarck's scheme to bring the states of Germany under the rule of Prussia. The largest obstacle to German unification had been eliminated by Prussia's success at Königgrätz and by the treaty of Prague of 23 August 1866, which gave a formal registration to the defeat of the Habsburg monarchy. Napoleon III's prestige suffered as a result. By 1870, *"L'Empire c'est la paix"* had become *"L'Empire c'est la baix"* and had won him the overwhelming hostility of the intellectuals of his day, from whose witty and pungent attacks he never recovered.

Nor was this all. At this point Napoleon III was also very sick, suffering for some months in the spring and summer of 1870 from cold, fever, tooth trouble, and, most outstandingly, from stone, as well as from the aftereffects of the drugs administered for the relief of these miseries. To mount a horse was torture; and, at times, coherent thought impossible. Stricken by these various *douleurs,* in acute pain at times almost past endurance, he suffered daily the take of telegrams and other official business brought currently up to his apartments and coped as best he could with the responsibilities that flowed from it all. By 1870 Napoleon III was, as was plain to all who saw him, a man gravely weakened by age and by illness—indeed a shadow of his former self. Physically he had the appearance of a man already dead. His left arm was paralyzed; his eyes were glazed and dull; he moved with a slow, shuffling walk and was kept going only by increasing doses of drugs. Sick and racked by pain, his judgment, though often still shrewd, was clouded by the languor that had always interrupted his moments of energy. The rare visits of the members of his government so obviously tired the emperor that the ministers often withdrew for sheer pity without having even attempted to broach the subjects about which they had come to see him.

The upshot of all this was that Napoleon III, in the last year of his reign, came to rely increasingly upon those members of his entourage for whom conflict with Prussia was considered unavoidable and, among these his wife, the Countess Eugénie de Montijo was the most notable. An auburn-haired Spaniard aged twenty-seven at the time of her betrothal to Napoleon III in 1853—a woman of passionate political temperament, inexhaustible energies, wide interests, and varied tastes—Eugénie cut an imposing figure at court. In August 1855, at a great ball in the Tuileries, Bismarck was presented to Napoleon III and Eugénie, and he was properly responsive to her grace and beauty; the empress was "more beautiful than any of the portraits I have seen," he told his wife, Johanna; not in general style, he added, unlike his sister, Malwine, though her face was longer and narrower and her eyes and mouth more beautiful.[33] Eugénie did not reciprocate Bismarck's deference; quite the contrary. Of all her enthusiasms and passions, the greatest and most consuming were her hatred of Prussia and of Bismarck and her longing for the day when France would avenge the reversal of 1866. She gloried in the reputation she derived from these enthusiasms. She shared with Napoleon III a deep commitment to the empire, and she combined with it a virulent chauvinism. She claimed that "real strength only comes from consistency"—a phrase that shows how drastically she differed from her husband. She pushed this view all the more strongly because she believed that "France is losing her place among nations and must win it back or die."[34] It is said that on 15 July 1870, after a vote approving war credits had been taken in the French legislature, she summoned two aides from an antechamber and described what was about to occur as *"ma petite guerre."*[35]

We know a great deal about Eugénie's activities during the last years of the Second Empire, most of which were based on her desire to bring about a crisis of relations with Prussia. Early in the year we find her recording the fact that the inspector-general of the Austrian army, Archduke Albrecht, was visiting Paris with a view to combining Austrian and French movements in time of war. This pleases her greatly: *"Il est, comme moi,"* she writes, *"passioné du désir d'une alliance avec l'Autriche."*[36] Nor was this all. In her dairy she pours out the resentments surviving from the confused and frustrating years between 1866 and 1870, and a most cynical and discreditable interpretation is given to the motives of Bismarck in blocking French plans to obtain control of the Belgian railways in 1869. Eugénie's influence mounted as the health of the emperor fell into a decline. It is impossible to believe that Franco-Prussian relations were bettered in any way thereby; in all her pronouncements and writings, Eugénie stands in marked contrast to her Prussian counterpart, Queen Augusta. Needless to say, her pernicious influence was not inconsiderable.

We have it from no less an authority than Halévy that the empress had set her face against the constitutional changes of 1870 because they represented the total defeat of her political views.[37] Years later, when she had calmed down considerably, she still recalled Napoleon III in the spring of 1870 as "practically counting for nothing because of his illness, yes; but particularly because he had surrendered the right to act arbitrarily against his ministers."[38] Of course, explanations such as these can be pushed too far. How many decisions would have been made differently had Napoleon III not been ill in July 1870? The record does not provide a single example. French policy was full of blunders, but through it all and even in the darkest hours, Napoleon III was animated by a deep faith in the cause in which he believed. The decision for war in 1870, as for peace in 1866, will be forever controversial, but neither can be chalked up to the state of Napoleon III's health, and

Eugénie, empress of France (From Comte Fleury, *Memoirs of Empress Eugénie,* 2 vols. [New York: D. Appleton and Co., 1920], 1:facing title page)

for one reason: these decisions were not made by Napoleon III alone. Good health was no guarantee of freedom from blunder, given the constraints that imposed themselves on the crucial decisions.

That said, it is undeniable that the unhappy imperial marriage did much to throw French policy into confusion. Napoleon had, during the time of the Crimean War, overcome similar problems of health and had learned to live with marital disappointment, though it can hardly be said that his escapades with a host of mistresses afterwards were vicarious or that they gave him the degree of comfort and security that he wanted and needed. For Eugénie, however, the cleavage with her husband had an unmistakable effect. It made her resolute for an independent course. She had little influence on the day-to-day formulation of French policies, but the contemptuous and offhand way that she characterized them undermined the consistency of application that they desperately needed. It is beyond question that she deluded the Austrians in this period about Napoleon III's intentions and about the strength of his diplomatic position. And in 1870, she was only too willing to throw out the liberal ministry whose prestige had been one of the overriding factors in bringing on the declaration of war. Worse still, her appraisal of the crisis after the initial defeats prevented the retreat to Paris for which Napoleon III was pushing and led straight to the disaster of Sedan.

By 1870 the Second Empire, which had been proclaimed with such great fanfare eighteen years earlier and was peculiarly the product of Napoleon III's mind, had fallen into a decline. Its prestige was going. With that peculiar ease that the French have for unloading upon an individual the shortcomings of a nation at large, blame for all that was wrong with it, all that was corrupt in it, was quickly heaped upon the man at the top, and upon his shoulders rested the whole weighty structure of the empire that he had established. As the years passed it became more and more evident that, should this main pillar ever be removed, the structure that it supported would instantaneously and irremediably collapse. And that pillar was crumbling.

Election results bore this out. In each successive election the opposition showed itself to be increasingly powerful, and in May 1869 the foremost group, the republicans, captured Paris and most of the big cities. The government faced a new political crisis of staggering proportions: half of the members of the lower house of the legislature, the Corps législatif, consisted of candidates who had rejected the official ticket and had campaigned for constitutional reform. By January 1870 the opposition finally forced Napoleon III's hand; he drew up a new constitution, summoned to the premiership the opposition's leader, Émile Ollivier, and with this proclaimed the advent of the "liberal empire," in which he agreed to rule "with the cooperation of ministers and parliament" and to share the initiative in legislation with both houses of the legislature. The new constitution was decked out with democratic trappings; in reality it was a bundle of contradictions. Ministers were "responsible," but to whom was left to speculation. And though the powers of the Corps législatif were increased, those of the upper house, the senate—still a nominated body—were increased as well, indeed more so: the senate was given a veto over legislation.

Above all, the "liberal empire" was brought about by the collaboration of Napoleon III with Émile Ollivier. Ollivier has a unique place in the history of the Second Empire, for he exercised crucial influence both on its domestic evolution and (to a lesser extent) on its foreign policy. Ollivier was a man of not inconsiderable political bent and sharp intellectual power; he had a multiplicity of gifts and interests, and he tried to cultivate them all and to sacrifice none to any single-minded pursuit. As a youth, Gambetta had seen in him a combination of "the passion of Fox with the political genius of Pitt"[39] but later abandoned him as being unrealistic—striking representative of that most execrable politician, the brilliant orator with a fascinating command of language but totally blind to the realities of the world.

Émile Ollivier was the son of a republican Carbonaro. In 1848, at the age of twenty-two, he was appointed prefect (state governor) of Marseilles; he was observant and active during the year of revolution, preaching the unity of all parties and the fusion of all classes, but his hopes foundered on the election of Louis Napoleon Bonaparte as president of the Second Republic in December of that year. In 1857 he was elected to parliament as a member of the republican opposition, but he was more intent than ever on avoiding a purely partisan criticism of the regime. He would not work for the captur-

Émile Ollivier, prime minister of France (From Émile Ollivier, *The Franco-Prussian War and Its Hidden Causes,* edited and translated by George Burnham Ives [Boston: Little Brown and Co., 1912], facing title page)

ing of power by his party as his first objective. His ideal was not Danton, still less Robespierre, but Washington. He was a passionate admirer of Italy on whose painting he had written several books. Politically he was an eclectic; the constitution of 1870 embodied the values he most respected. This republican's cult of imperial tradition and his attempts to combine republicanism with Bonapartism both in the Second Empire and in his own nature—these hold the key to Ollivier's character and were the source of much of the frustration and tragedy in his life. Even more than that, they explain why, even after 1870, he could never creep back into favor—despite the brilliant qualities that Gambetta had observed in him and despite his seventeen volumes of self-justifying memoirs, which (according to Arnold Toynbee) make him almost the equal of Thucydides as a historian of his own times.[40]

Ollivier's mind was, in its deepest instincts, freewheeling and not always predictable. He was one of the first to welcome Wagner's music to France; he was married to a daughter of the famous Württemberg economist, Friedrich List. On the one hand, he deplored Napoleon III's early foreign adventures in Mexico and in Poland; on the other, he was a strong partisan of the view that France needed a powerful executive and that Napoleon, if pressed by public opinion, could well become both the founder and the custodian of his country's liberties. Fundamentally, Ollivier wished to eliminate questions of power from international relations. The rights of nationalities could not be limited by the supposed necessity of maintaining the balance of power: "Balance is a fine word, just as order is, but a conventional balance established against the will of the people is no more balance than silence produced by despotism is order."[41] Ollivier had come to power a convinced advocate of nonintervention, disarmament, and friendship with Prussia. The Prussian ambassador in Paris noted that Ollivier had "a very marked sympathy for German culture and for German ideas in general. One day, in fact, I commented on this to him, and he replied that these sentiments dated from his first marriage when he had learned to know Germany from the distinguished Germans whom his wife, the daughter of List, drew to his house."[42]

However, there was another side to Ollivier's beliefs. A man who was not disposed to fight a war over the principle of power politics was perfectly prepared to fight one over the graver and far more emotional issue of national pride. It is the mark of the emotional intensity of Ollivier's national feeling that he could write as early as 1859 that he considered the "outraged honor of France" a just and worthy cause for war and an exception to his general desire for peace; that in a speech acknowledging the decisiveness of Königgrätz, he contrived to assert that he was not asking his country "to bow her head before a humiliation" and that, if she felt thus, she should put aside any doubts and at once take up arms; and finally, that he sought in January 1870 to persuade Lord Lyons, the British ambassador, to present disarmament proposals to Prussia as British rather than as French so that, in the event they were rejected, French honor would not be compromised.[43] Moreover, Ollivier was quite prepared to allow that a war was legitimate if it constituted a genuine expression of national will. He said in 1863: "A war is allowable if it is the voice of the people. Hurrah for war if it is desired by the whole nation—the instrument of passion!"[44] He came to power in 1870 convinced that what distinguished his regime from its authoritarian predecessors was that it represented the upwelling of deep, popular forces. Later on, he blamed the war of 1870 on the people of France; the cheering crowds, he said, gave the government no choice and drove them into war—an explanation, incidentally, that later historians have repeated. In July 1870 he announced to Prince Richard Metternich, the Austrian ambassador: "It is no longer men like Rouher and La Valette who give direction to the policy of France. It is I, minister of the people, originating from the people, a minister responsible to the nation, responsible for its dignity."[45] Thus Ollivier was pulled two ways. On the one hand, he was convinced that his government represented the best hope for peace, which was vital to the interests of France; on the other, he could, by his own admission, be won for war if it were popular.

Hence the many facets of Ollivier's behavior. Hence his extreme national touchiness; his preoccupation with symbols of national honor; his exaggerated concept of national dignity; his truculent sensitivity to the views of others. These qualities reflected Ollivier's political judgments and reactions, marked as they were by a love for the cadence of words, for the intricate, the indirect, the oversubtle, the allusive and, above all, the pretentious—all this in place of the blunt, often brutal, but usually incisive and vigorous facility of his German counterpart in going to the heart of things. As Lyons wrote, Ollivier "was particularly alive to the importance of not exposing France to the appearance of being slighted; in fact, he would not conceal from me that a public rebuff from Prussia would be fatal—*'un échec c'est la guerre.'* 'We who have to render an account to parliament and to the country are less than the former government able to put up with any wound to the national pride. Our main object is peace, but we must show firmness and spirit or we shall not be able to cope with revolution abroad and socialism at home.'"[46]

Ollivier must, therefore, bear some of the responsibility for the war of 1870. He admitted as much to himself. Though in his memoirs he declared his conduct to have been at all times beyond reproach, little jottings in a tiny notebook that he carried with him during the worst days of the crisis contain certain remarkable questions: "Did I commit no mistake? Did I bend under pressure? Why did you declare war on Prussia?—I did not declare it! It was Prussia who declared war on us. [A profound error of fact.] My only two mistakes were to have opposed the country's military reorganization when I was in opposition (but it's true that my exoneration is favored because I did not excite France against Prussia at the time) and not to have opposed the declaration of war so as to gain time to be ready. But I did not know that we were not ready."[47]

The shortcomings of Ollivier's character were made all the more dangerous because of a structural change of the first importance that had, with his arrival at the Tuileries, come over the Second Empire: the link that now existed between the cabinet and what we may call public opinion. The Austrian ambassador once remarked: "Louis Napoleon always will permit himself to be guided by what he believes to be the opinion, the interests, and the will of the country."[48] The French ambassador in Karlsruhe noted that any move on the part of the Prussians to force the Main would unchain a war much more easily than had been the case in the past, when Napoleon had to avoid the appearance of an active policy merely out of concern for the stability of his dynasty first and for that of France second.[49] No more: the new government could go to war in the belief that it was defending the honor of France and be confident that it had the support of the people.

The writer must stress this situation because only against this background can one understand the importance of the degree of dismay, bewilderment, and discouragement with which, in the middle of the month of May 1870, the Prussian rulers and those of other Powers of Europe generally learned of the appointment, as successor to Count Napoleon Daru at the French foreign ministry, of Antoine Agénor, duc de Gramont, and absorbed, upon his arrival, the first impressions of his person and his entourage. Their attitude was not unreasonable. Gramont was convinced that his appointment would atone for the blunders that had enfeebled French diplomacy since the days of Königgrätz. He arrived in Paris firm in the belief that alliance with Austria-Hungary, the power to which he had hitherto been accredited, was the answer to all French ills. Negotiations for such an alliance had been going on for some time, and Gramont made them his own after a pretence of constitutional reluctance: "The engagements would have had no significance if I did not accept them, but I accept them."[50] He was convinced that he had stumbled on to something vital to the French diplomatic effort. From that time on, no other purpose existed for him than to put the finishing touches on a Franco-Austrian alliance. A French general, Lebrun, was dispatched to Vienna to translate the alliance into practical terms, and though he achieved nothing important, he returned convinced that the alliance was made—and that if France invaded southern Germany, Austria-Hungary would mobilize at once and would tie down a large part of the Prussian army. Gramont's enthusiasm was more than redoubled—an enthusiasm that tapped to the deepest roots not only his unquestionable and implacable patriotism but also his anti-Prussian feelings (violent to the point of blindness), his innate suspiciousness, and his congenital eagerness to unearth and to bring to public knowledge a sensational diplomatic triumph.

Seldom does one encounter in the historical record anyone concerning whose general iniquity there is such unanimous agreement as that of Gramont. The verdict is indeed severe, but most certainly not unfair. Where patience was needed, he was bull-headed; where deliberation of utterance was essential, he was headstrong and unyielding; and where some measure of caution would have crowned his efforts with unequaled success, he overreached himself and lured his nation into catastrophe.[51] These characteristics reflected his origins and background. The son of émigré parents who had followed Charles X into exile after the July revolution of 1830 only to return three years later, whose ancestors in the Loire valley had accompanied

Antoine Agénor, duc de Gramont, foreign minister of France (From Émile Ollivier, *The Franco-Prussian War and Its Hidden Causes,* edited and translated by George Burnham Ives [Boston: Little Brown and Co., 1912], facing p. 88)

Henry of Navarre during the wars of religion of the sixteenth century, and related through marriage to some of the highest names in the history of France—Guiche, Orléans, Lesparre, Louvigny, Andoins—Gramont was a man of deep religious faith, inextricably bound to the Vatican and hostile to Italian nationalism only less than that of German. An excellent musician, a connoisseur of painting and of wine, Gramont commanded great devotion and inspired great respect. Upon the news of the February revolution of 1848, he appears to have fled to London, where he married an English-woman. Named as plenipotentiary first to Hesse Cassel and then to Würt-temberg, Turin, and Rome, he took up in January 1861 the post at Vienna. He became friends with the Emperor Francis Joseph and with the outstand-ing figures in the Habsburg court, where he drank in the anti-Prussian talk of the Austrian military circles and saw his star rise until, in the late afternoon of 14 May 1870, his hour came: he was summoned to the Tuileries.

All the same, the person of Gramont remains for the historian a singularly unflattering one. Not that one could have supposed this from his appearance: the only representation of him known to this writer (evidently a photograph of a drawing) shows a high forehead and cool, intelligent eyes, the mouth thin and tight, the cheeks covered by whiskers characteristic of the period. The Prussians, who no doubt collected the most information about him, ac-knowledged his ability but suspected the worst in him. Many anecdotes that have survived the time give color to his personality. He had, for instance, many friends from his days as ambassador in Vienna, and the record reveals that these were military people of generally high distinction with whom he was a great social success. He executed his duties at this delicate post with sensitivity and perception, and the same could be said about his tenure of the foreign ministry. His part in the negotiations of May 1870, for instance, for an alliance with Austria-Hungary shows him to be a man of high intelli-gence and competence, vigorous and masterly but also suspicious, intensely loyal to a few and, above all, dramatic to the last vein.

Daru, his predecessor, had favored compromise and a policy of cautious restraint. Gramont wanted action. His coming to power was an unmistakable sign that the policy of the Second Empire had been stood on its head and that there had come to the fore an anti-Prussian group whose object abroad was the destruction of the treaties of 1866 and whose object at home was to use that policy to prop up support for the regime. Gramont himself bore this out. He said upon leaving Vienna for Paris: *"Je serais Bismarck français."*[52] Bismarck himself was, according to the reports we possess from the Prussian records, under no illusion as to what the appointment meant. On the margin of the report dealing with the new minister, he penned the awesome comment: "War."[53] In Bismarck's view, the most likely target of French ambition was Belgium, where a crisis over railroads the year before was just now ending. But there was also (as we shall see below) the question of Spain, and the now very real possibility that France would lay there a rock across Prussia's path. As Lothar Gall has written, "A man such as Bismarck to whom the French scene was particularly familiar—for the last year he had followed it more closely than almost anyone—could be in no doubt about this."[54]

Gramont's difficulties were compounded by another, even more important factor. He was a career diplomat. He had been away from Paris for almost twenty years and was out of touch with opinion at home. It is said that he wrote to a friend for the name of a journal that could reliably reflect the thinking of the government and that could, if the circumstances required, bend itself to his own interests and policies.[55] Nor was this all. Though appointed by Napoleon III, Gramont was on close terms neither with him nor with Ollivier, whom he regarded as an upstart and a romantic. Gramont had no underlying tug of loyalty toward the new ministry and indeed much dislike of it, and he supposed that he would have little difficulty in tripping it up. His impatience soon urged him into a campaign against the government in the press. He was also being pulled hard in this direction by clericalist opponents of the emperor's policies. An unmistakable change came over French policy, and German opinion took alarm. At Hamburg, the French minister, Rothan, an astute judge of events, wrote: "Your accession has produced here a vivid impression that can hardly be expressed."[56] And in Paris the other German diplomats were hard put to improve upon the words of Cavour's old confidant, Nigra: "There is no other way of saying it; the nomination of Gramont is a prelude to war, nothing could be clearer."[57]

34

Ollivier and Gramont would, one must suppose, come to stand as the most popular targets of those bitter caricatures that would appear, in their own country, after the Franco-Prussian War—caricatures of ruthless imperialists and who, together with the generals and military men, led a supposedly innocent France into the dreadful slaughter of war. Is there anything that can be said in their defense? Not according to Henry Salomon, one of the best-informed students on the subject: "It is M. Gramont who is responsible for the innumerable faults [leading up to the outbreak of war], but it is M. Ollivier's political conception that enabled him to commit them."[58]

But that is not altogether correct. The liberal empire—the absence of cabinet government (with parliamentary majorities, ministerial unity, and responsibility independent from the monarch)—was hardly a shortcoming unique to the French system of 1870. Cabinet government had never taken root in France, neither during the restoration nor, as Charles Pouthas once pointed out, even under Louis Philippe, Napoleon III's predecessor.[59] There is a more important consideration. Both Ollivier and Gramont shared to the full the consciousness of national pride and of national identity that was a mark of that period. They believed in the prime importance of France and indeed in her indispensability as a component of European civilization. They considered her armed strength essential to the accomplishment of her historic mission. They were not aware—could not be aware, any more than could millions of their countrymen—of the damages and miseries that could flow from the colliding of the great industrial powers of the modern age. It fell to them, they believed, to arrest the decline into which French prestige had fallen. Had they not occupied the positions they did, others—presumably less qualified, possibly even less responsible—would have done so. Both found their personalities inextricably caught up in the dilemmas of the age. For nearly eighty years France had given the law to Europe in military matters, whereas Prussia, her antagonist, had, only ten years earlier, been the least of the continent's military powers—a sensation that jarred French opinion as had nothing since 1848.

Thus, the disasters that followed the activities of Gramont and of Ollivier cannot exclusively be laid at their feet. Yet the impression remains irresistible that the treatment accorded them both inside their country and without is, when all is said and done, by and large justified. All this was something that would not be brought fully home until the sad and terrible days in the autumn of 1870 when the government of the Second Empire, breaking up in chaos and horror, would fail, and fail so singularly, France and the French nation. Until that time the illusory belief in the power as well as in the persistent and apparently spectacular development of the French army would endure. Never for a moment would it be absent from their minds, nor from the minds of other statesmen, journalists, and patriots of every brand. Without it, the tale that follows—of the ways and stages by which both France and Prussia felt their way toward a fateful military confrontation—would be unintelligible.

2

Napoleon III and the Spanish Revolution of 1868

Spain in the summer of 1868 presented a bleak and melancholy picture. Internal anarchy and decay had cost her most of the power, cohesion, and independence that she once had enjoyed. The intrigues were endless, involving the court, the Cortes (legislature), the army, and the bureaucracy. Queen Isabella II, controlled by cliques and having neither an effective administration nor a sizeable standing army, was helpless to deal with the situation. Interminable ministerial changes, the decline of Spain as a world power, immense changes in management, science and technology, the growth of a republican movement—all of these boded ill for the first Bourbon queen of Spain.[1]

From 1834 on, Spain under Isabella II regressed socially, economically, and culturally compared to the other parts of Europe and increasingly lost the ability to defend her own frontiers and independence. Other states, especially France but also Great Britain, constantly intervened in Spanish affairs, threatening to assemble armies on Spanish soil, to march troops across her borders, and even to conduct military campaigns on Spanish territory. In Cuba, an insurrection against Spanish rule that began in 1868 was threatening to turn into a serious war for independence and was drawing the attention of the European powers, to say nothing of the United States. Affairs went from bad to worse, and the climax was reached in September 1868 when Isabella was overthrown by the leading officers in the Spanish army and fled across the border to France. A provisional government was set up, with Juan Prim (hero of the Mexican War) and Francesco Serrano as the strong men. The question of succession opened.

The revolution of 1868 threw into disarray the relations of Spain and the powers of Europe, doubly so those of Spain and the government of Napoleon III, upon whose goodwill the court of Isabella had counted so heavily. The Spanish question soon became the dominant topic in international relations and in western Europe the theme of passionate domestic controversy as well. There were two reasons for this. First, the question, though the product of struggles for power within the narrow circle of the royal families, their courts, and the small ruling élites, also had an ideological tinge and in time came to engage the sympathies of wider groups on the Iberian peninsula and elsewhere in Europe. Indeed, it would be no exaggeration to say that the revolution of 1868 would have some of the symbolic importance in Spain and in Europe that the Carlist wars had thirty years before and that the Spanish civil war would have a century later. Second, the contest came to be viewed and portrayed as an outgrowth of the fundamental division and clash between the two powers whose paths were to cross in 1870: France and Prussia. On the Prussian side, the revolution of 1868 was welcome news. Bismarck said that the movement in Spain, if it developed the way he hoped it would, "would be an effective poultice in favor of peace." And he added: "God will no doubt bless the love of peace which we demonstrated eighteen months ago [during the Luxembourg crisis] when we were obviously the stronger party, and if nevertheless they attack us, we are, with God's help, still superior to the French. . . . The Russians will hold the Austrians in check."[2] Urgent instructions advised the foreign office that it was in Prussia's interest that the succession question remain open and that a solution to it on terms desired by Napoleon III would not be in Prussia's interest: "Even if it should not last, what is decisive is that the fallen regime was hostile to us, the present one, friendly. . . . The Spanish question should remain a question mark."[3] When the news came of the flight of Isabella, Bismarck, like everyone else, recognized that Napoleon III's government was the most deeply affected. The real international significance of the Spanish revolution and of its course during the next two years was its bearing on France and on the problems (both domestic and international) that assailed her.

Spain bewitched Napoleon III. During the last two years of his reign, France pursued an interventionist policy there in part to avoid the dangers to the Second Empire that grew out of the Spanish revolution but more particularly to strengthen her own position in case of conflict with Prussia. Napoleon III's object was clear, though by no means easy of achievement: to assure in Spain a government that would be so friendly as to render France no anxiety. From September 1868 (when Isabella was turned off her throne) until the outbreak of war with Prussia in July 1870, France worked to twist the situation in Spain to her favor, for three reasons. First, the tension between France and Prussia after Königgrätz made Spain a battleground between the two opponents that ultimately produced the Hohenzollern candidacy. France could not suffer a member of the ruling house of Prussia to take the throne at Madrid; the prestige of the Emperor Napoleon III, indeed of the Second Empire itself, hung in the balance. Second, the French were anxious over their security. The frontier between France and Spain was turbulent, and the cost of defending it would be prohibitive. The French wanted to make sure that in the event of war in the east, they could be safe on their southwestern border and free of any obstacle that could hamstring the movement of their fleet between their Mediterranean and their Atlantic and channel ports. Third, France had become isolated. The clouds of war were lowering on the horizon, the realization growing that a trial of strength was coming on the Rhine. For this reason France dared not overlook any move that might strengthen her position. As relations between France and Prussia darkened and as the "liberal empire" made halting efforts to bolster a regime that sensed ever more keenly its decline and the rising potency of its rivals, it was natural—indeed inevitable—that France should take the lead in trying to turn the Spanish revolution to advantage.[4]

The diplomats of Europe were keen to speculate on the reasons behind Napoleon's reaction to the loss of his ally across the Pyrenees. They soon learned of his covert but unshakable devotion to the cause of the Bourbons, dismal though their prospects often seemed. No sooner had Isabella crossed into France than he was advising her to go back to Madrid to raise an army of royal troops. He continued to do so after she had arrived in Paris, but with an enthusiasm that was soon to wane. Still, it may be taken as symbolic that the personal relations between the Tuileries and the Basilewsky palace (where

39

Isabella took up residence) were most cordial. Isabella visited Eugénie often, and the members of her family more so. Eugénie's own Spanish origins gave her a special interest in that country's affairs, and she was kept informed of changes in the political atmosphere by well-placed friends. More than one observer of the French political scene—Lyons, for instance, most strongly— was unshakably convinced that court-to-court gossip, so abundantly culti- vated in the salons of reigning European royalty, had carried to Eugénie's ears snide remarks about Napoleon by her mother, the Countess Montijo in Madrid, whose lips abounded in such utterances.[5] A perceptive and intelli- gent but not overly scrupulous woman, a compulsive talker and a shameless intriguer, the countess was in the forefront of those who supported Isabella. She favored an aggressive French attempt to restore the fallen queen as soon as possible and believed that Napoleon was not doing all he could to bring this about. All this being the case, she was naturally anxious to insert herself as prominently as possible into the process of Franco-Spanish relations and to establish Isabella in the French eyes as the only architect of a lasting solu- tion to the succession question. In early 1869 she tried to use the troubles in Spain for such a campaign, offering to raise an army to recognize Isabella's claim if Napoleon III would publicly repudiate all other contenders. Her headquarters in Madrid soon became the focal point for collecting informa- tion about Isabella's opponents and a source by which a steady drum fire of pressure was kept up on her behalf.[6]

But Isabella could not go back. Her only support at home was from die- hard partisans—the clergy and the greater part of the nobility—brutal and obstinate men, impatient with opposition and unsuited to a nationalist age.[7] Gradually this became obvious to Napoleon III, and in February 1869 French policy was reversed. Napoleon determined to get rid of Isabella, who had become an intolerable nuisance, and to replace her with a new candi- date—the crown prince Alfonso, the prince of Asturias and Isabella's young son. Here was the perfect solution, one that would suit French strategy as well as her prestige. The French wished to keep the Spaniards dangling at the end of a string that only the French could pull. As Napoleon III put it in a letter to Mercier, the French minister at Madrid: "Alfonso is ideal for us; he is at an age when his personal opinions cannot count and can be brought up with modern views far from flatterers and in a way that is favorable to our cause. His age permits a regency which would probably be held by those men who have pledged most to the revolution. For seven or eight years this regime would resemble a republic, but only in name; its composition could be changed by a vote of the Cortes, and the prince would be a child occupying a post that no ambitious person could pretend to."[8] In Napoleon's vision of the future, Alfonso would be a tame figurehead, his regime firmly under Napoleon's control, strenuously anti-Prussian and ready to accommodate France. As time went on, the monarchy he would head would be securely pro-French, tied to France more than to any other foreign power or foreign cause.

The installation of Alfonso, however, presented the French with one gigantic problem. It could never be accomplished without the support of the count of Reus, Marshall Juan Prim, the man who dominated the destiny of Spain at the moment and whose high emotional pitch and delicate power of maneuvering had been in evidence since the revolution had triumphed. A popular general who had fought in the Mexican War, after his return to Spain in 1846, he had gradually risen to a position of preeminence at Madrid, and it was understandable that he should have done so. Prim was one of the ablest men Spain produced during the nineteenth century—a combination of aristocrat and democrat. His competence was based on extensive experience with Spanish policy in Europe and in America, including not only his service as a military officer in those regions but later responsibility as chief diplomat of the provisional government that was installed at Madrid after the revolution of September 1868. Prim was a modest, quiet, and scrupulously honest (if somewhat emotional) observer. Clear-eyed and perceptive, a skilled diplomat and an able statesman, he had not been opposed to Isabella at the outset of her reign and, indeed, had served as one of her closest advisers. By 1866 the intimacy between Prim and his royal master had been somewhat impaired by the strains of recent years; too often he had seen himself obliged to oppose or to obstruct efforts to thwart reform (particularly with respect to the clergy) that the queen was inclined to indulge. Finally, in 1866, the futility of Spanish politics drove him into opposition, and he determined to expel the Bourbons from Spain. For the next two years he toured Europe, seeking support for the anti-Isabellist cause. The year 1868, marked by the September revolution and by his installation as head of the provisional government, brought important changes to the international life of Europe. Prim would do his best to cope with these changes according to his lights, and the way he did so is a large part of the story that follows.[9]

Napoleon III, on his side, supposed that Prim would be no problem. In February a special agent was dispatched to Madrid with an irresistible offer: France would discard Isabella and back Alfonso to the hilt, and Prim would, if he threw his weight behind this move, be made regent of the kingdom. Prim refused to be drawn.[10] A few days later he revealed his true opinion when he provoked in the Cortes a discussion that left no doubt of the impossibility of any policy aimed at restoring the Bourbons to power as long as he controlled affairs. The offer to Prim had unhappy consequences for France, for she immediately fell under suspicion of blocking Spain's efforts to find a monarch elsewhere than within the exiled ruling family as well as of using her influence to drag out affairs.

Time, however, was not on Prim's side. The situation in Spain continued to deteriorate. The generals and the politicians who made up the provisional government regarded each other with increasing suspicion.[11] The civilian population felt that chaos was drawing nearer to them. In the winter of 1869, backed by the Countess Montijo, the Isabelionos stuffed the hotels in Madrid with sympathetic officers. In April royalist guns damaged the shopping streets in central Madrid. Nor was this the only problem. The Carlists—partisans of Don Carlos, the feckless and pathetically obtuse pretender whose fall in 1832 had triggered armed revolts throughout the country—and other revolutionary elements were making preparations for action, seeking to arouse their compatriots to armed rebellion in various parts of Spain, especially in the Basque provinces in the north. It might be supposed that the French rulers were unhappy about this since that the Carlists had no sympathy whatsoever for Napoleon III—and indeed much contempt for him. On the contrary, the threat of a Carlist civil war had high attractions in French eyes: it would take the pressure off Napoleon III and would pin down the provisional government at home and render it harmless during a European crisis. If all the Great Powers could be kept clear of Spain, the succession question would burn itself out beyond the pale of civilization, as Metternich had hoped would happen with the Greek revolt in the 1820s. Yet

Marshall Juan Prim, minister of war and president of the Council of Spanish Ministers (From Émile Ollivier, *The Franco-Prussian War and Its Hidden Causes*, edited and translated by George Burnham Ives [Boston: Little Brown and Co., 1912], facing p. 14)

Napoleon III continued to walk warily and avoided overplaying his hand—now closing his eyes to activity near the frontier, now intervening to remove insurgents to the center of France or restricting their movements in the country. No effort was made to hide the French origin of the arms that reached the Carlists; on the other hand, a ship in their service would be kept out of French waters or confiscated. Some prominent Carlists were, to be sure, ashamed to take money from imperial France, even on clandestine terms, and wished to rattle the saber of insurrection and civil war. Their objections were drowned out by their opponents. Still, the effect of the whole affair was to strengthen the hands of the French. La Valette, the foreign minister, wrote: "If the provisional government knows what is good for it, it will take care not to abuse our goodwill."[12]

In France Napoleon III's difficulties were made worse by new storms on other horizons. At the end of May 1869 parliamentary elections took place amid a chorus of complaints against the government. The campaign reflected the violence that invaded almost every aspect of political life during the last years of the Second Empire. The press, as soon as it was free from censorship and control, repaid the government for this liberty with unbridled and virulent abuse. The results of the election were irrevocable because they showed that the old system of managing the country was rotten and had collapsed. For example, the rise of the reds, of whom there were now thirty in the Corps léglislatif, could not but bode ill for the future. In July the minister of the interior announced a series of constitutional reforms by which the empire would be liberalized. The rapid implementation of these reforms would have afforded the government its one chance of success; instead Napoleon dawdled, in his fashion.

And there was more. In August 1869 the political situation in France changed yet again. Napoleon fell ill, and rumors about his impending abdication spread. At the same time, the great project of a triple alliance against Prussia—combining France, Italy, and Austria-Hungary—ended in empty talk. The discussion had been going on for some time, but the underlying cause of its failure may be summed up easily enough: the only real benefits would have come to the French. The Austrians wanted the alliance confined to the Near East—an entente that would thwart Russia in Rumania and would stifle pan-Slavism throughout the Balkans. The Italians, for their part, wanted to get French troops out of Rome; they knew that Prussian strength was their best guarantee both against Austria-Hungary and against France. No negotiation was ever more barren or hopeless. Bismarck was correct when he dismissed the talks as "conjectural rubbish" and said of the alliance in 1869: "I don't believe a word of it."[13]

These, then, were the domestic and international factors that drew the line in front of which French policy moved. On the one hand, Napoleon made use of the Carlists to add to the perils of the Spanish government; on the other, he continued to push the Alfonsist cause, whatever doubts his ministers might have had about its long-term prospects. It did not take the Carlists to make the French unpopular. The Alfonsinsos could do that by themselves. The Alfonsist press had too obvious a French bias and placed too many hopes on Napoleon III. On top of this, there was wrangling among the Alfonsinsos themselves, the top elements directing affairs in isolation and constantly sniping at their colleagues. Popular feeling against them grew stronger. Discipline crumbled in their ranks. Against the advice of those who knew better, they courted the politicians and ignored the military, without whom there was no hope of success. Mercier noted: "In such circumstances there is little I can do but temporize, watch the flow of speculation and rumor, and speak up whenever I see dangers to our interests."[14]

Meanwhile relations between Isabella and the French government ran downhill. Napoleon III's advisers had always regarded her as an expensive luxury, if not an outright embarrassment, and their attitude only hardened as the months passed. Isabella, on her side, continued to depend upon Empress Eugénie for encouragement and support—a dependence that all of the French ministers disliked and that most of them knew to be unreliable. There was no throne for her to win back in Spain, no support for her of any substance. Isabella could stomach everything that Napoleon III wanted except her own disappearance, and to guard against such a prospect she intrigued tirelessly. Isabella still had hopes of coming to an agreement with the provisional government; as late as September 1869 she even supposed that she could curry the favor of Prim through the duke of Seville, "the republican member" of the royal family.[15] To no avail. Nothing was pulled out of Prim except an expression of support for her abdication and some admonitions about her conduct if she ever returned home. Abdication papers were drawn up on 3 October, but Isabella rejected them out of hand. So the matter was to rest until June of 1870. The only result of the commotion was to destroy the unity of the groups around the queen, to persuade some of her supporters to join the ranks of the Carlists, and to plunge Napoleon III ever deeper into confusion.

In the winter of 1869 Napoleon III had other, more ominous things to worry about. This was the moment when another candidate might become king of Spain, one infinitely more displeasing to him than either Isabella or Don Carlos. Antoine d'Orléans, duke of Montpensier, was the youngest son of Louis Philippe, king of France from 1830 to 1848, and the husband of Isabella's sister, Luisa Fernanda. He had sunk into political obscurity after his father's dethronement in 1848 and, until the eve of the 1868 revolution, he had busied himself with increasing the large fortune left to his wife by Isabella's predecessor, Ferdinand VII, and with managing her estates in Andalusia. Over the years Luisa Fernanda and Isabella fell out, and Montpensier and his wife began to plot against the queen. In the spring of 1868 Montpensier stepped out of the shadows and offered himself as Isabella's successor. But a rock was soon placed squarely across Montpensier's path: Prim had made the revolution against a Bourbon queen, and he firmly refused to accept in her place a prince from the junior branch of that line—and one who had a Bourbon wife besides. The result was not without paradox: a fateful schism in the monarchist majority for the duration of the revolution.

Montpensier's supporters had long been conscious of the opposition of Napoleon III. It had been a matter of common knowledge before the overthrow of Isabella and was a prime factor in Prim's success in frustrating their ambitions. Napoleon III had solid reasons for opposing Montpensier. He had much to fear from the Orléanists in France, by whose attacks he was constantly being harassed. He had made that plain as early as 1867 when O'Donnell, then Spanish prime minister, visited Paris and broached the idea of replacing Isabella with her sister. In January 1868 one of Montpensier's partisans, emboldened by the duke's assurance that he had in France means of overcoming resistance there, went so far as to sound out the empress. He did not like what he heard. Eugénie promised that "France will oppose Montpensier with every man and musket in her possession."[16] She went further in her hostility. She released scandal against Montpensier in the foreign press. A story appeared in the Belgian papers to the effect that Montpensier's candidacy was being underwritten by Prussian money in return for Spanish neutrality in a war between France and Prussia. Metternich reported: "The empress has asked if she can count on the help of Austria to put down the schemes of Montpensier which she lays squarely at Bismarck's door."[17] Eugénie's maneuver attempted to discredit Montpensier both in Spanish circles and abroad. It flattered Isabella and at the same time laid bare the full importance of Spain in the relations of Paris and Berlin—a point not lost on Bismarck in 1870.

The hostility to Montpensier cut even deeper with the French ministers. Moustier, the foreign minister, was more against him than were Napoleon III and Eugénie. A month after the formation of the provisional government in Madrid, Moustier instructed Mercier to keep up a running stream of attacks on Montpensier from the intimate confines of the capital.[18] Mercier—the man on the spot—hesitated, pointing to the difficulties of avoiding discovery and expostulating that in view of the opposition to Montpensier in Spain already, there was no point in exposing France to fresh abuse. He spoke truly; several papers had already begun to stir up feeling against Napoleon III, some saying that he favored Alfonso; others, the empress, Isabella.[19] Mercier's objections found favor at home. For the moment Napoleon was content to be a passive spectator while the Bourbons consolidated their support behind the scenes with secret French help. Moustier's campaign was called off.

The French rulers soon found comfort from other, unexpected sources. The papacy had regretted the overthrow of Isabella and after the revolution continued to recognize her as the rightful sovereign. It had serious plans for Spain; it wished to prevent further revolutions and to show both Spain and Europe that it had a voice in the succession question. Unlike the devout Isabella, Montpensier was a liberal Catholic, and as such an impossible choice as successor. On 29 January 1869 Cardinal Antonelli, the papal secretary of state, announced: "The choice of Montpensier is one of those that would be looked upon with great displeasure by the Holy See."[20]

The British were even more resolute. They remembered the kind of cold war that they had had with France in the 1840s over the question of the Spanish marriages. They did not want any extension of Orléanist influence in southwestern Europe, doubly so because they feared that the Second Empire was teetering toward collapse. They were also absorbed by their fear of an Orléanist restoration in France and by the prospect of the union of the French and Spanish crowns in the same family—a contingency that had caused a panic in 1846. For these reasons Clarendon, the British foreign secretary, ordered Sir Henry Layard, his ambassador to Spain, to keep in step with his French colleague: "Avoid saying or doing anything that would create the impression that French interests on the question of succession are not our own."[21] Layard therefore duly supported the French in their opposition to Montpensier with an impressive, though quiet, display of words, and the friendship that he enjoyed with Mercier added to the effectiveness of their collaboration. This was a display of Anglo-French solidarity—a mocking echo of the days of victory in the Crimean War a decade earlier.

Throughout 1869 the feeling against Montpensier built up to a white heat. His resources, his popular backing gradually gave out. Mercier had been peremptorily instructed to leave the country the minute Montpensier was elected. French diplomats gave out that the fabric of Spanish society could not withstand an Orléanist at Madrid. In the summer of 1869 pamphlets from Paris denouncing Montpensier flooded the capital and the provinces, and Prim, resolute as ever, vigorously underwrote the French campaign. By the autumn of 1869 the die was cast. Even Montpensier's most insistent supporters convinced themselves that the opposition from Paris was too much. Near the end of January 1870 Montpensier was defeated for a seat in the Cortes in a by-election in Asturias. In March 1870 he caused scandal by killing his cousin, the duke of Seville, in a duel. On 7 June the Cortes carried a series of measures that made it impossible for him to go on. Montpensier thereupon yielded—as much to reality as to force. The French could thus breathe more easily. Against Montpensier they had, in Mercier's words, "done all that is possible to the point where we risked compromising our integrity and shirking our responsibility."[22]

Montpensier was not the only candidate to topple because of French opposition. Shortly after the September revolution feelers were put out to win for the throne of Spain the colorful Fernando, former king of Portugal and father of the present one, Luis. Prim, in particular, was keen on him. For one thing, there was nothing in Fernando's record that would estrange the goodwill of France; Iberian union accorded perfectly with Napoleon III's championing of nationalities, as the experiences of 1858 in Rumania and of 1859 in Italy had shown. Triumphs there had provided the French with a running stock of mounting prestige. Fernando himself was fifty-two years old, in good health, Catholic by birth and liberal by conviction, with long political experience and great interest in the arts and sciences—to say nothing of the Spanish language that he spoke like a Castillian.

But Fernando had heavy baggage too—so heavy, in fact, that the idea that he would ever be an acceptable candidate to the French was, to all intents and purposes, a wholly impractical and even fatuous one. There were four reasons for this. First, his candidacy bloomed just at the time when French affections for a Bourbon restoration were in full flower. Second there was a dynastic problem: if Fernando were to die, the throne of Spain would go either to Luis or to Antonia, Fernando's daughter. The Portuguese government would never allow Luis to combine the crowns of Spain and Portugal— Iberian unity was anathema to them. A female succession, however, would land in Madrid a woman whose husband was equally anathema to Paris— none other than the Prussian Prince Leopold of Hohenzollern-Sigmaringen.[23]

Third, Fernando's family connections outside Germany lay in Belgium, whose independence the French had just threatened by their plan to acquire its railways. The danger never matured into action, but it left its mark all the same. Napoleon III appreciated that the prevailing cry against French aggressiveness, reinforced as it was at this moment by alarms from Great Britain, was not likely to make Fernando a friend of France. Spain under Fernando could not be counted on for support in a war between France and Prussia, whereas Bourbon support was unlikely ever to slacken. The Second Empire was drifting into increasing difficulties at home, and the favor of

Candidates for the throne of Spain (*clockwise from left:* Leopold of Hohenzollern-
Sigmaringen; the duke of Montpensier; Fernando of Portugal; Prince Alfonso, Queen Isabella's
son) (From R. Olivar Bertrand, *El Caballero Prim,* 2 vols. [Barcelona: Luis Miracle, 1952],
2:near p. 225; used by permission of the Institut amatller d'art hispanic, Barcelona)

clericalist opinion in France was more important for Napoleon III than ever before. Napoleon III had no doubt where the Bourbons stood on the Roman question; here Fernando was, in the words of a French politician, "a question mark."[24]

Add to these a fourth, personal factor. Fernando himself was a slippery character, a man of high intelligence but without fighting spirit; fitted to be a politician rather than a king, he was determined that the politicians should not shift the decision from their shoulders to his. No sooner had he been approached than he made it a condition of acceptance that the Portuguese line be barred from succession in Spain—a device for saving the crown of Portugal for Luis. The French at once made a great cry and threatened to open up "an aggressive campaign" against Fernando's candidacy if it ever got off the ground—this despite the fact that it offered security against Montpensier, whose accession was (after that of a Prussian prince) the prospect that the French feared most.[25]

Still, Napoleon was aware from the reports that he received from his agents in Madrid that important groups of leaders and a considerable element of the Spanish population would not rest easily until Fernando was made their king. Indeed, if anything, they seemed to be more vocal and more numerous than were the supporters of Montpensier. The stirrings were everywhere. For example, a number of pamphlets pointed out how outlying dependencies (India, the island of Sardinia, Malta, and especially Ireland) were faring badly in the world, and then tried to contrast this with the benefits that they thought Scotland had secured from a union with Great Britain—an implied parallel to the potential Portuguese union with Spain.[26] Spanish diplomats, too, were active on Fernando's behalf. Early in January 1869 Fernandez de los Rios, a sharp-eyed and perceptive observer, made a secret trip to Lisbon to secure Fernando's assent. Napoleon did his best to wreck the mission. His attitude had been revealed already in a conversation that he had had at the end of 1868 with D'Avila, the Portuguese minister in Paris and Fernando's close partisan: "I can think of nothing worse for our relations."[27] Montholon, French minister at Lisbon, went further and frightened Fernando with the perils he said were certain to arise the minute he entered a country where all authority had broken down and where his very life would be in instant jeopardy. These strokes succeeded. Mercier reported: "The Portuguese minister has told me quite explicitly that encouragement from France was the absolute precondition of Fernando's approval, but that such encouragement is nowhere to be found."[28]

Just at this moment, however, French foreign policy received a sharp change. For reasons that remain obscure, Napoleon III seems to have permitted Olózaga, the Spanish minister at Paris and a stout champion of Fernando, to believe that he would not look with disfavor upon a Portuguese king at Madrid. In the middle of February 1869 Napoleon talked with the duque de Saldanha (whose pro-French attitude was well known) and gave an unsolicited, though tepid, endorsement to Luis, king of Portugal, for the Spanish crown—a means, he said, of averting the danger of a republic in both countries. Saldanha took the message to Lisbon on 25 February. On 4 March Napoleon swung round again, letting Olózaga know that Fernando, not Luis, had been his favorite candidate all along. Olózaga lit up: "An excellent idea. I shall go to Madrid at once and arrange for Fernando's selection."[29] This was the very moment when Montholon was busy spreading rumors that in the event of Fernando's accession, Spain would become another Piedmont—a pawn in a struggle between foreign powers—or else another Lombardy, ruled by a foreign prince and foreign army. In such circumstances merely becoming the king of Spain offered little prospect of remaining it for long. The sudden spread of such threats came as an unwelcome intrusion at a time when matters were already confused enough. It became difficult for Prim to get Fernando until it was known what the French attitude really was, and in March 1869 the French government did not know itself.

Olózaga returned to Paris. He did not yet despair. He was in constant touch with the more resolute groups in Madrid—including some members of the provisional government—and he still believed that Napoleon III could be swung unequivocally behind Fernando if his supporters in Spain pressed hard enough. Tessara, newly appointed ambassador to England, came racing up to Paris and tried to carry the day; there was a stormy meeting between him and Napoleon III, Tessara denouncing French hypocrisy as shown in the Carlist intrigues, Napoleon III reiterating his high principles. Tessara came home bitterly anti-French, as he remained ever after. The provisional government at Madrid was less dismayed. It still hoped to settle the problem between Napoleon III and Fernando, and it was confident that he would not put up a substantial resistance. Olózaga, too, was undaunted. He persisted in laying all Fernando's troubles at the doorstep of Montpensier and refused, against all evidence, to take into account Napoleon III's duplicity. He said to Ollivier: "It is the diabolical agents at Madrid whose attitude had determined the views of the emperor. But I am sure I can overcome these."[30]

He underrated another factor. Just at this moment, March 1869, French intelligence first picked up the scent of a Hohenzollern candidacy. No one then foresaw the deadly tangle over this issue that would absorb the diplomats of Europe a year later, but there were warnings. In February 1869 Edouard Count Vincent Benedetti, minister to Prussia, reported that certain representatives of the provisional government had put out feelers and had gone so far as to raise the question how Paris would react to a Hohenzollern at Madrid. His superiors responded as if someone had trodden on a sore corn. Napoleon III said: "If the candidacy of Montpensier is directed against my dynasty and can be handled, that of a Hohenzollern prince will be a dagger at the heart of the French nation."[31] The French press was aghast at the prospect and let out a huge discharge of hostile ink. Mercier was called back from Madrid to discuss it, as was Benedetti from Berlin. Back in Berlin, Benedetti expostulated; Thile, the secretary of state, denied his accusations with every display of offended honor, and the affair died away.

Still, this bare-bones account of the incident fails to indicate its real significance for Franco-Prussian relations and for the crisis of July 1870 in particular. First, Samuel Johnson's dictum about women preaching and elephants dancing applies here. Whether this attempt by the Spanish government to secure a Prussian prince for its throne—the first really official, organized, and concerted effort to do so since September 1868, and the first one to bring into contact on the subject duly accredited figures of the French and Prussian governments—was done well is less important than that it was done at all. It was the first time that the provisional government had taken soundings from Prussia at so high a level, and the latter's officials, from Bismarck on down, could not fail to take notice. Moreover, the consequences of the offer for Fernando's candidacy were immediate. Earlier that month the constitutional commission in Madrid had voted to restore the female succession to the throne. The connection between Fernando and Leopold was too obvious to overlook—a factor that explains Napoleon's objections to Fernando at the time and the latter's formal refusal, in May 1869, of Prim's offer. For two months the question slept.

In September it burst to life once more. Saldanha, now Portuguese minister at Paris, pushed on by Prim, again tried Napoleon. This time the situation was more favorable. Spain was sliding into collapse. Anti-French sentiment was building. Alfonso's chances of becoming king were fading by the day. The only safe course for the French was to temporize while trying to stave off a crisis that might push the Spaniards into some precipitous decision. As well, hostility toward France might be turned against someone else if it could be shown that Napoleon had not closed his mind to Fernando's chances. The risk was not, in any case, serious; the likelihood that Fernando would reverse himself was slim. Napoleon knew that and knew other things as well. For instance, the fact that the suggestion had passed through Saldanha's lips was sure to tell against it; Saldanha was anathema to the Portuguese government even more than to its king. Under the circumstances a sympathetic attitude toward Fernando could do no harm to France. This was the line that Napoleon III took when he saw Prim at St. Cloud on 14 September 1869.

It was an auspicious occasion—the first interview that the two men had had in more than a year. Napoleon III did most of the talking. He began with a general disquisition on the state of affairs in Spain; he left no doubt that he was not without sympathy for the difficulties in which the provisional government found itself. Prim was moved. He flattered himself that Napoleon III was now cured, by the opposition to them in Spain, of any Alfonsist longings, and he took the occasion to express his regret over the failure of his government to persuade Fernando—a ticklish subject because it had been the French who had done more than anyone else to wreck Fernando's prospects. Prim had hardly been unaware of all this. More generally, he had grown sick of French vetoes and had come to view Napoleon as an obstructionist. Still, he shrank from a break. He had been determined ever since taking power to promote Iberian unity by bringing Spain and Portugal under the rule of a single crown, and he could not afford to estrange Napoleon by pressing him too hard now. On his side, Napoleon III still feared war on the Rhine; this was the consideration that made him hesitate. The meeting became animated, free-wheeling. Discussion hopped from one question to another. The whole problem of the interregnum was gone over in painstaking detail, but no names for the throne were mentioned. Napoleon III came away from the meeting believing that French interests could best be achieved by a pose of friendliness, however formal, toward the provisional regime while he—and the French agents throughout Europe—took whatever steps were needed to avoid the selection of any monarch of whom they disapproved.[32]

The provisional government can be forgiven for continuing to emphasize the rewards that Spain would gain by following a policy that brought Fernando to the throne. Its real problem lay elsewhere: in its failure to carry the French sufficiently to shake Fernando's own resistance. Speeches by members of the Cortes carried little weight; Fernando had heard similar remarks over the months and knew what they amounted to. Nor was he encouraged by the prolonged negotiations with France and by the disappointment that these had brought. He underestimated Prim's resourcefulness. A Portuguese king still seemed to Prim a rallying point for patriotic and national opinion. He was mindful of the situation in France and not unsympathetic to Fernando's feelings, but he determined not to stand still and to let events slip through his fingers.

In the spring of 1870 Prim tried yet a third time. He instructed Olózaga to ask Napoleon for assurances that the French government would not frown on Fernando's selection. Napoleon acquiesced, though not, it is said, without some grumbling.[33] On 19 May Napoleon III wrote to Fernando, offering a half-hearted endorsement of his candidacy—the same day that Saldanha, now returned to politics at home, overthrew the ministry and took over the premiership. Here was another favorable sign. Saldanha was a staunch champion of Fernando's candidacy, and it was only to be expected that he would throw his weight behind it.

But Saldanha had feet of clay. His support of the candidacy was no asset in itself, and in any case influential Portuguese had convinced themselves that Napoleon III was an incorrigible liar who could not be trusted, a conclusion that was sustained by the tone of Napoleon's letter, decked out as it was with high sounding declarations but—much more important—also with temporizing and equivocating words. For example, Napoleon III announced that he would look with pleasure upon the willingness of Fernando "to assume the heavy burden of the Spanish crown."[34] The words themselves were window dressing—a throwback to those he used when endorsing King Luis in February 1869—and those who could read them in Portugal had no difficulty in knowing how much heavier the Spanish crown would weigh if French desires in Spain went unfulfilled. Prim, on his side, had no difficulty grasping this; still, he wished to remain on good terms with France. He thrashed around for some means of satisfying imperial prestige without injuring Spanish interests. Like Napoleon, he was playing for time and was using every means possible to ward off attacks from his opponents.

Napoleon III also needed time, for three reasons. First, the negotiations for a triple alliance (mentioned above) had reached deadlock. Second, the political situation in Spain had darkened; though he felt his own position at home strengthened by the plebiscite of 8 May 1870, the progress of his protégé Alfonso was no better, indeed worse, than before. Finally, intelligence from Madrid continued to be bad—very bad. Mercier's reports ran over with rumors of a Hohenzollern candidacy. For these reasons, Napoleon swallowed hard and prepared to accept Fernando as a *pis aller.*

He was too late. Fernando turned down the throne on 15 May, four days before the arrival of Napoleon III's letter. Both Prim and Napoleon were done in by their own words. Though both looked with favor on Fernando, they were now casting their nets in opposite directions—Napoleon still with Alfonso, Prim now with Leopold of Hohenzollern-Sigmaringen. That Napoleon III should have gone so far to gratify Prim at the same time the latter was preparing to run the candidate whom Napoleon most fiercely opposed is not without a touch of irony. In any case, French hopes that soft words might allay Fernando's suspicions, buy time for Alfonso, improve his position in Spain, and speed up a resolution of the question of succession—all of these ran into the sand. Prim, growing impatient with the situation and believing correctly that Napoleon III was too wedded to Alfonso to back anyone else, gave Mercier a veiled warning in June 1870 that Spanish patience had passed the point of no return. The French were soon to see exactly what he meant.

One final attempt was undertaken by the provisional government to find a prince—this time a prince from Italy—for the Spanish throne, the only attempt that was not hamstrung by the opposition of the French rulers. The attempt was to lead to many misunderstandings between France and Italy over the nature and the extent of each other's obligations in the days leading up to the Franco-Prussian War. The historian who feels the need to touch lightly and incidentally on the origins, the course, and the immediate consequences of this attempt faces a forbidding task, for the complexities of the unstable and constantly changing diplomatic environment in which all of this proceeded defy easy generalization. It took the late Federico Chabod more than two hundred pages and a number of documentary appendices to summarize, in a work of outstanding scholarly and literary quality, the main points of this story.[35] But since there are few readers who will have, at a distance of 120 years, much of this background in mind, the following is offered—with due apologies for its inevitable inadequacy—as a reminder of the major outlines of what occurred.

In the years immediately preceding the revolution of September 1868, relations between Italy and Spain were sour. Spain under Isabella was an undisguised champion of the pope and of the Neapolitan Bourbons. Spain had recognized the kingdom of Italy only in 1865; the Spanish Bourbons disliked and distrusted the house of Savoy, an excommunicate from the Church and an ardent supporter of Italian liberalism, and had only the liveliest contempt for a family that had overthrown the legitimate rulers of Parma, Tuscany, and Naples. On the other side, Italian pride was estranged over the disdain with which the Spanish regarded their Latin cousins, whom they considered beneath them both culturally and politically. One of the few elements of harmony between two countries existed among the republicans. In this instance even the harassed government at Florence could feel little repugnance, and much malicious gratification, over the subversive aid given by Italian radicals to a movement directed at overthrowing a crown so constantly at odds with its own.[36]

Isabella's opponents took full advantage of the opportunities to turn Italy from Spain. Prim had found time to make a trip to Florence in the summer of 1867. He appeared as the aggrieved party, unfolding his complaints against the government and offering concessions to Italian nationalism in

exchange for a repudiation of the Bourbon extremists. His mission succeeded. King Victor Emmanuel always believed that his house could provide
a successor to the throne that Prim hoped to make vacant. It was Prim, however, who laid down the terms for future cooperation. Italy was to look with
sympathy on the overthrow of Isabella; she was to look with sympathy on the
government that would take her place. To these proposals the Italians did
not object, and for good reason. The Roman question had just exploded. On
3 November 1867 the French had checked Garibaldi's advance at Mentana
and had gone on record in the Corps législatif that Rome was the pope's
forever; Italy could never have it. If the throne of Napoleon's ally were over-
turned, it would mean for Italian nationalism the removal on the road to the
Eternal City of one principal disputant.

News of Isabella's flight to Biarritz in the wake of the September revolution found the Italian government ripe for a forward policy. Almost immediately Victor Emmanuel put out feelers for Amadeus, his second son, the duke
of Aosta, and a favorite of the royal circle in Florence. He turned to Napoleon III for support. Napoleon refused it. Paris was at this time in no mood
to tolerate any candidate who might pose a threat to the return of the Bourbons. The French press wrote the candidacy down as "a Prussian maneuver,"[37] and it quickly died away. In the summer of 1869 it came to life again.
Political difficulties in Spain and the rising frustration over filling the vacant
throne combined to launch Prim and his colleagues on an effort to find in
Italy a king for Spain. This time, however, the candidate was no longer Amadeus but Victor Emmanuel's nephew, Thomas, the duke of Genoa. Negotiations dragged out tiresomely. Prim was not yet sure of the French attitude—
indeed, he did not raise the topic with Napoleon at his September 1869
meeting—but he had confirmed through his agents in France that the candidacy would not be disliked at Paris. At the end of September, he instructed
his minister at Florence to raise the question with Victor Emmanuel.

Just at this time, it will be recalled, Prim had used Saldanha to repeat to
Fernando the offer of the Spanish crown, after having induced Napoleon to
support it. Just at this time, too, Prim had permitted his agents in Germany
to take soundings from the Hohenzollerns. Prim's conduct can be explained
only by his determination to keep more than one iron in the fire. The Genoa
candidacy was a makeshift expedient without staying power—an idea hit on

by Prim without enthusiasm and with not inconsiderable qualms on his part about its reception by Spanish opinion. Napoleon III shared Prim's attitude, but his calculation was different. Whereas at first he shrank from endorsing the candidacy of Amadeus out of his belief that it would add too much influence to Italy, it now seemed opportune to give an endorsement to the duke of Genoa because there was not much influence to take away. The question thrust itself forward against the needs of high policy. At the time the negotiations for the triple alliance were hanging fire. On 24 September 1869 Victor Emmanuel, Francis Joseph, and Napoleon had, by a personal exchange of letters, taken the step that Napoleon hoped might lead to an alliance. In such circumstances, anyone could see that friendship between Victor Emmanuel and Napoleon III would be of value to France. To remove any doubt about his cooperation, Napoleon, in early November 1869, answered a question from Madrid: "The emperor is prepared to recognize a legally elected sovereign and considers himself sympathetic to the candidacy of the duke of Genoa."[38]

There was one great flaw in this calculation: it rested purely on monarchial solidarity; it was hamstrung by the opposition of the Italian government. The Italian cabinet was overwhelmed by pressures against a rapprochement of any kind with France. Lanza, who became prime minister in November 1869, was an abler man than his predecessor, and Sella, the minister of finance, was abler still. Sella was the strong man in the Lanza cabinet; basically liberal in outlook, he knew something of the situation in Spain and was not bemused by Prim's offer, still less by Victor Emmanuel's hope to prop up his shaky throne against republican agitation by doing deals behind the backs of his responsible ministers. In Sella's view, the practical need was to get French troops out of Rome; only then would gains pour into Italy's lap. Sella was firmly convinced that there existed in France a well-considered plan to tie Italy to Napoleon's apron strings and to drag her into a war against Prussia that could only be executed at Italy's expense; if this calculation were right, the acquisition of Rome would be pushed further and further away.

Sella knew that he held a strong hand, and together with Lanza he persuaded the king to give up his attempt. This was no mean achievement, for Victor Emmanuel was deeply attracted to his nephew's candidacy, which (according to the British ambassador, Paget) "oddly enough he appears to consider complimentary to his family." Moreover, it was a fact that the king "doesn't like Lanza and can't bear Sella who, when he was last minister, showed a certain determination to curtail the royal expenditure and to reform the royal morals"; all the same, Paget was impressed by the common sense and constitutional propriety that the king showed in the end.[39] For the time being, Victor Emmanuel's interest in the Spanish throne waned. On one important point, however, Victor Emmanuel scored a private victory, and this no doubt explains why he was prepared to accept Lanza's and Sella's wishes: he did not tell the new ministers the most important fact of all, namely, that he had made a conditional pledge to fight alongside France and Austria against Prussia. He believed that when the time came they would have no choice but to accept the fact that he had committed the country to war, Spanish throne or no.

This suited Napoleon III. He determined to keep up good relations with Victor Emmanuel in the hope that a change of ministry might force the Italians to adjust their attitude. His position on the Genoa candidacy was another matter. It is difficult to believe that his heart was ever in the idea. For one thing, there was a danger in having at Madrid a Savoyard king should the Roman question raise its head. France would then have to choose between the twin evils of backing down completely on the protection of the papacy or of countering the impatient forces of Italian nationalism. A Savoyard prince would bring none of the advantages that would accrue to French policy with the installation of a Bourbon—it was better only than a republic. There was little chance that a Savoyard could restore order; he would be faced by the hostility of the Spanish people. Yet these reasons, far from deterring Napoleon III, instead drove him on. It was good policy for him to let the candidacy go unopposed in the safe and sure hope that it would never come off—a calculation that was immediately proved correct. In January 1870 the candidacy was, with great fanfare and solemnity, announced to the chancelleries of Europe. Thereupon it died. What proved decisive was not the opposition of the Italian government—that had been known all along— but that of the duke's mother, to say nothing of the Italian press. This time France escaped blame. At the last minute the French minister in Florence put in a kind word on the duke's behalf. At no time did Napoleon III issue a veto, as he had with every other candidacy.

By now, however, an ominous note was again intruding into what had become merely academic discussions. On 17 May Mercier reported: "I have been assured that Prim very secretly had some *demarchés* made to the house of Hohenzollern in order to obtain the consent of a prince of the Sigmaringen branch to enter the lists, but here he seems to have encountered difficulties. Thus a foreign prince is, at least for the moment, completely out of the question."[40] There remained, however, a growing uneasiness. The rumors about Leopold refused to go away. During June Mercier was besieged by orders from Paris to find out all there was to the story. Mercier continued to profess optimism, writing on 24 June: "Though I think Bismarck quite capable of snaring a Hohenzollern on the throne of Spain, I really cannot understand why he would risk such an adventure where, after all, he has so much to lose and so little to gain." He went on: "I foresee a Hohenzollern will have trouble implanting himself in Spain, but one must be on one's guard. Later we shall be able to think of the candidacy of Alfonso." No sooner had the crisis over Leopold's candidacy broke than the French began to plead with Fernando—whose prospects had been wrecked by France a year earlier—to take up the running once again in order to pull Leopold's fangs. In the word of the hapless Mercier: "You can save Europe from a war and Spain from herself."[41] By this time it was too late; Fernando rejected the offer out of hand. The damage had been done.

An ordinary politician might be baffled by the incongruousness and irreconcilability of Napoleon III's multiple policies. Not so Napoleon himself. But it was precisely these inconsistencies that make it hard for the historian to follow his tracks. From the private correspondence of his closest ministers, however, one does derive the impression that if he had one principled aim throughout the Spanish throne problem, it was not so much to settle it once and for all on terms beneficial to France as to stop the progress of any candidate not tied to France completely, in the hope that this would clear the way for the candidate he wanted most, Alfonso. His difficulty in pursuing this particular aim was simply that he always had to keep up appearances of a quite different sort. The members of the provisional government had to be reassured that France had no desire to dictate to Spain her choice of monarchs, while the members of the imperial government had to think the reverse; politicians at Madrid had to be persuaded that Napoleon III was not averse to a Portuguese candidate at the same time that those in Lisbon had to believe that the Spanish crown was too heavy a responsibility to bear; Prim had to be lured by the vision that France wanted good relations at the same time as he and the rest of his countrymen had to be made to fear that a Carlist insurrection, encouraged by France, would lead to a civil war that would tear down everything they had been trying to build up; the Italians had to be convinced that Napoleon III was a good friend, clericalist opinion inside France that he was no such thing. It was indeed a sign of Napoleon III's skill and dexterity that he contrived to keep up these more or less contradictory appearances by artful deceit at the same time as he gradually edged himself into a position where he could once more command and be obeyed. Even if people had now learned to distrust and to disbelieve his motives, they were still likely to be confused and confounded by a smoke screen on this scale, and behind such a screen he could arrange his policies and adjust his positions until his opponents fell down from exhaustion. This was, as we shall see, a drama of which there would be a repeat performance in July 1870.

3

Bismarck and the Hohenzollern Candidacy

On 12 March 1870 the Prussian crown princess—as unfortunate a political bungler as her son, the later William II—wrote a letter to her mother, Queen Victoria of England, on the subject that was uppermost in her mind: the possibility that Prince Leopold of Hohenzollern-Sigmaringen was about to be elected to the vacant throne of Spain. Under no circumstances did the Prussian government want the rulers of France to know about it, she said in this *"most profoundly secret"* letter, "but the King, Prince Hohenzollern, Leopold, and Fritz [the Prussian crown prince] wish to know *your opinion* in private."[1] As it was so great a secret, the crown princess asked her mother to bring up the subject orally with Lord Clarendon, and then only in the strictest confidence. Clarendon advised the queen to withhold her opinion on so delicate a matter; he had little doubt that the proposed arrangement would produce an unfavorable impression in France.

The crown princess had touched on the subject that would dominate the counsels of the Hohenzollern family in the first half of 1870. In these counsels, Bismarck, with much anguished effort and great strain on his nerves and health, pressed strongly for the candidacy of Leopold, urged its acceptance upon King William, and in effect lit the fuse of the time bomb that was, after many vicissitudes, to lead to the Franco-Prussian War. Up to the point at which this narrative has now arrived, the incentives as well as the impediments to Leopold's candidacy had lain overwhelmingly (though not exclusively) in the familial-dynastic field, but by the beginning of 1870 political considerations—specifically, Bismarck's attitude toward the candidacy and the whole subject of Franco-Prussian relations in general—became a fundamental factor, vitally affecting virtually all persons involved. The big question, which no document has been able to answer, is this: Why, in the end, did Bismarck go to war with France at all? For the more we look at the background of the conflict, the more we wonder, as does Norman Rich, why Prussia at least did not do everything in her power to avoid it.[2]

No sensitive observer in 1870, surveying from a distance of four years all that had transpired in Europe since the battle of Königgrätz, could have failed to have been impressed not only by the inordinate increase in the power of Prussia but also by the extensive decline in the rival powers that confronted her across her eastern and western frontiers. Not only had Austria been thrown out of Germany, the states of south Germany—allies of Austria in the struggle just ended—tied themselves to Prussia by treaties of alliance through which, among other things, they agreed to place their armies under Prussian command in time of war. The international situation had been unsettled as long as Prussia and Austria had been at each other's throats in central Europe; now the tide seemed to have turned decisively in favor of Prussia. So many of the obstacles on the road to national unification had been pushed out of the way that a trial of strength on the Rhine seemed utterly unnecessary to accomplish this ambition.

There is, of course, something to be said on the other side. A strong current of opposition still ran throughout Germany against the extension of Prussian influence south of the Main. Particularists, ultramontanes, and princes anxious to resist further infringements of their own sovereignty were still licking their wounds over the defeat that they had experienced in 1866 and had deep-seated and powerful grievances against the Prussian rulers. It was not to be expected, in an atmosphere buzzing with rumors of a possible Prussian sweep south of the river Main and with crises brewing up with France further west, that their duties and interests could long remain detached from the political excitements of the moment. It was indeed not long before these excitements began to demand Bismarck's attention. Elections to the German customs union in 1868 returned an ominously high number of antinationalist members, and the Bavarian elections of 1869 only underlined further the strength of the particularist tradition. Everywhere beyond Germany's borders, but especially in the states south of the Main, the medley of complaints on the part of Berlin's enemies was fast swelling into a uniform chorus—against its military system, against its system of conscription, against its system of taxation by means of which all of this was established and maintained. So strong was the opposition to Prussia in south Germany that some historians believe that Bismarck's entire policy between 1868 and 1870 can be understood only in terms of the stagnation of the national movement. According to this view, Bismarck launched a war against France to quicken the pace of the national movement and to forge a new German empire in the heat of the fulminations that war against an age-old antagonist would provoke.[3]

The thesis is persuasive, and it may indeed have been uppermost in Bismarck's calculations. Yet between 1868 and 1870 he had, times without number, expressed his satisfaction over the national question and the speed by which it was progressing. On more than one occasion he had had to rein the impulses of the German nationalists who regretted the failure of Prussia to throw her net over south Germany and who now called upon her to take up arms against France. Bismarck's answers to these complaints are famous, not least for their many political reactions, often expressed in biting aphorisms and witticisms—appealing to some readers, infuriating to others, but always striking and provocative. Consider as one example a letter of 24 February 1869 to Werthern, his minister at Munich, answering some of his southern supporters and military leaders in the north who had become critical of his policy and who were expressing the view that the cause of unity would be lost unless there was an abrupt reversal of policy. The letter has come down in history as one of his greatest political-literary efforts and acts of statesmanship. Space does not permit a complete summary of it, which is a pity, because his entire outlook and policy in that agitated winter were reflected in it. Concise, pithy, beautifully organized, an invaluable analysis not only of recent political developments in Bavaria and in France but also of the military and religious trends that supplied the backdrop for them, the letter is also replete with interesting and often penetrating observations on individual matters, and it may stand in its entirety as one of the most eloquent and compelling pleas for recognition of the folly of modern war and for the essential need for international peace not just in Europe but everywhere in the civilized world ever penned.

Bismarck argued, first of all, that he was unconvinced that war with France was really inevitable. But he could not be brought to concede that even if at some point it should appear inevitable, this would necessarily mean that one should initiate it at any particular juncture—even one that appeared favorable from a military standpoint. The course that appeared most favorable from the purely military standpoint was not always, he maintained, the most favorable one from the political standpoint. Beyond this, Bismarck was not willing to concede that even a war against France that could be expected to end successfully in the military sense was necessarily desirable. What would Germany's objectives be in such a war? The conquest of new territory? But the Germans wanted no French territory. The destruction of the French armed forces? But the destruction of them was not possible. Nor would any such destruction be permanent, for a military humiliation of France would only rouse the other powers of Europe to intervention and produce new opponents to join the one Germany had to her east, down the Danube. This was a plain description of fact. Though neither Great Britain nor Russia was on good terms with France at this time, neither was likely to relish the prospect of the general upheaval that would be unchained by the creation of a national Germany—and nor would Denmark, still in the throes of recovery from the defeat sustained at the hands of Prussia six years before.

Never, surely, was the issue more clearly drawn than here between the duty of the statesman to avoid, if possible, the horrors of war in the modern industrial age and the perennial tendency of military leaders to see as inevitable any war for which they are asked to plan and prepare and to wish to begin that war at the time, and in the circumstances, most favorable to their side. Bismarck ended with a brilliant word picture of the principles by which his statecraft was guided, and, despite its length, the passage is too striking and illuminating not to be quoted in full.

> That the unification of Germany would be enhanced by policies involving force, I think is self-evident. But there is quite another question, one that has to do with the precipitation of a violent catastrophe and the responsibility of choosing the time for it. An arbitrary intervention in the course of history, on the basis of purely subjective factors, has never had any other result than the shaking down of unripe fruit. That German unity is an unripe fruit today is in my opinion obvious. If the time that lies ahead works in the interests of unity as much as

in the period since the accession of Frederick the Great has done, and particularly the time since 1840, the year in which a national movement was discernible for the first time since the wars of liberation, then we can look calmly to the future and leave the rest to our successors. Behind the wordy restlessness with which those who do not know the trade search after the talisman that will produce German unity in a trice, there is generally a superficial and, in not a few cases, impotent lack of knowledge of real things and their consequences.[4]

All of the above having been said, the importance of this communication (and others like it) for the diplomatic situation of July 1870 cannot be overemphasized. That Bismarck did not want a violent solution to the German question; that he did not wish to impose Prussian rule on south Germany by force; that he was fully aware of the difficulties faced by the national unification movement; that he knew it would have to go through transitional stages lasting five, ten years, perhaps as much as a generation—is clear. All the same, he was confident that the final unification would be realized in the fullness of time: "We can set our watches but the time will not go any faster, and the ability to wait while a situation develops is one of the prerequisites of practical politics."[5]

Rather than antagonizing France, Bismarck wished to demonstrate to European opinion, and to French opinion especially, that a unified Germany could be realized without resort to war. At all events he wished to avoid exacerbating the French government by any flagrant violation of the terms of the treaty of Prague, and he therefore determined to prevent any such violation from taking place. It was for this reason that in February 1870 he rejected out of hand an appeal from Baden, the most liberal of the southern states, to join the North German Confederation. With Prussia even more unpopular in the south than she had been before the war, and with the pro-union forces weak, dispirited, and disorganized, such overtures were, in his view, singularly premature. He did not want to alarm south German opinion, but above all he did not want to provoke a crisis with Ollivier's new government in France, "as it signifies peace for us."[6] He was again correct. The Second Empire had begun to shake. Its prestige was going. The intentions of Napoleon III were too inscrutable to be relied on; thus, for the time being a policy of restraint and moderation was called for. Bismarck said to his minister in Baden: "You know how firmly we have kept our common goal [of

German unification] in view, but you also know how carefully considered the motives are by which we choose our course and measure our pace."[7]

It is one of the great ironies of history that the day after Bismarck laid down these instructions to his minister in Baden, in eloquent and compelling words that reformulated his opinion about the need to avoid war and to reduce the speed of the unification movement, he embarked upon a campaign to secure for the throne of Spain Prince Leopold of Hohenzollern-Sigmaringen, a step that could not be achieved without a crisis of relations and the real possibility of war with the French government.[8]

The contradiction that Bismarck's policy presented here can be dealt with most easily by flicking aside, as many historians have, all arguments that he made about a peaceful solution to the German question as a smokescreen for his real ambitions. Maybe they were nothing more than that, for Bismarck was a master at verbal manipulation. But the beneath the cloud of phrases were hard realities. Prussia had every reason for wanting peace. She had just been hammered together and was not ready for war. Time was required for the Prussian bureaucracy to organize the north, for the general staff to impose Prussian organization on the federal forces and to tune them up to the Prussian concert pitch, for Germany to accustom herself to the presidium of the Hohenzollern monarchy, and for Bismarck himself as federal chancellor to acquire the moral prestige over the north that had taken four hard years (from 1862 to 1866) to acquire in Prussia herself. Bismarck was not one to take risks unnecessarily, particularly to achieve ends that were in themselves not absolutely urgent. Everything pointed to delay, but a halt implied that meanwhile everything must be done (by practical administration and cautious diplomacy) to improve conditions that made for the ultimate acceptance of the Prussian solution by the south. The chart of the future was studded with rocks—many of them sunken, many of them just awash when the national tide was at its height—but Bismarck's navigation in the next three years was masterly and, as we shall see, he followed the advice he gave in his letter to Werthern.

There was a more important consideration still. Bismarck had every reason for fearing the effect of a Prussian military victory on his own position. Would a victorious war not create heroes who could shake his prestige and his authority? Was it not likely to involve opposition of one kind or another at home? And what of the experiences of his own during the Austrian war? Despite his military tunic, Bismarck was a civilian, and—by no means unimportant—a father with two growing sons. He had said on the battlefield of Königgrätz: "It makes me sick at heart to think that Herbert may someday be lying here like this." And later: "No man who has looked into the eyes of a dying man on the battlefield will go lightly into war."[9]

Why then did Bismarck take up the Hohenzollern candidacy? According to one view, his motive was to shake himself free of domestic troubles: he had been backed into a corner by the paralysis of the German unification movement in the north, to say nothing of the need to control it in the south. This view is, on the face of it, plausible. The Austrian war and its outcome had turned the political situation in Prussia upside down. The parties on both the right and the left split up. The majority of liberals formed the National Liberal Party—liberal in outlook and favoring a faster pace over the question of unification. In the words of Otto Pflanze: "To avoid further compromise with the liberals he had to make progress in the national question. . . . German affairs had reached an impasse from which, as so often in the past, the only possible egress appeared to be a crisis of relations with France."[10] The problem with this view is that it exaggerates the link between the National Liberals and Bismarck. Lothar Gall and Klaus Erich Pollman have warned against the dangers of overestimating the connection during this period, and Eberhard Kolb has demonstrated that their strictures can be extended to foreign affairs.[11] The National Liberals were parliamentarians; they wanted a parliamentary government that would attract their counterparts in the south. Not so Bismarck, who wanted the opposite; for him, a parliamentary majority was merely the means to strengthen the power of the state, the Prussian monarchy. Despite setbacks, things were moving in the right direction, and when the means of achieving German unification short of war still existed, why go over to that course?

Antagonism between Bismarck and the clericals has produced a thesis of a different sort. The Hohenzollern candidacy had, it is said, a defensive or even a preemptive purpose: an obsessive fear of the Vatican and of the Catholics of south Germany. The thesis certainly has weight. The German Catholics had been bewildered by the defeat of the Habsburgs. Some of them became federalists; a few even advocated the further extension of Prussia, in the belief that the Roman Church would have greater freedom there than in the small, liberal states. The Catholics in the North German Bundestag took opposite sides on nearly every question. Gradually they became committed to south German particularism, rather to their surprise. They resisted Bismarck's attempts to turn the Zollverein (customs union) into a parliament and became obstructionists in the Landtag, the lower Prussian house.

However, the real Catholic threat to Prussia's interests lay south of the river Main. The situation in Bavaria was, in particular, disturbing. There was, first of all, the historic connection between Bavaria and Austria. There was the obsession of the Bavarian king—that passionate intriguer, Ludwig II— with the questions of prestige and power; Ludwig's house, the house of Wittelsbach, had ruled Bavaria since 900; no princely house in Europe, the Habsburg not excepted, was more ancient. There was also the strategic location of Bavaria. Bavaria was, of all of the states south of the Main, the one most receptive to French influence and French intrigue. In February 1870 Bismarck spoke of his desire to prevent Bavaria from becoming "a base for Austrian-French ultramontane efforts against us."[12] Bismarck had voiced his resentment over the time when his family had been feudal vassals of the Wittelsbach house—curious, in that the estate for which they owed service was one of which they had been deprived by the Hohenzollerns. A united Germany was inconceivable without the second largest German state—the largest state south of the Main, the key to Bismarck's south German policy, and a state that, as James J. Sheehan has pointed out, possessed aspirations to the leadership of Germany well into the nineteenth century.[13] Even if—as was no doubt the case—by 1870 Bavaria had fallen under the shadow of Prussia, she still acted independently in significant ways. She still had her own army—two crack corps, as a matter of fact—without which success in war might be impossible. And there were, throughout the last half of 1869, unmistakable signs that Bavaria was breaking away from Prussia's control.

On 18 February 1870 a calamity happened at Munich: the pro-Prussian cabinet of Hohenlohe resigned, and the particularist Patriot Party took power. Werthern reported: "The extremist members of the ultramontane party have overwhelmingly captured the Bavarian ministry and will do everything in their power to make trouble for us—especially if they are to find common cause with the democrats of Württemberg on matters like the military question."[14] A Hohenzollern candidacy would be the answering call to these untoward events. It would be a blow against German clericalism. It would be a blow against German particularism. In a word, it was a preventive maneuver, and a fairly desperate one, not to provoke war with France but to prevent a Bavarian defection into the arms of Austria and the chamber of horrors that this would unlock for the German question: an Austro-French alliance, a Catholic League, trouble in the Near East, and the specter (feared by Bismarck ever since 1866) of being compelled to take Russia's side against another Crimean-type coalition.

Against this view, however, there is also much counterevidence and one decisive argument. Bismarck was no doctrinal zealot. He was, to be sure, a religious man who never ceased to seek the guidance of God in his statecraft (and not infrequently, as Ludwig Bamberger jeered, found the Deity agreeing with him), but he was singularly unmoved by confessional differences, much less by the rather superstitious abhorrence of Rome espoused by people like the historian Heinrich von Treitschke. Throughout the spring and summer of 1870 and beyond, he maintained cordial diplomatic relations with the Vatican, and for a time during the war with France, he even gave serious thought to providing an asylum to the pope in case he became forced, as a consequence of a takeover of Rome by the Italian radicals, to flee abroad.[15] Not only this. The view that the Hohenzollern candidacy had its origins in Bismarck's inordinate fear of the Roman Church assumes a unity among the German Catholics that did not exist. The Catholics of Germany were not a single block, a solid lump among whom differences were nonexistent or irrelevant. As Jonathan Sperber has written, the Bavarian Catholics were far too suspicious of all Prussians, no matter what their confession, to join with them in any common political cause—throughout the 1860s, for example, they refused to participate in political organizations run by Prussian Catholics and wished to be no part of a mass base for any associations that were dominated by elites north of the Main.[16]

71

Why then did Bismarck take up the Hohenzollern candidacy? Perhaps he wanted the Hohenzollerns to think of themselves as rulers of a Great Power and no longer as obscure princes in north Germany. He may have had an eye on Spanish trade. There may also have been the various motives referred to earlier. The domestic and the Catholic situations may have played a role. It is indeed possible that Bismarck had come to the conclusion that the movement for unification was slithering into decay, that all peaceful means for achieving it had been exhausted, and that a national war was necessary to break the deadlock and to keep up the drive. And finally it is possible that he wished to prevent the election of a Bavarian or Habsburg prince, the rise in prestige of these rival houses, and their enrollment of Spain in an anti-Prussian coalition. All these are weighty enough considerations, but even taken together they are not sufficiently convincing to explain Bismarck's abandonment of a safe and eminently sound evolutionary approach to the German problem and his adoption of what only a few years ago would (to adopt Norman Rich once more) be described as a policy of brinkmanship.[17]

In sorting out his motives, one must bear in mind one overriding fact: for Bismarck, politics was at bottom an expression of power, and at the time the power center of opposition to Prussia lay not in Munich nor in Stuttgart. It lay in Paris. Bismarck might applaud a constitutional regime in France; he might hope that French statesmen could, in the fullness of time, accustom themselves to the idea of a united Germany; but he also knew that a united Germany was inimical to French national interests and that sooner or later every French government of whatever political stripe would feel itself obliged to resist the prospect with all the strength of which it was capable. It is, therefore, safe to assume that Bismarck took up the Hohenzollern candidacy not for domestic political purposes, not for reasons having to do with unrest and instability in the south German states, still less to ward off a threat from the ultramontanes of Europe, but overwhelmingly (if not exclusively) as a counter in the power struggle that he had, for the last four years, been waging against France.

This is not guesswork. It is demonstrated beyond peradventure by Bismarck's diplomacy in dealing with the Spanish crisis in its infancy, when a revolution first threatened to chase Queen Isabella off her throne. He defined his attitude in a letter of 27 September 1868 to the vice-president of the Prussian ministry of state, Freiherr von der Heydt: "I do not believe that the Spanish revolution will ignite a European conflagration even though there are, throughout Europe, parties who would like nothing better than to intervene on behalf of the present regime."[18] The revolution was developing successfully, and its triumph would be a surety for peace. Why this would be so Bismarck did not explain, but it is clear from his letter that he expected the new government to be anti-French and that an anti-French regime on the other side of the Pyrenees that would act as a brake on any aggressive pretensions the French might harbor. For this reason he kept a sharp lookout on France while the revolution was unfolding and envisaged the possibility that France might fall upon Prussia while free of any threat in her rear, "but for the moment with the Spanish fly on his neck, Napoleon cannot of course think of a war with Germany."[19]

When the revolutionary party in Spain installed itself in power and set up a provisional government on 5 October 1868, Bismarck at once grasped that the Prussian government should do everything it could to convince the party that Germany had for it nothing but goodwill. He said to William I: "We must do everything we can to aid a regime whose sympathies for us cannot, unlike those of its predecessor, be doubted."[20] Saurma, chargé d'affaires at Madrid, had complained that the new government might lead to complications and was in a hurry to mature conspiracies against it. Bismarck rebuked him: It is only natural that Saurma should be concerned about the overthrow of a monarchical regime, wrote Bismarck, but the sole concern for Germany should be German interests, and the regime that was overthrown had to be counted on the side of Germany's enemies. "Its overthrow is therefore a desirable event for our policy."[21] On 28 October he took a further step. Peremptory instructions were sent to Canitz, the regular minister, to cut short the leave that he had taken and to return at once to Madrid. Bismarck pulled out all of the stops. He believed that the government that replaced Isabella was a strong new card in Germany's hand. He said as much himself in a letter at the end of May to Max von Forckenbeck, the National Liberal member of the Prussian chamber of deputies: "The Spanish revolution saved us from war."[22]

Greater opportunities were not long in coming. Even before the approach of the revolution, feelers had been put out in Prussia that in the event of Queen Isabella's overthrow, Leopold of Hohenzollern-Sigmaringen would be very much in the running for the Spanish throne. The origins of this story are curious. In the fall of 1866 Georg von Werthern attended a dinner party at Biarritz, a fashionable resort (beloved by Bismarck) in the south of France, where the famous of Europe came to politick and to frolic. Werthern had been secretary of the Prussian legation at Madrid from 1850 to 1851 and returned there for a brief stretch in 1864. Among the guests at the party that he attended were prominent members of the Liberal Union, the dissident reforming faction that had just broken off relations with Isabella the previous July and that now wished to chase her off the throne. Isabella's days were numbered, they said. Conversation then turned to possible candidates, and among those mentioned were the names of the members of the royal families of Belgium, Portugal, and Italy. The discussion pulled Werthern up short. He said to the guest across the table: "Why, my good man, have you not overlooked the best qualified candidate of all?" The guest asked: "Whom could you be talking about?" And received the answer: "Leopold of Sigmaringen. Who could be better qualified? He is the husband of a Portuguese princess—a union that opens up the possibility that some day his heir might succeed to both thrones, achieving the Iberian union of which many Spaniards dream; more than that, he is related to the Bonapartist family in France and to the royal house of Prussia. Most of all he has several sons to carry on the line."[23]

The name of the guest to whom these remarks were addressed was unknown to Werthern at the time and remained so until he was, some two years after the event, told that it was one Don Eusebio Salazar y Mazarredo, *bon vivant,* conspirator, future deputy to the constituent Cortes, councilor of state, and close confidant of Prim—the head of the government that would replace Queen Isabella. Imaginative, nimble, high-powered, and persuasive, Salazar was, in his ideas and efforts of diplomacy, strongly pro-Prussian, and he therefore listened as Werthern spun the crystal, peered into the future, and laid down the terms for a deal. The first condition of acceptance would be the consent of the French rulers. If Napoleon could be persuaded to convince the king of Prussia that the Hohenzollern dynasty would be a guar-

Prince Leopold of Hohenzollern-Sigmaringen (From Émile Ollivier, *The Franco-Prussian War and Its Hidden Causes,* edited and translated by George Burnham Ives [Boston: Little Brown and Co., 1912], facing p. 54)

antee of European peace and stability, and if King William gave his consent—then and only then could the question of acceptance be considered. Salazar left Werthern with the understanding that the agreement of Napoleon would be sought: "To avoid every possibility of danger for Prussia we will endeavor to make the candidacy acceptable to the emperor."[24]

This is, at any rate, the account of the conversation that Werthern gave to Bismarck in a letter of 25 July 1870, soon after the outbreak of the war with France. As to the literal accuracy of this account, one must reserve judgment; the claim on the part of historical personages to recall at a later date the exact words used by themselves and by other parties in long conversation is bound to inspire a certain uneasiness in the historian. But the description, whether literally accurate or not, may safely be taken as reliably reflecting Salazar's views on the subject in question.

As a matter of fact, Salazar never approached Napoleon III or the French government. Napoleon III, on his side, never approached the Spanish government on its position on the Hohenzollern question. These were astonishing oversights. Leopold was a Roman Catholic and more closely connected by blood with the French emperor than with the king of Prussia. He was married to a daughter of the former king of Portugal and also closely related to the Bonapartist house of Murat, and his younger brother had become king of Rumania—on French nomination. In the spring of 1869 (as mentioned in chapter 2), Napoleon instructed Benedetti to sound the Prussians on the Spanish question and to let them know that the interests of France would never tolerate a member of the Prussian royal family on the throne of Spain—this in spite of the dynastic connections just mentioned. Why did he not stress these objections to his German relatives? Neither the French nor the Sigmaringen archives have shed any light on this subject.

In any case, Prim and the Spanish government were too absorbed by events in Italy—namely, by their decision to offer the crown to the duke of Genoa—to follow up on Salazar's initiative. Not until the latter's candidacy collapsed on 2 January 1870 did negotiations with Leopold resume. On 17 February Prim wrote officially to Prince Leopold offering him the Spanish throne. At the same time he wrote three other letters: one to Leopold's father, Prince Karl Anton; a second to King William I, head of the house of the Hohenzollern, and a third to Bismarck. It was Salazar who placed these letters in his pocket (or on his person) and carried them to Germany.

On 27 February 1870, shortly before eleven o'clock in the morning, Salazar delivered Prim's letter to Bismarck. There is no evidence that before this time Bismarck was involved in the question, but by now his involvement was crucial.[25] Upon receiving Prim's letter from Salazar, he instructed his assistant, Keudell, not to let anyone else in; he needed time to think the question through. By the following day he had made up his mind: he would accept Leopold's candidacy. He dictated a long memorandum to Keudell outlining his reasons for acceptance.[26] On 9 March he presented these arguments in an even longer paper to the king.[27]

In presenting to the king his case for acceptance—a communication written with exceptional force and eloquence—Bismarck drew attention to the political and economic benefits for Germany that would result from closer ties to Spain. He pointed out, moreover, that in the event of war between Germany and France, France would have to divert a division of troops to the Pyrenees. The central part of the memorandum moved away from economic and political questions and dwelt instead on the consequences that would result from a refusal by Leopold to accept the Spanish offer. If that happened, the crown would fall into the hands of a member of the house of Wittelsbach. This would not only destroy Prussia's ascendancy in Germany, but would also establish a dynasty in Spain that would look for support to France, Rome, and the anti-nationalist elements in Germany. This was by no means the only danger: a refusal might lead to the establishment in Spain of a republic, and the resulting spread of the republican virus to Italy and France might have the effect of bustling the French emperor into some precipitous action. Leaving nothing to chance, Bismarck wrote: "Acceptance would ensure the safe development of the Spanish question. . . . For France it would be of great value if the Orléanist candidacy in Spain appeared to be eliminated."[28]

Did this memorandum represent a change of heart on the part of Bismarck? Had he now decided that war against France might now be necessary? By no means. It is impossible to take the reasoning of this document at its face value because it is remarkable for the insubstantiality of the factual premises on which it is based. It was a document of advocacy, and (as Gordon A. Craig has noted) its arguments clearly were carefully selected and intended to appeal in the main to the dynastic cast of William's mind.[29] Many of its conclusions—to which the king affixed marginalia indicating disagreement—were completely flimsy. That Bismarck seriously believed that a pro-German Hohenzollern on the throne of Spain would be a source of security for France is, for example, not only difficult to believe; it is preposterous. In building up the other arguments, Bismarck's main purpose may have been to obscure the importance of the Hohenzollern candidacy as it related to France and the possibility that it would provoke a crisis of relations with that country, for the king could be expected to object vigorously to any policy that ran the risk of war. Bismarck made the strategic dimension of the matter clear enough: a pro-German government in Spain would compel the French to defend their Spanish frontier and would mean the difference between one or two army corps that the French would muster in case of war with Germany. But this too would be a service to peace: "France's desire for war or peace with Germany will always rise or fall in direct relation to the hazards of war. In the long run, we cannot look to the good will of France for preservation of the peace but to the impression created by our position of strength."[30]

William remained unmoved by Bismarck's arguments. He refused to consent to the project. He would not stand in the way if Leopold wanted the throne and determined to accept it outright, but he could never command it. He made one concession: he agreed to let Bismarck present his arguments in the presence of the members of the Hohenzollern family. Such a meeting took place on 15 March 1870.

The king began by reminding the guests that he had called them together to discuss a momentous question but that no decision was to be taken until later. He was, he said, fully convinced of the importance of the matter. He went on to tell of the offer by the Spanish government, and of how similar offers made during the course of 1869 had been rejected because of the unstable political situation in Spain. At William's instruction, Bismarck then read out letters from Prim to Karl Anton, Prince Leopold, and himself. There then ensued four hours of agitated and intense discussion—such discussion as only the Germans can conduct and endure—between the participants. To this discussion, Karl Anton devotes over 4,000 words of notes.[31] They are not uninteresting, but they need not detain us. The central point emerging from the meeting was that Bismarck won over a majority of the participants—not only Roon and Moltke, whose presence Bismarck specifically had requested, but also Delbrück, the able head of the chancellor's office, and Thile, the secretary of state.

The opinions of the "most experienced and weightiest" advisers of the crown moved the Sigmaringen princes. Since their names have already come up, and since they will come up at many points in the remainder of this account, it may be well to take note now, if only briefly, of the personality and character of these most curious and fascinating of men. Young Leopold was, at the time of his selection for the Spanish throne, thirty-four years old. Though there were conflicting views among his contemporaries (as there have been among historians) about his character, the weight of the evidence reveals him to be a healthy, honorable, and courageous young man—the product of a German military education, with all of its advantages and drawbacks, full of life, straightforward, manly, and all in all an attractive character. The same can generally be said of his father, Karl Anton, though here the imperfections were more numerous. Judged from the standpoint of intelligence and administrative talents, Karl Anton was certainly in the front rank of his family members of the time. Tact, on the other hand, though he did his best to muster it on a number of occasions, was not his strongest suit, and he frequently allowed himself to be overly impressed by emotion and by hubris. Ambitious and intensely rank-conscious, he also showed at times an exaggerated and unwise concern for the outward prerogatives of title and of position. His conduct was supported by a stubbornness that was as fortunate when directed to hopeful undertakings as it was calamitous when addressed to unpromising ones. The reader who attempts to pass judgment on his performance and on that of his son in their ordeal would do well to bear in mind, as many of their contemporary critics failed to do, the appalling complexities—and in many instances insolubility—of the problems with which they were faced and the simultaneous and conflicting pressures to which they were subjected.

For the moment all seemed lost. The support of the ministers did the princes little good. William stood impregnable. On 20 April Leopold and his father sent the Spanish government a letter declining the offer that was made to them. Bismarck had no trouble diagnosing the situation. He said to

Karl Anton of Hohenzollern-Sigmaringen (From K. Th. Zingeler, *Karl Anton, Fürst von Hohenzollern* [Stuttgart: Deutsche Verlags-Anstalt, 1911], facing p. 108)

Delbrück: "The Spanish affair has taken a wretched turn. Indubitable reasons of state have been subordinated to private inclinations of princes and to ultramontane female influences. Irritation over this has, for weeks, been placing a heavy burden on my nerves."[32] The whole project, it appeared, had fallen apart.

That it did not fall through appears to have been entirely due to Bismarck himself. In order to assuage the anxieties of William, Bismarck dispatched to Spain two agents to keep the door open. The first of these was Lothar Bucher, Bismarck's trusted aide; the second was Major von Versen, a Prussian officer named by Moltke. According to the Spanish documents, Versen was sent along with the object of negotiating a Spanish alliance.[33]

There was one remarkable omission in all of the arguments that Bismarck had made to the king and his advisers: they made virtually no mention of the situation inside France, but there is reason to believe that French political affairs were very much on Bismarck's mind at this time. Bismarck did not believe that Napoleon III, whom he had known since 1855, wanted war, but the same could not be said of the hard-liners in the French government: Empress Eugénie, Rouher, the vice-emperor, and influential ambassadors like La Gueronnière at Brussels and former officials like Drouyn de Lhuys, who were bent on a revival of imperial prestige and revenge for Königgrätz. As we have seen, Bismarck was not worried by their attempts to secure these opportunities by diplomatic combinations—as his comments on the projected Franco-Italian-Austrian alliance attest. He was aware, too, of other constraints. He knew, for instance, that the bar to improved French relations with Austria was the Magyars (who had just become partners in the Dual Monarchy) and the Germans temporarily ascendant in "lesser" Austria. Napoleon's hopes for improved relations with Italy were hamstrung by the presence of French troops in Rome. Anglo-French relations had fallen into a decline since 1869, when a French company tried to get control of strategic Belgian railway lines. And Bismarck had succeeded in driving a wedge between Paris and St. Petersburg by the promise that he had made in 1868 to support a Russian attempt to tear up the Black Sea clauses of the treaty of Paris of 1856.[34] All the same the French were drifting into difficulties at home, as Bismarck, ever vigilant, bore witness when he remarked: "A king of Prussia can make mistakes, can suffer misfortunes, and even humiliation, but old loyalties remain. The adventurer on the throne possesses no such heritage of confidence. He must always produce an effect. His safety depends on his personal prestige and to enhance it, he will want to start a dispute with us on some pretext or another. I do not believe that he personally wants war, but the insecurity of his advisers will drive him on."[35]

Bismarck had good reason to worry about French politics. In May 1869 there took place in France the third general election since 1852, and the results were a setback for the imperial government. On 2 January 1870 Napoleon yielded to popular feeling and launched the "liberal empire" with Ollivier at its head. Ollivier was a man in whom Bismarck placed high hopes, and not without reason. Bismarck had calculated that Napoleon III could not afford to see the Prussian program carried out in Germany without ruining his dynasty, but he also believed that the "liberal empire" and Ollivier especially would shake Napoleon's personal rule as much as would parliamentary opposition. He noted: "It will be possible to remake Germany peacefully without war if a constitutional regime continues in France."[36] For this reason he turned down the Badenese petition for membership in the German confederation. He knew that acceptance would foretell a sudden change of direction in German politics and would cut the ground from under Ollivier's feet.

Bismarck had sized Ollivier up to a nicety. Ollivier had come to power firm in the view that continued French opposition to Prussia was futile—the discredited politics of his war-mongering predecessors. If Prussia were bent on annexation of the states south of the Main, he resolved that France should not stand in the way. There was one awkward point: south Germany retained an independent international existence. Even here Ollivier was far from outright resistance to Prussia: "As far as the Main goes it has been crossed a long time; German unity has already been made against us; what remains is political unity, and that is important only to Prussia to whom it will bring more difficulties than she cares to imagine." Napoleon III was more cautious: "It would be wrong to state in advance what France will do in the event Prussia crosses the Rhine." On the one hand, Ollivier's policy called for passive acquiescence; Napoleon's, for watchful waiting. By the winter of 1870, French policy tilted more and more in the direction that Ollivier wished it to take. He recognized this himself. He said to his minister in Stuttgart: "The unification of Germany would, we must admit, make a stir in political circles; it might even cause embarrassment; it could rouse passions on the right, but that's about all."[37]

Thus Bismarck was on solid ground when he surveyed the situation in France. He believed that Ollivier's desire to improve relations with Berlin was real. In the course of the next two months, however, events stood this view of French policy on its head. On 8 May the plebiscite discussed above invited the French people to judge the liberal reforms effected since the constitution of 1870, and they resolved the issue overwhelmingly in favor of the imperial government. When the results became known, one of Napoleon's opponents said morosely: "The empire has been given twenty years of life."[38] There was soon a further alarm. In the spring of 1870, Napoleon III quarreled with Daru, his foreign minister; on 15 May he dismissed him and put Gramont in his place. Bismarck was not long in diagnosing the significance of these events. Together they spelled the end of caution in French foreign policy—the end of the "liberal empire" that Bismarck had regarded as the best guarantee of good relations with France. Together they were a sign—an unmistakable sign—that Napoleon III was again moving toward action in German affairs.

In the meantime Bismarck's agents in Spain had been busy. Bucher arrived in Madrid on 13 April, went immediately to see Salazar, and "though he had not taken off his clothes for five days and was feverish" talked matters over with him until midnight. On 20 April he saw Prim. Prim was rattled. To his own amazement (and that of William I when the latter was told about it), Bucher had some difficulty in interrupting the torrent of words with which his host inaugurated the discussion, but he finally managed to break in long enough to explain why he had been sent to Madrid and what was expected of him. Prim cut him off. Pacing up and down like a caged lion in his office, he poured out to Bucher "with the liveliest sincerity" his innermost thoughts on the succession question. Bucher had the impression that Prim sensed his impending death and that his long and passionate monologue represented a species of political testament. It amounted to this: Spain wished to remain deaf to any and all threats from France, and for this Prim had done all he could: "I can do no more." The discussion went on, we are told, for four solid hours, Prim doing most of the talking—more than talking, in fact: pouring out his complaints, trying to explain his position, pleading that Bucher use his influence in the direction of immediate acceptance, even (according to Bucher) embracing the embarrassed emissary two or three times in the exuberance of his emotion. Prim ended by stressing practical concerns: "We are sure of a majority of two-thirds, but every additional day threatens some loss. Many deputies are going home to take care of their own businesses. By 20 May the heat will be too great; everything must be completed by then: the official acceptance received; the constitutional provisions for the founding of a new dynasty passed." Anti-Prussian pressure was marked and growing: "Our press is . . . susceptible to influences from outside; there are some papers that love gold even if it comes from France."[39]

Bucher presented an account of his mission to William I on 30 April. To no avail; William remained unmoved. On 12 May it was Prim's turn. Even before his answer from Fernando had been received (discussed previously in chapter 2), Prim inquired of Bucher what was going on. Bucher pleaded for delay, and for good reason: Bismarck had fallen ill. Frustrated, fatigued, and depressed, with a bad case of jaundice into the bargain, he was in seclusion at his estate in Varzin, out of touch with events. He had intended to remain there about five days but his condition worsened, and it was not until the second week of May that he began to think of returning to the capital.

In reality, the situation was not as gloomy as Bismarck supposed. Gradually, almost inexorably, the ice that had for weeks frozen all of the progress of the Hohenzollern candidacy was beginning to break up, and in this Bismarck's agents played no small part. Versen and Bucher were untiring in their approaches to Karl Anton and Leopold and overwhelmed the royal pair with effusive descriptions of the glorious future that awaited Leopold in Madrid. Karl Anton's attitude toward the project, under the weight of these arguments, now underwent a swift change. In a letter to his son, Prince Charles of Rumania, he announced: "There is great anxiety about what would become of a Spain *which we have spurned.*" A republic established there would pose a great threat to Italy, where "the secret societies have already prepared the ground." Rumania, too, would not be free of danger "since such political revolutions are doubly contagious among peoples of Latin stock."[40]

Versen was also busy. In the middle of May he won Crown Prince Frederick William for the project. In further conversations, he tried to make clear to officials of the German foreign office the nature of Prim's anxieties over the situation in Spain.[41] The upshot of all this was that there took place, in the middle of May 1870, a sharp campaign to change the mind of William I. William was, as ever, reluctant and upset that the affair was still going on; on the other hand, he now had evidence from Versen that Leopold wanted the crown and was acting on his own volition. Here was the new element in the situation. Not only that, in the last part of May Bismarck reappeared on the scene. On 21 May he returned to Berlin, bearing in mind all that had happened during the month—the return of his envoys from Madrid, the results of their talks with Karl Anton and Leopold, and, not least, the new developments in France: the plebiscite of 8 May, the chauvinism that the vote was sure to instill in the imperial government, and, worse still, the coming to power of Gramont a week later. A new wind was blowing, and Bismarck was too astute a man not to detect it. On 28 May he wrote to Karl Anton: "Today no less than before I feel no doubt that Germany has a vital interest here, and at critical moments the pointer on the scales might well register differently according as we know Madrid to be a friend or an enemy." Bismarck had raised the subject with the king once more and had received the assurance that the latter would not oppose Leopold's acceptance of the Spanish offer. That was all; the king, Bismarck told Karl Anton, would never command a member of the royal house to undertake a mission of this nature.[42] Shortly after receiving Bismarck's letter, Karl Anton accepted the Spanish throne on behalf of his son.[43]

After discussing the question with Bismarck personally, Karl Anton reported to Leopold that the chancellor was now "triumphant and *coleur de rose.* If another refusal had come from us, we would have had to answer for it, for the Spanish throne question is a big factor in Bismarck's political calculations."[44] Versen also saw the chancellor at this time and asked what support Leopold could expect from Prussia after he went to Spain. Bismarck answered: "He can expect nothing at all from Prussia; he has to be a German in Spain; he is stationed in a Prussian warship."[45] Bismarck only regretted that the more energetic Prince Friedrich Karl, who had been mentioned as a candidate, had not been offered the Spanish throne: "We could have counted him as offsetting three French army corps."[46]

Still, though the candidacy had been organized and pushed forward by Bismarck, war with France was far from his thoughts. There is powerful evidence for this. From 1 to 4 June 1870 Bismarck met with Tsar Alexander II and William I at Ems. Bismarck expressed disapproval of Habsburg policy in the Near East and tried to persuade the tsar that the south German princes would make a better bargain with William than if they waited to be swept away by a more democratic wave in favor of a liberal successor. There was talk of affairs in Rumania. That was all—no hint of the coming war, no request for Russian support on the one side, no pledge of Russian support or even neutrality on the other. Indeed, France was passed over in silence. Bismarck, on his side, showed no signs of increasing hostility toward France. On the contrary, he made repeated gestures of friendship with Napoleon. He pressed hard for a plebiscite in north Schleswig, where the Danes were in the majority. This would please Napoleon III's nationalist principles, and Bismarck favored it also—against William's objection. He announced: "It is harmful that a hostile nationality should live in the same community with the Germans."[47]

The maneuver was put into operation. Alexander II wrote to his uncle, reminding him of his promise for a plebiscite. William was furious, and Bismarck had hard work preventing an angry answer. Not only that: at this very time, according to Fritz Stern, he pressed for French investment in Prussia. He wrote to his banker Bleichröder: "I would consider it an important success if we could attract French capital to any appreciable extent in this country. Along the Rhine, this has already been the case for a long time and, in large measure, to the great advantage of industrial enterprises."[48] As to Germany, it is likely that Bismarck planned some national stroke in the south to smooth the way for military discussions in the federal parliament; it is probable that he anticipated protests both from France and from Austria-Hungary, but this would not necessarily unleash a war. German-Austrian and Magyar affairs still dominated opinion in the counsels of Vienna, and Bismarck still hoped that the "liberal empire" would make Napoleon III more pacific—and that Leopold would arrive at Madrid before anyone knew what was happening.[49]

But that was easier said than done. On 1 June Salazar was notified of the developments of 28 May. On 5 June Bismarck returned to Berlin. He at once dispatched Bucher to Madrid; Versen, on his side, hurried off to Leopold in Bad Reichenhall. In the meantime, there were repeated attempts by Thile to keep up support for the project. Versen's appearance rousted Leopold out of his holiday, and the major found him out of sorts. Leopold wished to enjoy the quaffs of mineral water before assuming his new dignity. But Versen insisted that he mount the horse that he had been summoned to ride. Before the Cortes could act, the terms of acceptance had to be negotiated with the Spaniards. Hohenzollern family law, moreover, laid down that William's consent had to be requested and given. Leopold wavered. He wanted to have his cake and eat it—somehow to assume the crown of Spain and yet not provoke a storm. Versen determined not to yield. Leopold gave way, bowing to Versen's arguments that the question should be settled behind the scenes and without delay. Leopold caught the train to Sigmaringen, and there with Karl Anton he drafted a letter of request. Salazar, who had joined them, sent off a telegram to Zorilla, president of the Cortes, that Leopold would accept the crown and that only William's consent was needed.[50]

In the meantime, Thile reported a fresh burst of royal indignation. The crown prince, now a convert to the candidacy, had blurted out to William at Ems the news that Bucher was in Spain, Salazar in Germany, and Versen roaming around the countryside despite the fact that he had been ordered by the king to return to his post at Posen. William was in high agitation. On 12 June he wired the foreign office of his amazement that "this sort of thing could be going on behind my back." Thile wired at once to Bismarck: "While anxious not to irritate your nerves, the king demands to be informed of everything that Salazar brings by either by word of mouth or in writing before any action is taken." In the margin of the telegram Bismarck vented his fury.

This beats everything!

So His Majesty wants the affair treated with royal interference?!!

The whole affair is possible only if it remains the limited concern of the Hohenzollern princes; it cannot turn into a Prussian concern; the king must be able to say without lying: I know nothing about it.

The exchange is a salutary reminder that Bismarck often had difficulties with William I that were not easily overcome and that he was not always responsible for German policy. For the moment, their differences seemed not to matter. On 21 June the royal assent was finally obtained, secured by the indefatigable Bucher—though not, he reported, without difficulty. William wrote to Leopold: "You have taken a decision that you—rightly in my view—previously rejected out of hand. Now you regard the political views put forward in the winter of this year by Minister Count Bismarck as justified and incontrovertible from the statesman's point of view. Had that been my view originally, I should not so decidedly have approved of your rejection of the Spanish crown."[51] Still, these words did little to dim the enthusiasm of those who backed the project. Leopold would, it now seemed, at last wear the crown of Spain.

By 21 June 1870 the final negotiations between the Spanish envoys and the Hohenzollern-Sigmaringen family had been completed, and on that day Versen left Sigmaringen for Berlin bearing with him two telegrams from Salazar informing the leaders of the Spanish government of Leopold's decision. At last, on 23 June, Salazar triumphantly dispatched his critical signal to the president of the Cortes: he would arrive in Madrid with Leopold's formal acceptance of the crown, and the terms would be approved by the Cortes on about the 26th.

Critical because it went wrong. A cipher clerk in the legation at Madrid blundered; "about the 26th" (of June understood) came out "about the 9th" (of July understood); he thus passed the message that Salazar would return in the middle of July. It made no sense to keep the deputies, already anxious and out of sorts, hanging around in the sweltering heat of Madrid for another seventeen days, and on 23 June Prim prorogued the Cortes until 1 November. When Salazar returned on 26 June he found Madrid deserted. Prim agreed to summon the Cortes but had to reveal why it was being summoned. With the decoding error, all of the wonderful calculations built around the Hohenzollern candidature melted away. In Berlin the question immediately became: was the error an unhappy slip or an outright falsification? Bismarck, ever vigilant, had no doubt whatsoever as to the answer. He wrote to the crown prince: "Our knowledge of events makes it hard to believe that such a fateful error could be chalked up to accident,"[52] and his attitude was not unreasonable. The diplomatic files showed that the correct version had indeed been received at Madrid. What had gone wrong?

Canitz, the Prussian ambassador, was on the spot. Pressed for an explanation, he loaded onto the shoulders of Kleefeld, the chancellery clerk, all responsibility for the incident—"about the 9th" seemed as reasonable to Kleefeld as "about the 26th." Kleefeld had an explanation of his own: no mistake had occurred, he insisted, but rather a outright deception on the part of Canitz, who from the start had regarded with the liveliest skepticism the Hohenzollern candidacy and who had taken the opportunity to destroy it once and for all while he had the chance. Kleefeld's explanation is supported by a good deal of circumstantial evidence. Canitz and Bismarck never saw eye to eye: Bismarck regarded Canitz as a nincompoop; he had packed him off to Spain as ambassador so that he would not have to give him a more sensitive post and had, like a steamroller, flattened one after another of Canitz's objections to the Hohenzollern candidacy on the grounds of grand strategy.[53] Seldom did Bismarck trouble to conceal an opinion about one of his ministers, especially if that opinion was unfavorable, and such sneering condescension may have unnerved Canitz. The German diplomatic staff was a thoroughly professional operation, but it was not without its share of frustrated officials whose style of operation is best described by a long word, *Geltungsbedürfnis* (one of those assembled gems of German lexicography), which literally means "the need to be appreciated, the desire to show off." Whether Canitz contrived to falsify the telegram of 21 June cannot be said for sure, but as Norman Rich (who understands this affair best) has observed, he could not have been unaware of its importance. More, time was on his side, for after he had received the telegram from Kleefeld, he had three days to decide what he was going to say. That he applied for a leave of absence the day after the error was uncovered is astonishing, since he was well aware that important events were about to transpire for which his presence would be urgently needed.[54]

There is, of course, no direct and absolutely conclusive evidence against either man. Public officials who sabotage their own government do not normally leave for posterity documentary evidence confirming such conduct. Kleefeld and Canitz corresponded clandestinely throughout this period, and Javier Rubio, in his admirable study of the Spanish role in the origins of the Franco-Prussian War, cites leading figures in Madrid as sources for his opinion that neither man can be held exclusively accountable.[55] Some of these figures were not always reliable authorities, but on such matters they were likely to be well informed; in any case, Professor Rubio has had more extensive access than has the writer of these lines to the Kleefeld manuscripts and to the Spanish foreign ministry archives at Madrid. All the same, this writer is unable to overcome the impression (shared, incidentally, by Norman Rich) that the evidence, though confused and circumstantial, tells much more strongly against Kleefeld than it does against Canitz and that during the most sensitive stages of the affair—particularly the last week of June, when the question of war or peace seemed to hang in the balance—all of the deception and duplicity in the relationship between the two men proceeded overwhelmingly from Kleefeld's side.

The most detailed account of what really happened and the one most likely to be closest to the real facts is that given by Kleefeld's own private papers, which emerged in 1911 when a Spanish source fed them to a certain Herr Bohnen, a shadowy German businessman in St. Petersburg.[56] Kleefeld's papers include a series of highly confidential notes that he had taken on the Hohenzollern candidacy, a careful scrutiny of which reveals them to be copies of the telegrams exchanged between Bismarck and Salazar in 1870. Kleefeld apparently had purloined these documents from the legation at Madrid. The papers also contain a series of letters in which Kleefeld presents himself as a liar, a professional swindler, a blackmailer, and, not the least sensationally, a spy—an agent presumably not only of Montpensier but also perhaps of the crown prince of Asturias, both of whom were rival claimants to the Spanish throne. The most conclusive evidence of Kleefeld's guilt, however, is found in a private letter written by his wife—herself a Spaniard, related by blood to the deposed Queen Isabella—to a friend on 15 September 1883. Here she expresses anxiety over the possibility that Kleefeld might be forced to return to Germany; if this were to occur, the German foreign office might revenge itself on her husband by producing as witnesses against him other employees of the legation who had since returned—Kleefeld was a man who had a real talent for making enemies—and thus force him to reveal what had happened. This alone would appear to explain the fact that although now grievously discredited and taken seriously by almost no one, Kleefeld was to remain in Spain until his death in Valladolid at the end of 1885.

In any case the decoding error meant the ruin of the *fait accompli* that was the basis of all of the hopes about the candidacy that Bismarck had managed to build up. Salazar returned to a hot and deserted capital; no election took place; and by 3 July the French were beginning to fight back. Spanish policy was thrown into disarray. Prim insisted to Mercier that his one consolation was that the whole affair had been arranged behind his back by his enemies. All of the evidence suggests that he was lying to escape the wrath of France,[57] but in the hugger-mugger of rumor and speculation it made no difference.

The more interesting question is why Bismarck decided to organize the candidacy at all. The answers by historians have gone up and down over the years. One of the most lively and provocative ones appeared in 1981 in an essay—one of four he has written on the subject—by Josef Becker, who managed (with the assistance of officials of the Biblioteca of the Real academia de la histoira in Madrid) to procure the original of a vital document of 25 June 1870, said to have emanated from the secret files of the Prussian government and purporting to show the tactics that Bismarck wished to adopt when Leopold's election became known in France. Written in French, first published and translated in abbreviated form in 1876 by the Spanish historian and archivist Antonio Pirala and brought to the attention of students of the problem in 1909 by Pirala's German counterpart, Richard Fester, the "letter of instructions" (as it has come to be known) is a hot potato, and it has burned the fingers of several historians who have handled it. Lawrence D. Steefel, writing in 1961, took the view that the letter came from the pen of Bucher, not Bismarck, and his argument is not unpersuasive.[58] We have seen that Bucher was enormously impressed by the significance of the negotiations and that he threw himself with single-minded intensity into amassing all that he could in a brief time. Becker, in any case, accepts Bucher's authorship, but he goes on to argue that this is irrelevant because of Bucher's close intellectual proximity to Bismarck and—a more important point—that the letter conclusively demonstrates not only that Bismarck did not expect his posture of noninvolvement to be accepted by the French government but also that he was (at least after 1868) aiming at a crisis of relations, if not a preventive war, with France.[59]

About these claims three things must be said. First, the letter of 25 June 1870 was not a detached work of political statecraft written in the calm of Bucher's (or Bismarck's) study. It was written in haste for a particular group of people—the Spanish leaders whose nerves had been frayed by the delay of nearly two years in finding a king and whose anxieties Bismarck may well have wished to calm. The very language of the letter points this up: "It is possible that we may see a passing fermentation in France and, without doubt, it is necessary to avoid anything that might provoke or increase it."[60] Still, in this instance, Becker's verdict is sound. It cannot be seriously maintained that Bismarck failed to anticipate the reaction of the French; to do so would, as Otto Pflanze writes, "place him behind an amateur like Karl Anton who from the outset predicted a wild reaction in anti-Prussian Europe."[61] But that is really beside the point. The French had been expostulating against Leopold's candidacy since April 1869 (when Benedetti had his first contact with Thile); by June 1870 it was a rumor of long standing, and everyone in Madrid was talking about it. By July it would be secret no longer, and the French were waiting to blow it open.

A second and more important point. Though it is always dangerous to speak with too great assurance about Bismarck's motives, it is simply not true that he believed in preventive war, still less that the letter of instructions of 25 June 1870 can be taken as evidence that he did. Becker runs off the rails here. Throughout his life Bismarck was an opponent of preventive war,

maintaining once that it represented an monstrous intrusion into the workings of Providence and in any case made as much sense as putting a gun to
one's head because one was afraid to die.[62] Many a lifelong teetotaler has
got drunk once; the most faithful spouses occasionally stray; and this rule of
conduct for Bismarck has to have that *clausa rebus sic stantibus* attached to
it like all others. But his pretty consistent opposition to preventive war makes
resort to it here much more unlikely and therefore demands convincing (indeed overwhelming) evidence, which is not forthcoming, to convince anyone
of it.[63] Indeed, in the spring of 1870 he made it clear on more than one
occasion that if the trumpets of war were to sound, France would have to
sound them, and—as we shall have occasion to note—right down to the
middle of July he was confident that Napoleon had not the ears for such
music nor the means to conduct it. Bismarck's overriding motive in backing
the Hohenzollern candidacy was to check the new aggressiveness in French
policy before it had a chance to move forward. It is, of course, true that the
possibility of war with France was always present in Bismarck's mind, if only
because there were few possibilities that were not present in it. But to say
anything more definite than this about Bismarck's reasons for the scheme is
to make assertions that do not hold up.

Third and finally, the readiness to make war on France if necessary had
doubtless been there since 1866—the readiness, not the decision. The decision to have war in 1870 was made in 1870 and, as we shall see, only after
the Hohenzollern candidacy had collapsed.

Nor is this the only theory about Bismarck's behavior in the Spanish question. A convincing case can be made—Jochen Dittrich has made it—that
Bismarck used the Hohenzollern candidacy not to provoke war *with* but
rather revolution *in* France. On more than one occasion he had pointed to
revolution in France as one of those disturbances that would hurry Prussia
along the path to unification. The Hohenzollern candidature had been arranged behind France's back and with a view to presenting her and everyone
else in Europe with a *fait accompli;* Napoleon III and his entourage thus
would be faced by the fact that their honor and prestige (on which their
regime had come to rest) had suffered yet another crushing blow. It was only
to be expected that this latest manifestation of incompetence on their part
would unchain of series of upheavals that would tie France's hands and allow

Prussia to take control of south Germany without having to worry about interference from Paris or from anywhere else.[64]

The fallacy of this argument is that it begs the real question: What means had Bismarck of knowing how a revolution in France would unfold? A long revolution would certainly turn France inside out, aid the Prussian cause, and push up the momentum for unification. But the last three revolutions had been quick, almost bloodless affairs. What possible good would there be in exchanging a creaky and ineffective Napoleon III for a republican regime that, by virtue of the very conditions that it gave it birth, would feel itself compelled to take a stronger and more vigorous line with respect to the unification problem than its predecessor had ever dared to adopt? After all, Bismarck believed—rightly—that the empire was the form of French government most favorable to Prussian interests, and indeed he went on trying to restore Napoleon III even at the beginning of 1871. He sometimes thought that a French revolution would lead to war; it was quite against his intentions that war would lead to a French revolution.

Nor was this all. Bismarck had every reason to think that Napoleon III, weak and ineffective, would, if it came to the point, shrink from war. His record from the time of the *coup d'état* on 2 December 1851 supported such a belief. Napoleon III was, when it came to the point, a man of caution. He had shrunk from war with Russia in 1854. He had shrunk from war with Italy in 1859. In each of these wars he was pushed into action by his allies and in each of them he had made a peace that they considered hasty, ill-advised, and premature. He had pulled out of Mexico in 1867 rather than run the risk of a confrontation with the United States. After 1866 he had tamely submitted to a series of humiliating reversals. What Martin Luther once said about sexual temptation—that one could not prevent birds from flying over one's head, but one could keep them from nesting in one's hair—applies with equal force during this time to Napoleon III. There were many Franco-Prussian crises between 1866 and 1870, so that temptations to war often flew over Napoleon III's head; they never nested in his hair. Bismarck himself once said to Bucher that if Napoleon III had wanted to go to war with Prussia, he already had ample provocation.[65] This calculation was wide of the mark—how thoroughly wide Bismarck was soon to find out.

4

The Negotiations at Ems

In the diplomacy of late-nineteenth-century Europe, midsummer tended normally to be the doldrums; but never, it seemed, was there a summer more languid in this respect than that of 1870. The crisis over the Belgian railways had reached its culmination in 1869 and then died away, leaving France and Great Britain on cool terms. No other major complication was visible on the horizon. All over Europe weary statesmen took off from their capitals for their watering-places or for their *villégiatures.* Paris was no exception: Ollivier was somewhere in the country having an agreeable time, and most of the other ministers were away too. All of the generals were on vacation. Gramont and Napoleon were the only figures of substance to remain in the capital.

In Berlin a similar situation prevailed. King William was at Bad Ems, where he could shed the cloying attentions of his bodyguards and courtiers, enjoy the delights of relative anonymity, and take his annual cure through the medium of the incomparable spas of that city. Bismarck, too, liberated by the departure of his royal master and only too happy to escape the dust and heat of Berlin, the intrigues of the foreign office underlings, and the boring interviews with foreign envoys, moved at the end of June to Varzin, his Junker estate in Pomerania. There, with Bucher, his alert and experienced aide, he planned to bury himself for two months—five hours by slow train from Berlin, and then forty miles on rough roads. There were no visitors and virtually no social life. Varzin was covered with trees (overburdened with them, in fact), and Bismarck could do what he liked: ride in the woods from morning until night, gorge on the beef and hams that he had hoarded in the estate's great cellars, and—by no means the least of his pleasures—

wash down his gigantic meals with copious quantities of "black velvet," the mixture of stout and champagne that he had invented.

Similarly the diplomatic community in Berlin. The foreign ambassadors, finding themselves with no one to talk to at the foreign office, now also fled this summer-bound city for their respective vacation haunts. Thus Benedetti got ready to depart for the resort at Wildbad; Loftus, his British counterpart, and Oubril, his Russian one, headed for the shores of the North Sea. There remained in the chanceries of the embassies and the legations only the chargés d'affaires and the second secretaries. These, if their wives and children were away (as they usually were in the summer), were left to open the dusty offices, to yawn over the translations from the local papers, to doze in their chairs after the heavy diplomatic luncheons, to grind out the occasional dispatch to show that they were still alive, and to go out, perhaps in the early evenings, to the parks, where people strolled under the poplar trees in the twilight of the warm summer air.

All this was changed by the impact of events in Spain. Shortly before noon on Saturday, 2 July, there came to the Quai d'Orsay from a certain Viscount Walsh—a pronounced and somewhat eccentric legitimist with excellent connections to highly placed sources in Madrid—a short and cryptic note that Gramont later claimed produced upon him an impression deeper than anything that his ambassadors, in all of their dealings with foreign governments, would be able to report.[1] The source of this document, whose authenticity Walsh steadfastly guaranteed, remains a mystery, though presumably it emanated from Carlist figures in Spain who claimed to have dealt freely and extensively with the principals involved. The letter announced that Prince Leopold of Hohenzollern-Sigmaringen had informed his aunt, Princess Marie of Baden, that he had accepted the Spanish crown and that she, excited and alarmed, had telegraphed the news to Vevey, home of the wife of Don Carlos, pretender to the Spanish throne.[2] These words were confirmed belatedly at twelve-thirty in the afternoon on 3 July in the form of a telegram from Madrid.[3]

To those in charge of French policy, this seemed a stunning reverse: a shock that produced an effect comparable, said one historian, to the removal of a pin from a hand grenade.[4] There is not much to this. Leopold's decision, far from being the riveting sensation it was later made out to be, was (as we have had occasion to note) a fist that the French had seen on the horizon for a long time. Nonetheless, the French rulers were alarmed, and for good reason. Leopold's election would mean that the royal house of Prussia would rule on both sides of France. In a Franco-Prussian War, the French would have to keep an army on their southern frontier. William I's acquisitions north of the Main, together with his expulsion in 1866 of Austria from the German confederation, made the cup of Prussia's power, almost bone dry only ten years before, seem suddenly dangerously near to spilling over. For this reason, the rulers of France resolved to bring to bear at Madrid such pressure as to make the Spanish government withdraw the offer it had made to Leopold; they resolved to protest at Sigmaringen to the Hohenzollern family in the hope that his decision would be reversed. Some of Napoleon III's ministers developed a higher and more urgent aim: they wanted to humiliate Prussia and to restore French prestige throughout Europe.

Gramont personified this sentiment. Late in the afternoon on 3 July, he went to St. Cloud to see Emperor Napoleon III. Gramont knew before he left that the whole question of the Hohenzollern candidacy and of France's attitude toward it would come up. Yet he made no preparations: Ollivier was out of town, and Gramont did not seek advice from anyone else in the government. Nor did he inquire of the general staff (a practice he rarely followed). His lack of precise information, however, did not handicap him. As soon as Gramont outlined his strategy for the problem, Napoleon III endorsed it. This strategy represented the logical extension of Gramont's view that France must appear as the aggrieved party, unfolding her complaints and making no attempt to disavow her belief that Prussian policy, and the policy of Bismarck in particular, was behind the affair.[5] The strategy that emerged from St. Cloud consisted of four clear steps.

The first step was taken immediately after Gramont returned from St. Cloud: to attack the candidacy officially both at Madrid and at Berlin. Mercier became the recipient of a flurry of alarmed warnings from his superior that Leopold's presence at Madrid would be an intolerable offense against the honor of France and that he must be brought to renounce the throne at once. Gramont laid down: "In order to reverse this excruciating turn of events, you must use all the prudence, the energy, and the imagination that you can muster. Allow yourself to be intimidated by no one. Take care to use your contacts in the press and elsewhere without, of course, compromising yourself."[6] One has in this statement the epitome of the innermost feelings of Gramont as well as of many other highly placed people in Paris for whom Mercier was an intellectually shallow figure with little if any weight of his own to throw into the scales and who had been less than diligent in unearthing the candidacy in the first place. Hence the pedantic character of Gramont's instructions. All the same, the dispatch that he sent off to Mercier on the night of 3 July was not of the fire-eating character that would characterize his dispatches to the Prussian government later on. The difference in tone and style was considerable.

Gramont now turned to Berlin. He telegraphed to Le Sourd, the chargé d'affaires at the embassy, at ten-thirty at night on 3 July, warning the Prussian government not to proceed with the candidacy. The telegram was intended to make a stir, and it did. Its two vital sentences ran: "We cannot, without some chagrin, see a Prussian prince seating himself on the throne of Spain. We should, of course, prefer to learn that the cabinet of Berlin was not privy to this intrigue; if the contrary were the case, its conduct would suggest to us an attitude of too malevolent a nature to define in a telegram."[7] An interesting statement, this, showing quite clearly from the first how little Gramont was deterred from the motivation impelling him toward a confrontation with Prussia and how strongly he was swept away by his belief that only strong words, not a request for assistance, would compel the Prussians to give up the enterprise on which they had embarked. Far from hesitating and saying, "This is a plot of Bismarck's to catch us in a war," Gramont—if a trap it were—dug it deeper and then jumped straight into it. He welcomed it precisely because he was convinced that the French government had an unshakable case.

Precisely at this time Gramont took his second step. He sent out to the French envoys at the various leading diplomatic capitals of Europe a series of alarming messages suggesting that France was in immediate peril.[8] Reports of these messages were duly leaked to the local diplomatic communities and to the presses of the various countries concerned, and these had the effect of heightening the wave of alarm that was now spreading through Europe. They also had the unfortunate effect of evoking from some of the French representatives, as ministerial instructions are apt to do in all foreign services, dispatches back to the ministry designed to reinforce the views (in this case the fears) that the minister had expressed.

Gramont's third step followed closely on the second. He began a campaign to prepare opinion at home for the prospect of a confrontation—indeed, the real possibility of war—with Prussia. This he did through the medium of the newspapers in the capital. Paris was now rocked in those days (as was much of Germany) by the appearance in rapid succession—in the *Constitutionnel,* which was universally considered to be reasonably close to the foreign ministry, and in Prince Napoleon's *Opinion National,* which was generally a more liberal organ—of articles reflecting in overwhelming degree the Gramont line on the question rather than that with which the more cautious of the French ministers were thought to be associated.[9] It was the article in the *Constitutionnel* that, in view of the known reputation of that sheet as an official mouthpiece, caused the greatest stir, especially in the other capitals, where the paper was widely read in diplomatic and in journalistic circles. The other presses of Paris were less vocal in their support of the government, but Gramont was determined to drum up enthusiasm everywhere he could. Rival editors in Paris found their work aided instead of hampered as it had been before, and they provided information all the more zestfully as a result of official encouragement. Defiant columns came out expressing indignation on the grounds of high principle. The *Temps,* a sheet of moderate republican persuasion, was on the offensive. The *Patrie,* a little further to the right, demanded the immediate withdrawal of the candidacy. There was a clear stir, though not (as Gramont later alleged) to the point of war. Indeed some papers—the *Siècle* and the *Journal des Débats,* the one republican, the other Orléanist—refused to go along.[10]

It is fashionable today to argue that moral judgments constitute no part of the task of historians and that historians should dismiss from their minds all conscious thought of them. Still, these pages abound with exceptions to that dictum, and some remarks on the consequences of Gramont's actions seem called for. Actually, the judgment pronounced 125 years ago by Albert Sorel is hard to improve upon: that by moving at once into a campaign of public propaganda, Gramont revealed himself to be a singularly inept and short-sighted diplomat and leader; that the campaign was conducted in such a way as to ensure that events would develop along the most energetic and uncompromising of lines; that it was undertaken before the first French ex-postulations had been presented at Berlin; that it was one thing to ask the Prussians to call off the candidacy, quite another to ask them to admit that they were responsible for the designs attributed to them in the French press; and that nowhere in Gramont's strategy was there a request for the Prussian government to use its good offices to end the affair—an astonishing omission in view of the official Prussian line that Prussia had no involvement in the matter whatsoever. Even more important, however, was Gramont's failure to consult his colleagues before he began his campaign in the press and before he drafted his instructions to Le Sourd and to Mercier. Perhaps he doubted— rightly, Sorel suspects—whether the more moderate members of the gov-ernment were solidly with him and therefore decided to act at once in order to commit them beyond redemption. Probably there was no design at all, only the workings of Gramont's incorrigible impatience, which constantly urged him into a war of words. To him there seemed no alternative between humiliation and defiance. The verdict is indeed harsh but surely not unjust: Gramont displayed, by the tenor of his various undertakings in those initial days of the crisis, a singularly heavy and unhappy touch in the supremely sensitive and delicate matter of relations with Prussia.[11]

Gramont's fourth step was more sensible. On 5 July old Baron Karl von Werther, the Prussian ambassador, came to the foreign office for an urgent conference. Aristocrat to the core, a thoroughly honest if somewhat impres-sionable diplomat of the old school, Werther was liked and greatly respected both by Gramont and by Paris society, and he was only too aware of the danger to the improvement of Franco-Prussian relations posed by the Ho-henzollern candidacy. Gramont seized on this fear and exploited it to the fullest: "The selection of a Hohenzollern prince has produced an extremely painful impression upon French opinion. France will not tolerate it. She will oppose the candidacy with every means at her disposal." As for Spain, its glittering image was only a mirage. France held, over the long run, too many cards—indeed she had a lay-down hand. Leopold would be lucky to last six months. The conversation dragged on for two hours. Gramont ended by expressing the hope that William I would withhold his approval of the candidacy, thereby ending "an unfriendly proceeding on the part of Prussia."[12] There was an empty chair in Gramont's office; neither he nor Ollivier (who had in the meantime rushed back to the capital and had joined the meeting) thought to bring in Napoleon III. An appeal from one sovereign to another would have been a powerful card. A year earlier Benedetti had made known to the Prussians Napoleon's opposition to a Hohenzollern in Madrid—with salutary results. And Gramont would bring in the idea eight days later, when the stakes were much higher. No such appeal took place; no one thought to make it at the time.

All the same, Werther had been "hit on the head." The tension that resulted from the outcry over the candidacy was not calculated to moderate the workings of his naturally nervous temperament. The result was immediate. Werther was about to leave for Ems, where King William was taking his mineral waters; bewitched and anxious, he promised to unfold the French complaints to his master—no small service to the cause of peace. From the time of his arrival at Ems on the morning of 6 July until he departed for Paris three days later, all the influence that he possessed was consistently exerted in the direction of a withdrawal of the candidacy on terms that would suit the French book.

For the moment this did not matter. On the afternoon of 4 July, Le Sourd delivered to Thile the message that Gramont had composed the night before. Thile received the inquiry with the greatest of courtesy (though not a little embarrassment), but he firmly refused any suggestion that would expose the Prussian government to any charge of impropriety in the Hohenzollern matter. He rebuffed Le Sourd's query firmly, saying (as Le Sourd later reported) that *"le gouvernment prussien ignorait complètement cette affaire, et qu'elle n'existait pas pour lui."*[13] Thile's reply has been much criticized by later historians; though entirely false, it was, in fact, the only alternative. Any response less categorical would have excited the French beyond measure— as Gramont's message made clear. Given the tendency to sweeping exaggeration that dominated the convictions of Paris at that moment, it would have been portrayed as a virtual admission of Prussian guilt and complicity. God alone knew what would follow. Le Sourd attempted to draw out the conversation, but Thile would not be moved. Very wisely he decided that, before making further replies to Gramont's inquiry, he would refer the question to Bismarck. This was the news that Le Sourd telegraphed to Gramont at half past four in the afternoon on 4 July.

In the meantime, Gramont continued to move cautiously in his dealings with Madrid. He said to Mercier: "Act with all due respect, with all due tact, with all due deference that is owed the nation." Further telegrams emphasized that the Spaniards were masters of their own destiny and that France "today as before" would respect their sovereignty. Gramont supposed that the provisional government at bottom had disliked the Hohenzollern candidacy all along and would like to get out of it. He wrote on 6 July: "Those who bring it up and advise Spain to accept it assume a not inconsiderable responsibility before their country and before Europe; we have no desire to infringe the liberty of the Spanish nation, but the ordeal is a stain on our honor."[14]

Just at this moment important events were taking place at Varzin. Bismarck was not much troubled when news of the first French remonstrances flashed across Europe. His initial intention had been to refuse to discuss the matter with the French and instead to refer them to Madrid and Sigmaringen: the candidacy was an affair of the Spanish authorities and of a private individual with which the Prussian government had nothing to do. Thus he gave his full approval when he learned what Thile had said to Le Sourd. Bismarck knew from the outset that the French would not be fobbed off by official disclaimers of Prussian knowledge of the affair, but it is a far cry from this to asserting (as have some historians) that he supposed that they would use these disclaimers as a pretext for war. He fully expected French opinion to be indignant, but as long as the Spaniards remained firm, what could the French do? The louder the protest, the more discredit would ultimately fall upon the heads of those making it—that is, on the war party in Paris. To protect his own position, Napoleon would have to shift his weight behind his more moderate ministers, and the prospects for a peaceful resolution of the problem would improve. While it proceeded, the explosion would have the effect of stimulating national opinion in south Germany. If the war party proved more successful than Bismarck expected and took France into war against Prussia, Bismarck had no doubt that the Prussian army would rise to the occasion.[15]

Bismarck's maneuvers during this period have been overlaid with endless controversy. He is sometimes seen as the implacable enemy of France, bent on provoking the showdown that alone could complete the unification of Germany. This is Bismarck's propaganda—witness the statement in his memoirs that he always believed "that a Franco-German War must take place before the construction of a united Germany could be realized."[16] Like many other claims in that dazzling but willful volume, this need not be taken seriously, and in any case belief in the inevitable was not characteristic of Bismarck. On the other side, some historians, seeing how complicated and devious Bismarck's moves were during the first half of 1870, have sometimes ascribed a similar complexity to his aims and calculations and have supposed that uncovering his hidden agenda would enable them to explain them. This, too, will not do. Bismarck's central purpose in 1870 is not a mystery at all: contrary to his intentions, the candidacy became public before Leopold could formally be chosen king. None of the developments that took place from this time on could have been foreseen by him, because he had not intended them. There had been no election in the Cortes, only a proposal by the provisional government—that was what France was reacting to. There is a strong suspicion that during this phase of the crisis Bismarck, having seen that the whole thing had misfired, behaved as if he had nothing to do with it solely because it had misfired and not because he was trying to maintain an appearance of innocence—which nobody in Europe believed anyway. One thing was sure. With Bismarck away in Pomerania and the matter being handled at Ems by the king, the end of it was bound to be the withdrawal of the candidacy, which had been William's aim all along. The world would be presented with the unusual spectacle of the French scoring a resounding diplomatic success at the expense of Prussia: a triumph also in which European opinion was, on the whole, favorable to the French. Bismarck made no move to go to Ems until 12 July 1870, when the crisis seemed over. He was willing to use any means to prevent a French diplomatic triumph, and, as we shall see, Gramont's devices fit Bismarck's needs to the letter.

Bismarck's aim drew the underlying pattern in front of which Prussian policy, during the next eight days, moved. The basic argument of the dispatches that he sent off from Varzin was that vacillation and discord would not work at such an uneasy moment. He therefore determined to tone down Werther's voice. On 5 July he wrote Abeken, the king's factotum at Ems: "The firm and fearless attitude that we have always hitherto adopted in the face of every disturbance at Paris is the most essential feature to which we owe the preservation of peace. France, in my opinion, fears a breach more than we; however, should we give ground for the belief that we are more aloof, French insolence will leave us no other choice than war."[17] Bismarck's motives at the time are not hard to figure out at all. His object was simply to keep Prussian policy on a straight course.

On 6 July he took two other steps that seemed to suggest a conciliatory line. In his view, the darkening cloud of estrangement might be settled by a "confidential understanding" between the two governments. He wrote to Abeken that Leopold "should be informed of the attitude of the French rulers and should seek to win the confidence of the Paris ministers in order to avert the danger that the money and influence of France will be spent on conspiracies in the Spanish army."[18] In another, more direct way Bismarck did his best to keep on good terms with the French. On the same day he also addressed himself to Frederick William, the crown prince of Prussia. He emphasized the pacific intentions of Napoleon III and invited Frederick William to use his good offices to persuade the British government to break down the emperor's suspicions and to effect a tame ending to the crisis.[19]

Bismarck had chosen his ground well. Frederick William was married to Victoria, the British royal princess and the favorite daughter of the prince consort. The approach gave Bismarck some hope (belied in the event) that the offices of the British government might be called in as a restraining influence on the French. It is sometimes said that Bismarck's moves were stalling tactics to keep the French busy until 20 July, when the Spanish election would take place and Leopold could pose as the choice of the people. This is not so. Bismarck was angry over the French demands and suspicious of

Werther, but there is no scrap of evidence that he was at this stage aiming at war with France, still less that he viewed war with her as inevitable. He genuinely believed in the pacific intentions of Napoleon III. Unfortunately, as he suspected all along, Napoleon III controlled French policy not nearly as firmly as he controlled that of Germany.

As on other occasions, Bismarck concentrated on the task at hand and dealt with the future only when it arrived. His immediate object was to keep his hands on the king and Werther away from events. For the time being he got his way. William disliked to withdraw under fire (as he had shown as crown prince in 1848), and he did not care for the hectoring tactics in Gramont's message to Thile. His main concerns were different—the glaring weakness of the provisional government, the dissention and division in the Cortes, and the unfavorable reaction that the offer was likely to encounter in foreign capitals other than Paris, to say nothing of the pain that was likely to be inflicted upon members of the Hohenzollern family as a result of the separation from it of one of its proudest sons. But he resolved not to bow before pressure. Coached by Abeken (himself a fighter) and inspired by the very realities of which Bismarck was afraid he might lose sight, he, on 6 July, addressed a long letter to Karl Anton, inquiring as to the latter's reaction to his son's candidacy in light of the developments in France. The storm was about to blow and to involve him even more than the Sigmaringens. To ward this off, he recited Bismarck's proposal for a consultation with Napoleon III and threw out the suggestion that Leopold, if confirmed on 20 July, might proceed to Madrid by way of Paris in order to reassure Napoleon and the French ministers of his intentions—as if strange chance could arrange that he would be welcome there.[20]

As for Bismarck, he remained buried at Varzin, frustrated and ill. He was indignant that William was listening to the French complaints. His favored concepts of policy toward the question were now beginning, as we shall see shortly, to be shattered. He would continue for the next six days to stand uneasily at the helm of the ship of Prussian foreign policy, but only in order to guide it unhappily, as best he could, among the dangerous shoals and currents into which, left to himself, he would never have brought it.[21] For this reason the reader must not look to him for the same constancy and firmness of touch that he displayed up to now. He was a man buffeted by the winds of contrary fate, and he sometimes swayed with those winds. The running was now taken up by his sovereign, who was taking the waters at Bad Ems.

William's proposal was made to Karl Anton on the assumption that the French rulers, and Napoleon III in particular, were anxious to avoid war. This assumption was mistaken. Napoleon III certainly wished to avoid war, but he was constantly being urged to raise the stakes by the more extreme of his supporters, who were driven on at any sign of compromise. A most unfortunate consequence followed. Gramont had been annoyed and exasperated over the refusal of the Prussian government to discuss the situation; he now determined to answer this defiance by a dramatic appeal to the people of France from the tribune of parliament. On 6 July he delivered a statement to the French chamber in words so vivid and striking that they must be quoted at length:

> It is true that Marshall Prim has offered Prince Leopold of Hohenzollern-Sigmaringen the Spanish throne and that the prince has accepted it. But the Spanish people have not declared their will, and we do not yet know the details of a negotiation that has been concealed from us. A debate cannot, therefore, end in any practical result. We invite you, gentlemen, to adjourn. We have not ceased to manifest our sympathy for the Spanish nation nor to avoid the appearance of any intervention in the affairs of a great nation carrying out its full sovereign rights; we have not departed from the most strict neutrality towards the candidates for its throne and we have not shown any of them either preference or intervention. We will continue this line of conduct.

These last two sentences were, in light of what has been said earlier, the purest nonsense: the main reason why a candidate for the Spanish throne was not found was that the French, and especially Napoleon III himself, frustrated every hopeful effort at a solution, particularly because no such solution could bring the defeat for their opponents and the victory for France that Napoleon III and imperialist prestige demanded. But truth was not the issue. Gramont wanted to give the members of the chamber, the French people, and the powers of Europe a jolt—and so he did. The chamber was duly alarmed, and its members kept grumbling more loudly at intervals during his declaration. Accusations against Leopold were voiced, much to Gramont's delight. He went on:

> We do not believe that respect for the rights of a neighboring people obliges us to endure that a foreign power seating one of its princes on the throne of Charles V may upset to our disadvantage the present equilibrium in Europe and place in jeopardy the interests and honor of France. This situation will, we hope, not come to pass.

This was not the end of the speech. Gramont raised the question what the French government would do if Leopold refused to stand down, and himself returned a defiant answer on the grounds of high principle: "We shall count on the friendship of the Spanish people and on the clear-sightedness of the German people. If it should prove otherwise, fortified by your strength, gentlemen, and that of the nation we know how to fulfill our duty without hesitation or weakness."[22] Here was a clear affirmation that the Prussian government was behind the candidacy and that France would fight if Prussia did not get Leopold to withdraw his acceptance.

Why did Gramont raise the stakes so persistently and so dramatically? Was it merely to swing the weight of opinion in Europe behind the French government? Or did he hope that such a tone would bustle the Prussians into confessing their role in the affair? Probably a little of both. There was also a more personal element: fighting was his natural response to any challenge. Gramont was the leader of those who wanted a showdown, and he may have hoped to establish himself as "the man of the hour" in the eyes of French opinion.

But Gramont alone was not responsible. He was also being pulled hard in this direction by Ollivier. Unlike Gramont, Ollivier had no deep-seated hostility toward Prussia—indeed much sympathy for her; on the other hand, he was convinced that a strong stand at the outset would put things right. So far Gramont had crowded Ollivier from the center of the stage, for the crisis had caught Ollivier unprepared. He, like other Frenchmen at the time, was fully aware that Leopold was the favorite for the throne; where he erred was in his belief that France still had a chance to succeed in Spain—if the right tactics were adopted. Hence his shocked incredulity at the news of Leopold's

107

decision. Alarmed and angry, he rushed back to his offices in Paris and stormed over to the foreign ministry, where Gramont briefed him. Ollivier did not hesitate. He urged a strong line—Leopold must be made to stand down at all costs, even at the cost of war.[23]

There remains, though, the mystery as to why in the first days of July none of the news concerning Leopold got through to Ollivier. Here one can look for explanations only in the general lethargy of the French bureaucratic operations, the absence both of Ollivier and of many other figures of importance from the capital, and the refusal of his underlings to burden him with rumors that might or might not turn out to be true. In any case, he had not been back to Paris for three hours before he found ways of involving himself personally in the declaration to the assembly that Gramont was preparing. The declaration was already hot and strong, and Ollivier made it hotter and stronger. French opinion had to be given some dramatic encouragement; Gramont invoked the ghost of Charles V and the scourge of universal monarchy bound by family ties, but it remained for Ollivier to promise that the French nation would take up arms if the ghost were not excised. It was thus he who penned the final sentence, in the hope of raising a fighting cry from the chamber and the nation. Gramont himself had a more pressing concern: the date of 20 July, when the Cortes was to meet in order to "undo all we were trying to accomplish."[24]

The response was immediate. The commotion with which the assembly received Gramont's speech was so great that the sitting had to be suspended for a while. Sentiment was not all one way. Enthusiasts on the right supported the declaration with excited acclamation; on the center left and part of the center right, the reaction was more apprehension than anger; and on the left it was one of downright hostility. Leading figures accused the government of acting on the basis of misleading or erroneous information and on unspoken assumptions that were wholly untrue: an exaggerated image of German aggressive intentions, probably influenced by imperialist fears and needs; a very poor understanding of the obligations of the other powers, particularly Italy and Austria vis-à-vis France; and a wildly inaccurate picture of Bismarck's intentions with relation to south Germany. A deputy rushed forward and exclaimed: "But this is war! This is a challenge that you are hurling at Prussia!" Gramont replied: "It is peace if peace is possible;

it is war if war is inevitable." The exchange continued until Ollivier cut in: "The government wants peace, passionately wants peace—but peace with honor." He rejected the view that France, in taking up the challenge, was threatening to drag the country into a European war. On the contrary, if she wanted peace she had to prepare for war: "When France shows herself firm in pursuit of her legitimate interest as has, time and again, happened before, she has had the moral support and approval of all Europe."[25]

Thus, it could hardly be said that Gramont's declaration—and, even less, the debate to which it gave rise—united the French assembly behind the government's policy. On another and perhaps more important front, however, the speech achieved its desired effect. The opening gun in what might be called the explosion of public opinion had been fired, and the press reacted accordingly. It roared. The articles that appeared in the newspapers, invoking the names of the most outstanding figures in the governments of France and of Prussia, set tongues wagging and accusations flying for fair. Between 4 and 5 July the campaign against Prussia had begun to wear thin; the newspapers of Paris were still hot with indignation against the candidacy, but not even the most bellicose suggested that war might be imminent if it were not withdrawn. By 7 July this attitude had changed; Gramont's declaration produced a great surge of outraged patriotic feeling; all lesser emotions were laid aside. Ollivier later claimed that "the declaration that France received, in great majority, with impassioned appeal, stirred up neither surprise nor shock in Europe except on the part of a few timorous diplomats who were scared of everything that rose above their usual chatter."[26]

It would be difficult to find in the contemporary records evidence of any kind that gives a scintilla of support to this attitude. The French, to be sure, protested the affront to their security, and the attention of the powers was caught—but hardly in the way that Gramont had intended. The arrow launched by a politician who wished to shape opinion turned around and landed in his own breast. The governments of Europe were driven to near panic by the prospect of war. Even Granville, Clarendon's starchy and colorless successor as British foreign secretary, took alarm. He said to the French ambassador: "Her Majesty's Government very much regret the language by the duke of Gramont in his speech to the French chamber and wonder whether so strident a tone will lead to complications more serious than the incident itself."[27] As in London, so in St. Petersburg: On 7 July General Fleury received secret instructions from Napoleon III to stir up the suspicions of Alexander II and his foreign minister, Gorchakov, against Prussia and—a more ominous point—to warn the two of them that "if Prussia insists on going through with the candidacy of Leopold, this means war."[28] Napoleon III hoped that this threat would bustle the Russians into action. The hope was disappointed. Fleury minuted: "Prince Gorchakov has told me that, while understanding the sensitivities of France, he regrets the communication made to the French chamber by the duke of Gramont because he believes that it will widen the gulf between France and Prussia and add to the difficulties of accommodation."[29]

These two dispatches, excerpted from scores on this subject in the records of the foreign offices, show how wide of the mark the French ministers were. There had been much sympathy for the French case in the capitals of Europe before the declaration of 6 July—and there continued to be. But the effect of Gramont's declaration was to raise the stakes ruthlessly and dramatically, to commit France to war if the candidacy were not called off, and to make it more difficult for her to pull out of the setback with the rest of Europe on her side. The French ministers were, it must be noted, singularly slow to grasp this; neither Gramont nor Ollivier appreciated how disastrous the language of the declaration was to be. Not only did it stir up outrage against France all over Germany; not only was its tone objectionable, with its deliberately invidious distinction of Prussia, as near a neighbor as Spain, as a "foreign power" instead of as a "neighboring people"; not only was Gramont moving ahead of the evidence available to him and contradicting the formal denials of Thile when he accused Prussia of having engineered the plot. His last words threatened Armageddon. They were fatal. Accusations of aggressiveness could now legitimately be laid against France rather than against Prussia. If the further ineptitude of Gramont's policy had not a few days later plunged France into war, there would still have been the declaration to explain, and Bismarck (as he more than once remarked during the week that followed) was ready to demand an explanation of it so humiliating that France could be relied upon to fight instead. No affair better illustrates Talleyrand's dictum: *Pas trop de zèle.*

At this uneasy moment—uncertainty at Madrid, denials at Berlin, a whirl-wind of activity in the capitals of Europe—the French came up with a new and seemingly more rewarding approach. They decided to protest to the king of Prussia, head of the house of the Hohenzollern. Benedetti was re-called from Wildbad, where he had gone on vacation, and was instructed to present the case against Leopold to King William I at Ems. This seemed a promising line. From the start William had been at best tepid in his support for the candidacy; his whole political and religious outlook was against it. He regarded Spain as a country corrupted by Roman Catholicism and by Latin sentimentality. Moreover, at Ems, he was away from Bismarck's influence and free to disregard intransigent advice. His overriding concern was not some high issue of strategy but rather to remain faithful to the tools of his trade.

Gramont appreciated this—or rather his instructions did. He wrote to Benedetti on 7 July:

> If the head of the house of Hohenzollern has up to now been indifferent to this affair, we believe he can remain so no longer, and we ask his intervention, if not in the form of a direct command, at least by friendly advice and counsel to the person of Prince Leopold. . . . For our part . . . we seek the good offices of His Majesty in this unfortunate affair as the means by which we may realize the object of our ambitions, and we believe even more strongly that, by his involve-ment, he will have performed an inestimable service to the cause of peace. For that reason, you are to invite the king to take measures whose effect will cause the prince of Hohenzollern to reconsider his acceptance and to withdraw it with a minimum of difficulty and delay.[30]

Gramont appeared to have chosen his ground well. Here seemed a delib-erate stroke of cool diplomatic ingenuity—an appeal to William's deep sense of moral responsibility. In this guarded language, there seemed a grasp of the deeper realities that might have spared the French government much anguish later on. This conciliatory approach immediately crumbled away. A private letter to Benedetti that he drew up on the same day announced: "It is absolutely vital that you obtain from the king a categorical declaration that flows from the force of the present circumstances. The government of His Majesty is to declare that it no longer approves of the candidacy and disavows it. No equivocation or delays are to be permitted, and in case of a refusal, *c'est la guerre*."[31]

The letter was instructive—striking illustration, if one were needed, of the limitations on Gramont's negotiating skills. It is a commonplace of diplomatic practice for a foreign minister to use a private letter as an escape hatch to keep open a line of retreat if it appears that retreat is necessary. Gramont's letters reversed the traditional pattern: his private letter represented a hardening of the more moderate demands that he had put into his official instructions. Gramont was, as ever, convinced that he was racing against a two-week deadline; he was mesmerized by the date of 20 July. He never thought to attempt to give himself—or the Prussians, too, for that matter—a breathing space during which the run toward war could be slowed down. Quite the contrary; he talked himself into believing that "the government cannot wait much longer" and that his patience was nearing exhaustion, as if patience ever had been the outstanding feature of his character and career. France was, he supposed, in immediate danger of attack from Prussia and so could spare little time for negotiation. He told Benedetti that if the king failed to make the decisive concessions, troops had to begin moving in two days—otherwise the Prussians would throw sand in their eyes.[32] This was a desperate strategy.

When Edouard Count Vincent Benedetti, *ambassadeur extraordinaire* and minister plenipotentiary to the king of Prussia, boarded the train to Ems from Wildbad shortly before eight o'clock in the morning on 8 July 1870, he must have been greatly anxious over the consciousness of his own importance, for the mission that he was about to undertake was one of the most difficult and sensitive diplomatic assignments of all time. He was the bearer of a message of supreme importance from a French government whose foreign minister was singularly averse to negotiations. He had but a few days,

Vincent Comte Benedetti, minister plenipotentiary to Prussia (From Émile Ollivier, *The Franco-Prussian War and Its Hidden Causes*, edited and translated by George Burnham Ives [Boston: Little Brown and Co., 1912], facing p. 132)

maybe even only hours, to secure Leopold's withdrawal. The figure to whom his efforts would be directed was the king of Prussia—a sovereign whose writ, quite unlike that of his counterpart in France, ran unchallenged throughout the realm; a commander who had under his hand one of the greatest engines of war the world had ever known, an army that was still basking in the throes of the victory it had won over Austria just four years before and whose generals, with Moltke at their head, were only too impatient for a fresh trial of strength on the Rhine.[33] Finally, he had to carry out his duties while the king and his entourage were buzzing with resentment over Gramont's defiant speech of 6 July. The news of that declaration reached Ems the same day and brought to the highest intensity the resentment that had been building against France since the crisis began. The situation into which Benedetti now stepped was, in a word, precarious.

Theodor Fontane has drawn a marvelous little sketch of Ems in the last days of June 1870. Never, it seemed, had the city been more beautiful, more pristine, or more composed. Mountain peaks floated peacefully against skies in which the bright blue of summer made way for drifting clouds. In the courtyards and on the promenade, sunshine varied with brief gentle showers. The spa's waters fairly sparkled, and from all over Europe—from as far away as Russia—the most polished royalty came to the city to take its incomparable cures. Little groups of passersby assembled periodically at the marketplace to see the famous take their walks and gathered hourly in the city's square, as they had for centuries, to watch the saints make their appointed rounds in the clock of the town hall. Flowers, music, and laughing voices were everywhere. There were parties every evening. Amidst a shower of bouquets and banquets, William I had arrived at the spa on 20 June; for the next two weeks, free from the press of everyday business, he could do nothing but relax, stroll each morning in the gardens outside his residence, take tea with his British relatives in the late afternoons, and go out nightly to watch the plays and listen to the various concerts and symphonies that were being performed in his honor.[34]

By 7 July all had changed. The quaint garb of the city appeared positively museum-like, detached from the realities of the moment. The days were now tense. Europe had taken its farewell, it seemed, of nearly everything that the Ems hallmarks represented. The Gramont declaration, the first French volley in the war of words, resounded across Europe like the crack of doom. Werther seemed to capture the spirit of the moment when, stepping off the train, he said to one of the king's adjutants: "The devil is loose in Paris. It looks very much like war."[35]

And it did.

Benedetti arrived at Ems at six-thirty in the evening on 8 July, and he saw William I at three o'clock the next day. The meeting was more friendly and successful than either man expected. William I had been taken aback by the stridency with which Gramont had formulated his demands to the French chamber; all the same he took care to articulate, calmly and courteously, the basic thesis that he intended to use against the French position. He admitted to Benedetti that—as head of the house of Hohenzollern, not as king of Prussia—he had approved Leopold's decision and had kept Bismarck posted at key points; however, he had taken no part in the negotiations. While insisting that he would not command Leopold to give up the throne, he revealed that he was at this moment trying to size up the intentions of his relatives at Sigmaringen. In the king's words: "I am awaiting their decision and will discuss the matter more fully with you when word of it arrives."[36]

Benedetti was not discouraged by this conversation. He telegraphed to Paris at nine o'clock in the evening on 9 July: "I see, for my part, nothing objectionable for the king to first take soundings from the Hohenzollern princes before making their decision known to me."[37] Benedetti's reading of the situation was not inaccurate. He was on good terms with the outstanding figures of the Prussian government—he had been the French minister at Berlin for six years— and by them known to be an honorable and sensitive official of substantial experience, a person with whom they could do business.

For all that, however, his dispatch was not liked at Paris. Gramont said: "The negotiations are off to a bad start."[38] In his view, William I was not bargaining in good faith; he was less than forthcoming in meeting the overriding French objective that the candidacy of Leopold be brought to an end once and for all. It was no good for Benedetti to argue that commanding

Leopold's renunciation cut across royal dignity. This was a moral conception that Gramont regarded as of little importance in a crisis so supreme as this. With his ear cocked to public opinion, he began at once to batter away for some dramatic admission that would tell decisively against Prussia. Throughout the morning of 10 July, Gramont conferred with his secretaries at the Quai d'Orsay, groping for some device that would push William forward. At 1:25 he telegraphed to Benedetti: "Send me as soon as possible some communication that I can deliver to the floor of the chamber that the king of Prussia has *explicitly authorized* the acceptance of the throne by the prince of Hohenzollern and that he has requested your good offices in negotiating with him."[39]

Here was a decisive turn in the history of the crisis. Benedetti was instructed not merely to seek the withdrawal of the candidacy but to prop up support for the French government. In other words, any answer from Ems that was not a straight "yes" or "no" was now regarded by Gramont (and not by him alone) as proof that the king was stalling. It has been said that the greatest test of a statesman faced by a crisis is to slow down the march of events. Gramont would not have passed this test. There is other proof of this. On the night of 10 July, William I met Benedetti on the promenade at Ems. This was a curious conjugation; William I merely happened to be out for a breath of night air. He conveyed the news that the negotiations were still proceeding at Sigmaringen but added, with a little annoyance, that he was having difficulty reaching Leopold, who was on a walking tour of the Austrian Alps and out of touch with events. Nevertheless, William let Benedetti know that he was expecting an answer and indeed took pains to indicate that one would not be long in coming.

Benedetti did not mistake the import of what he had just been told. William's revelation, though much in the nature of a casual aside, was in Benedetti's view solid evidence that the king was at the center of events—where the French wanted him, determined to work his influence on his relatives in a salutary direction and intent to see that things kept moving along. As Benedetti observed later: "After all, what sense would it have made for the king to seek me out merely to tell me that there was nothing to report?"[40] Shortly before midnight, 10 July, Benedetti wired Gramont with a suggestion that the French try to relax the tension of the moment.[41] Gramont wired back his rejection: "You must redouble your efforts. Time is running out."[42] At midday on 11 July, Benedetti again met with William I. Badgered by Gramont, he was pushed into saying that the king was not doing enough; preparations were going forward to welcome Leopold at Madrid—a statement that in fact was not true—and the king had to take action at once if peace were to be preserved. William I remained unmoved. Benedetti's demand for an answer, pressed to the point of impertinence, evoked the same response as before: a promise not to stand in Leopold's way if he wanted to withdraw; a firm refusal to bring about that withdrawal by royal command.[43]

Underneath, there was, to be sure, a considerable change. William I was using all his influence at Sigmaringen to prepare the retreat that Bismarck had feared all along. Benedetti reported: "After having interrogated me at several points during the interview, the king ended by authorizing me to telegraph to you in his name that he was in contact with the princes of Sigmaringen, that a reply to his inquiries was imminent, and that he had every reason to believe that this reply would be definitive, final." He added more significantly: "A delay of two or three days will not make things worse."[44]

At Sigmaringen the way was being paved for Leopold to depart, however respectfully, from the political scene. Werther, who was about to leave once more for Paris, was forthright in this opinion. He said to Benedetti on 11 July: "The French government is likely to get what it wants," and Benedetti was too astute an observer not to pass along what he was told to Paris. He added more significantly: "I am absolutely convinced that Werther's return is good news for us and that it could have no purpose other than to demonstrate the goodwill of the king."[45] And again in a longer letter the same night: "From what has been said to me by the king, by those in his entourage, and, still more important, by M. de Werther, I am of the opinion that the Prussian monarch believes that the prince of Hohenzollern will renounce the crown that has been offered to him, that he will do so without delay, and that His Majesty the King of Prussia will not hesitate to give his full backing to a decision that he has himself played no small part in making."[46] These were not the words of a man who was whistling in the dark. No report from any other minister at a single European capital contradicted Benedetti—indeed, all reports confirmed, almost to the letter, what he was saying: that time was needed to effect the result that the French wanted to achieve; that the king of Prussia was doing all he could to bring this about; and that, because of all this, bluster at so tense a moment was singularly unwise. But, of all this, Gramont—inspired by the lively imaginations of his more bellicose journalists, themselves egged on by the military planners—was not to be persuaded, and the result was that the literally scores of pages of the *Origines diplomatiques de la guerre de 1870–1871* are taken up with accounts of his efforts to drive the powers of Europe, Britain and Russia most of all, into ringing declarations of public support—efforts that were, it must be added, not particularly welcome at the London and St. Petersburg ends and to which the responses of Granville and of Gorchakov were decidedly tepid.[47]

Benedetti's letter reached Paris on the night of 12 July. Did its optimistic conclusions make any difference? Not much. The ministers had another, seemingly more urgent problem on their hands. William's refusal to give way on 9 July had caused an uproar in the chamber of deputies. Members complained that they were being left in the dark, and for this predicament the government had only itself to blame. Gramont's decision to take to the public platform on 6 July led straight to the dilemma faced by the ministers five days later: once a flamboyant campaign of public propaganda had been launched, the French rulers faced an onslaught of demands for more information— from opponents both on the right and on the left. The complaints could not easily be ignored, and now the ministers feared that internal disturbance would raise its head against the deadlock at Ems. There had to be a new justification for the government's line of policy. On 11 July Gramont sounded the national appeal once more. He again appeared in the chamber. He thought to get through the session by asking members to rely on "their patriotism and good sense" while the ministers "deliberate before the emperor."[48]

He received cold comfort. The deputies wanted information. Information was what Gramont could not provide. A great row followed. The parties of the right and of the left tumbled into a bitter dispute over how far the government intended to go. Emmanuel Arago, an oppositionist on the left, demanded to know whether "considerations apart from the candidacy of Leopold had been raised."[49] Protests from both sides cut him off. A vote of cloture was carried. Gramont went home, unable to explain his policy. Ollivier, who had accompanied him, went home too. The row left deep marks. The overriding impression was that the forces of opposition would soon sweep away the ministry. On the night of 11 July, Metternich was moved to declare that Napoleon III had made up his mind to order mobilization the next day if the French demands had not been completely satisfied.[50] Ollivier—whose recognition of the gravity of the crisis manifested itself, he tells us, in chronic insomnia, for the remedy of which he now taking ever heavier doses of sleeping powders—confessed himself helpless before the awful drama. Agonizing like Hamlet over the cruel dilemmas and exigencies of a time out of joint, he shrugged his shoulders and said to Lyons: "Any cabinet—any government—that acquiesced in this affair would be overthrown. The very honor, the very greatness, of France is at stake."[51]

Other prominent Frenchmen, it should be noted, saw the dangers in so rigid an outlook. Adolphe Thiers, a former prime minister, stood at their head. Though keen to see the candidacy of Leopold dissolve, he was estranged by the blustering tone of Gramont's declaration of 6 July and supposed, with sharp foresight, that the bottom was likely to be knocked out of the French case abroad if it were pressed too ruthlessly at Ems. Thiers spoke with the voice of experience; he had been in much the same position when he defied Europe thirty years before and had paid the price of humiliation. His immediate concern was with the crisis in parliament. In Ollivier's words: "On 10 July he expressed himself of a view that was the exact reverse of most of the deputies. He declared that the withdrawal of the candidacy would, in whatever form, be a victory of dimensions so great for France that we would be fools not to content ourselves with it."[52] Thiers appreciated that the prevailing cry against the candidacy, reinforced as it was at just this moment by uproar in the chamber of deputies, would drive the ministers over the edge and so ensure the outbreak of war. He therefore offered his assistance and asked for a consultation with Napoleon III. Napoleon rejected the request.

Thiers's voice was drowned out by the tumult of the ongoing political crisis. Ollivier and Gramont returned from the chamber faced (in Ollivier's incredible words) with the naked choice between *"war and abdication as a*

Great Power."[53] Ollivier seems to have inclined toward the former if the king did not soon give way. Gramont, on his side, was much more clear-cut. In his view, the outburst in parliament against Prussia was part of a larger pattern of national indignation.[54] The view was not without substance. Leading politicians were stumping Paris, winning popularity for themselves and implanting the passions of war in the breasts of their audiences; bellicose journalists were pulling in odd pennies by writing jingoistic pieces; reports of the government's agents in the country bore out the expectation, held as an article of faith by Gramont, that the conscience of France had been shaken by the candidacy of Leopold.

Here again, however, the historian can only note that much of this outcry was of the government's own making. It was the declaration of 6 July that provided the momentum for this outlook and that led Gramont to exaggerate its influence. On 10 July he wrote to Benedetti: "Public opinion has burst into flames, is being brought to white heat, and is going to overwhelm us."[55] It was exasperating for Gramont that Benedetti had not breathed unquestioning defiance to William I, had watered down the blunt hostility to the candidacy expressed in his own declaration of 6 July. Gramont vented his exasperation in a letter to Benedetti on 11 July: "Up to the point at which we have now arrived, I cannot hesitate to inform you that your language has, with relation to firmness of tone, not represented the position assumed by the emperor's government. You must today make it more emphatic. We cannot admit the distinction between the king and his government that has been suggested to you. We demand that the king forbid the prince to persist in the candidacy."[56]

The rebuke was undeserved. Benedetti was far from wishing to weaken the French case. On the contrary, he did more to improve it than any other single man in the whole of the crisis. He had been sent to Ems to extract concessions from William I; this could only be done by tact and deliberation of utterance—qualities, one must add, for which his superior in Paris was not noted. In Benedetti's own words: "War could be avoided only if France and Prussia made clear their determination to maintain peace. . . . If, upon arriving at Ems, I had laid down an ultimatum, I would have caused us to lose whatever advantages we might otherwise have had."[57] It was to Benedetti's credit that he had opened the negotiations—no mean achievement after Gramont's blustering—and that he had wheedled from the king valuable admissions. At bottom, his mind fathomed with little difficulty what William I had in mind: the aims of freeing himself and his government of responsibility for the candidacy, of leaving the Sigmaringen princes full liberty to make up their own minds but at the same time striving to bring them to take the step he would afterwards sanction. This was the note Benedetti repeatedly struck in his reports to Paris. At all events, his patience—unlike that of Gramont—was far from exhausted.

William I was in difficulties. After authorizing Leopold to accept the throne of Spain, he was now called upon to retract that authorization. His personal dignity was offended as well—especially as the French government had addressed him in threatening terms in parliament. All the same, he preserved a moderate attitude. Did he regret giving his personal consent? Or did he look with alarm at the prospect of war between France and Prussia? Probably a little of both. At any rate, he did his best to accommodate Benedetti. What he seemed to desire was that his self-esteem should be considered and that he should be given time to make arrangements. But the time was out of joint. Tired, overcome by the heat of midsummer, he had come to Ems to relax and take his mineral cures. Instead, he found himself weighed down by the wearisome business of politics. Telegrams were pouring in at the rate of four or five an hour. Audiences had to be granted. He could not see Queen Augusta. The endless consultations and fatiguing diplomatic maneuvering had taken their toll on his patience and on his congeniality. His temper was short, his emotions sensitive, his communications conducted in a hugger-mugger of haste and confusion.

William's mood turned sour. The French rulers were surrendering to popular outcry and obstruction. From Sigmaringen there was nothing, silence. The letter that he had written to Karl Anton on 6 July had been intended to paint a clear picture of the difficulties that Leopold would face as king of Spain and thus to make it easier for him to pull out. The Sigmaringens had, as yet, showed not the slightest willingness to do so. William I feared that in the heated atmosphere of the time, nothing would come of his intervention. Still, his resolve was unshaken. He said to his wife: "I will not spend a thaler to buy a vote [in the Cortes]."[58] And a little later: "I hope with all my heart that Leopold is not elected."[59] In the meantime, Benedetti could only report that the king's desire for a peaceful outcome was unquestionable and that he was redoubling his efforts to contact his cousins.[60]

The news of all of these events, fortified by a stupendous volume of rumor and of speculation, had, by 12 July, created a state of the highest uneasiness in Paris. Leopold's refusal to stand down had brought Gramont's temper to a fever pitch. There were wild counsels in the chamber calling for immediate war. The Rhine could easily be crossed; the Prussian capital could be occupied by the French in a matter of days; the war would end with a new Jena. In light of these circumstances, the leading officers in the army were now given a greater voice in the proceedings. On 12 July Gramont talked with the French commander, Le Boeuf, and was told by him that war should begin at once; any delay would be disastrous.[61] In the heat of the moment, rumors of impending Prussian mobilization were flying thick and fast in the journalistic and diplomatic centers of the city. Unfortunately, such rumors found credence in the most strategically placed and influential of the French ministers.

In the meantime the international situation was changing. Italy was the weakest of the Great Powers, both in economic resources and in political coherence. She was estranged from Prussia by resentment that she had not received her due share of war prizes in 1866; she missed her cut of the Trentino and was fobbed off, after much complaint, with Venetia. Still, her enemy was Austria-Hungary, not Prussia, still less France. Two premises underlay the calculations of the Italian government. The first was that Italy could not afford to become involved in a war, no matter how or why it started. The second was that if war did break out she might be dragged into it despite herself.

An examination of the available evidence concerning the origins, the course, and the consequences of the efforts undertaken by Italian diplomacy at this time would in itself constitute a scholarly exercise of major proportions and would far surpass the limits of the present study, to which it is only incidentally related. Suffice it to say for purposes of this narrative that with the possible exception of one or two figures whose actions are recounted below, these efforts could never have yielded fruit but for the immense exactions of a single man: Emilio Visconti-Venosta, foreign minister since December 1869. S. William Halperin has called Visconti-Venosta one of the most level-headed foreign ministers in Italian history, "calm, cool, reflective, and clear-sighted," and the description is apt.[62] Visconti-Venosta was a strong character—a match for Bismarck in diplomatic skill, the equal of Ollivier in high-minded aspiration, and master of all in romantic utterance.

On 5 July, when news of the Hohenzollern candidacy first came through, Visconti-Venosta urged King Victor Emmanuel and the cabinet of ministers that Italy could not stand entirely aside. She must show that she was involved. But how? A public protest to Berlin would be too provocative, especially when it was not known whether the candidacy could be called off by the intervention of King William. A promise of unequivocal support to France without first securing a French evacuation of Rome would commit Italy too much. But what about private warnings to the Spanish regency? This would show that Italy was not sleeping. At the same time, it would be an assurance toward France that Italy had good intentions. The French ambassador, Malaret, welcomed this idea; on 8 July he cabled Gramont that, in the event of a Franco-Prussian war, Italy would not be found among France's enemies.[63] Beyond this, Visconti-Venosta was unwilling to go. He was, like the rest of the Italians, less concerned to be on the side of France than to keep his powder dry.

Precisely at this time the Aosta candidacy, dormant for seven months, was receiving new support. Sir Henry Layard, the British minister at Madrid, was a perceptive observer, vigor personified, ready to do anything to keep Leopold off the throne. He sympathized with the French grievances, however much he disliked Gramont's way of voicing them. In Layard's view, peace was more important than justice, and the lesser power must yield, however humiliatingly, so that peace could be preserved. Granville, too, thought that the regency needed to be shaken. On 7 July he telegraphed to

Emilio Visconti-Venosta, foreign minister of Italy (From *Enciclopedia italiana di scienze, lettere ed arti,* edited by Giovanni Trecanni, 35 vols. [Rome: Istituto della enciclopedia italiana fondata da Giovanni Trecani, 1937], 25:449; used by permission of the Istituto della enciclopedia italiana fondata da Giovanni Treccani, Rome)

Layard: "Use every pressure which will not offend the Spanish government but which, in your judgment, will promote the abandonment of the Hohenzollern project. You will say nothing that would provoke them to adhere to it."[64]

Layard duly complied. On 10 July he saw Moret y Pendergast, the minister of colonies, who inquired "whether, in the event a way could be found by which the candidature of the prince of Hohenzollern could be put aside, the English government would be disposed to help the Spanish government to find another candidate for the Spanish throne, as this was an absolute necessity—for instance, would they endeavor to obtain the consent of the duke of Aosta to accept the crown?"[65] Layard quickly drew the deduction: the duke of Aosta was again in the running for the Spanish throne.

The problems with the Aosta candidacy were revealed almost immediately. For one thing, it suffered from there being cabinet opposition to it. Sella vowed publicly that it would never take place as long as he was in office, and Lanza was of the same opinion—a view that had not changed since the Aosta candidacy was first aired in November 1869. Fortunately for his government, Lanza's budget had left the Italian army in a miserable condition— "barely sufficient for internal security"[66]—so that the more astute of the foreign observers realized that the French were expecting too much from Italian assistance (though this did not much matter in the heat of the moment).

A second problem was more decisive. Victor Emmanuel was known to be a fire-eater, aggressively pro-French and anti-Prussian. He had not forgiven Bismarck for making a premature peace in 1866, and he longed for the day when Italian prestige could be redeemed, not by peace but by war. He wished to shake himself free of all ministerial restraints and to use the crisis as a launching pad for a new burst of activity in the Italian question. Vanity, lack of credibility, unreliability—all of these had their part to play in the fiasco that was about to take place. Victor Emmanuel was by no means unaware of the size of his previous follies or of the weakness and limitations from which he suffered. (He is said, for instance, to have believed that his highly erratic and unscrupulous behavior in the war against Austria in 1866 had condemned Italy to a sterile and inconclusive peace and left his country no alternative but to stick with France through thick and thin.) So obvious, in fact, was the connection, in many instances, between his own anxieties about his past conduct and the humilities and exactions he inflicted on others, and so clearly were his pretensions to international eminence concentrated in areas where he knew his shortcomings to be greatest, that the student of his life could, without difficulty, find in the demands he placed upon others, something like a perfect index of the blunders he really committed and of the weaknesses of which he was really conscious.

The first news of the crisis arrived while Victor Emmanuel was at his hunting lodge at Valsvaranche, in the mountains of the Val d'Aosta. He stayed there ten days longer, which suggests that he did not know quite how to proceed. Meanwhile, the "promises" to France for which he now took personal responsibility were revealed in the absence of his ministers. He ominously remarked that "in this grave situation I do not want to find myself embarrassed by objections from the cabinet."[67] No doubt he feared to be present when the ministers were apprised of the situation. Possibly he wanted to be near Turin and Lanza's enemies, with whom he was now said to be having secret talks; possibly he wanted to be far away from Florence while a parliamentary attack was organized by oppositionists aimed at replacing Lanza with one of the king's friends. When this plan miscarried, he rebuked Napoleon that more warning should have been given so that he could have launched his plans for a *coup*. Paget had some inkling as to what was afoot and commented that "Victor Emmanuel is no joke under the present circumstances."[68]

Thus, while Visconti-Venosta pushed for peace, Victor Emmanuel pulled for war. On 8 July Victor Emmanuel conscripted Vimercati, his close friend, to act as intermediary between himself and Napoleon III. The essence of his proposal was this: Napoleon III should withdraw his troops from Rome; Italy would march into battle on France's side. On 9 July Vimercati wired the king: "A Franco-Italian pact will be completed at any moment."[69] Victor Emmanuel had opened these negotiations, one will not be surprised to hear, without any knowledge whatsoever on the part of the foreign minister. Thus, in the middle of an international crisis, the most severe he was ever to face, Visconti-Venosta had to contend with his own sovereign as well as with his counterparts in Paris, London, and Berlin—not an easy assignment.

No one could accuse Visconti-Venosta of a lack of energy. On 9 July he instructed Cadorna, the Italian minister at London, to sound out Granville on the possibility of joint action by the two powers not only at Madrid but— a more important point—also at Berlin. Italy and Britain would combine,

Victor Emmanuel II, king of Italy (From Alfredo Comandini, *Vittorio Emanuele II* [Turin: Ditta G. B. Paravia E. Comp., 1911], facing title page)

press for the withdrawal of Leopold's candidacy, and run Amadeus instead. Granville temporized; while stressing the need for plain language in Berlin, he insisted that efforts from outside to bring about a peaceful settlement be concentrated at Madrid. Moreover, though professing his delight that Italy and Britain shared similar views, he saw no reason why they should not express them separately.[70]

Here was the old British aloofness from Europe. It was uncommon for the British to conceive of any organization of Europe for its own sake rather than simply for British purposes of a balance of power. For seven years past, the British had followed a policy of detachment from Europe. Their relations with the continental powers, though intense and sometimes hostile, had been shaped by events outside Europe. Most of the cabinet had little interest in European affairs; they took the view that the European powers balanced each other out and that whatever happened would basically not make any difference (as it had in the Napoleonic times seventy years before, under a single ruler) in such a way as to endanger Great Britain. Nobody wanted to invade them. In their view, it was useless to try to distinguish between France and Prussia (or, for that matter, the other European powers) on the basis of how enlightened or benighted, scrupulous or unscrupulous, they were. If a verdict must be delivered, it would come straight out of the Old Testament: "They are all gone astray, they have all become as an unclean thing; there is none that doeth good, no, not one."

Still, Granville had no doubt that whatever the rights and wrongs of the matter, it was Spain's duty to give way. Some infringement of Spain's independence was better than a European war. He therefore agreed to warn the Spaniards that Great Britain would not support the choice of Leopold for the throne.[71] That was all. A useful distinction can be drawn here between the British and Italians on the score of their depth—how much of the crisis and how many of its dimensions their policies seriously dealt with. On this score, it is clear that the British were less European than any of the other Great Powers.

While the British and the Italians were debating the merits of the Aosta candidature, the negotiations for an alliance between France and Italy were moving forward. On 10 July Napoleon III received Vimercati at St. Cloud. Napoleon was bent on consolidating a united front against Prussia, and for the moment he seemed to succeed. He chipped away the last anxieties of Vimercati over Rome and pledged that French troops would withdraw as soon as the alliance was signed. Vimercati and Napoleon resolved to work together against the candidacy of Leopold until Amadeus had been put in his place. Vimercati added that he had refrained from discussing the alliance officially with Napoleon's Italian confidant, Nigra, lest the latter be distracted from the effort (in which the Austrians were likewise involved) to prevent the outbreak of war.[72] This was an impressive display of words, though rather late in the day when so much had changed already.

Did Napoleon mean what he said? He had promised to pull French troops out of Rome, but in truth he also had to worry about the opinion of the French clericals for whom *Roma capitale,* the battle-cry of the Italian nationalists, was anathema. All the same, Vimercati received a powerful reinforcement from Napoleon's now-bellicose sentiment. If the reply from Prussia, expected to arrive from Ems the next day, were less than satisfactory—less, that is, than an unequivocal withdrawal of Leopold's candidacy—all would be lost: Benedetti would be withdrawn from Ems, France would mobilize her troops, and war would follow. If this came to pass, Napoleon would notify Visconti-Venosta that France was relying on the *"anciennes promesses"* of the Italian government—an impression that he carried forward from his dealings on the subject with Victor Emmanuel the year before. The French garrison would be withdrawn from Rome "as soon as possible," and the Italian government would be called upon to dispatch via Vienna 100,000 men. The military cooperation of Austria, indispensable for an invasion of south Germany, was taken for granted. During the negotiations and later, France and Italy would differ sharply over how the Italian war effort was to be conducted and the precise terms for its operations, but this did not matter in the explosion of impatience and frustration of the moment.[73]

On 10 July Vimercati wired Victor Emmanuel at Valsvaranche with news of Napoleon's scheme. Victor Emmanuel snatched at it. A member of the house of Savoy would take the Spanish throne at Madrid; Rome would become Italy's capital, and Victor Emmanuel a hero in all Italian eyes. Victor Emmanuel's defiant attitude barred the way against any attempt at temporizing, and of course, the more the king pushed for a quick solution to the Roman question, the more suspicious Visconti-Venosta became. Victor Emmanuel did not repine at this; he liked to make differences sharper where Visconti-Venosta had sought to smooth them over. Victor Emmanuel took a ferocious line in foreign policy and in all else; he had long groaned under Visconti-Venosta's drift and delay. He was impatient with words and phrases, whether those of his foreign minister or all that structure of pact and treaties on which the French had in the past relied. In any case he now believed that he had Napoleon III in the palm of his hand.

Against this, Visconti-Venosta determined to remain the steady diplomat. Wiser than Victor Emmanuel, he did not want to settle things at a rush and believed that to do so would be a blunder of the first order. His fundamental concern was the future of Franco-Italian relations. In his view, even tolerable relations between France and Italy, not to speak of a rapprochement or an accord, was out of the question as long as imperial troops remained on papal soil in defiance of the convention of September 1864; as one of the negotiators of that treaty during his first brief tenure of the foreign ministry, he wished to see it reactivated, and its reactivation was impossible unless France fulfilled her part of the original bargain and ended unconditionally her illegal occupation of Rome. At the same time, he was becoming worried over the possibility of an imminent outbreak of hostilities between France and Prussia; only hours before, he had received reports from Nigra about an early French mobilization. If war came, the fate of Rome would have to be decided immediately; the question would have to be taken up by the Italian cabinet. The king's presence, however unwelcome from almost every other point of view, was therefore indispensable. At six o'clock in the evening on 10 July, Visconti-Venosta steeled himself and took the plunge, telegraphing to Victor Emmanuel that he must come down from his hunting lodge in the mountains and return to Florence. A confrontation between the king and the cabinet appeared imminent.

This did not trouble Victor Emmanuel. He regarded a Franco-Prussian war as a heaven-sent reward for his years of private diplomacy; in Florence he could stir up opinion against his weak ministers and perhaps replace them with his friends. As a consequence of this, a general state of anticipation and apprehension swept over Visconti-Venosta in the final hours of 10 July 1870. He was seriously disturbed by the king's pending arrival. The history of Italian diplomacy contained too many examples of double-dealing and of the simultaneous pursuit of conflicting policies by different parties for him to rest easy. All this, together with other disturbing symptoms of behavior in Victor Emmanuel, produced in Visconti-Venosta a distrust of the king and his policies that he was never able to overcome. From now on he would see in Victor Emmanuel an unreliable sovereign, to be watched closely at every turn. And things were only made worse for him by the fact that Victor Emmanuel was, at this moment, far from being the only problem. There were others—very serious ones—with which Victor Emmanuel's duplicities had now to be taken in conjunction.

One such problem was that no one had yet been able to find Amadeus, who (like Leopold) was somewhere in the Alps and unaware of what was going on. Another, more ominous problem had just unfolded at Ems: just before midnight on 10 July Visconti-Venosta learned that William I had admitted to Benedetti that he had approved of Leopold's candidacy and had added that he was trying to arrange a conference with the prince. This revelation came as no surprise to Visconti-Venosta.[74] For all its drama, it brought a reprieve of sorts. Most of the courts and diplomats of Europe had hit on the idea that a withdrawal of the candidacy would be a way out—a means of avoiding war between France and Prussia. The provisional government at Madrid, too, was at last moved to act. On 10 July it sent a special representative to Sigmaringen to beg Leopold to take back the acceptance that it had for months urged upon him. The king of Belgium (at Napoleon III's request), Beust, and Queen Victoria also had written to urge the Hohenzollerns to reconsider their position.[75]

Such pleas were not without effect on William I. On 10 July he again talked with Abeken. He brought out all his old arguments—Spain was threatened with revolution, wracked with social discontent; a long civil war was in the offing; at best, the country could be tamed only by inordinate efforts, lasting for years and tearing it to pieces.[76] It is not hard to understand why William I took the line he did. He wanted the Sigmaringens to respond—and to respond quickly—to the points he had put to them. That hope was disappointed. On 8 July Karl Anton had finally stirred himself to action. He sent off to Ems a telegram expressing a wish to obey a command from the king but refusing otherwise to renounce the Spanish throne. The answer drew blood from William I. He said to Queen Augusta: "My cousin is much impressed by the turn of events in Paris, but thinks he cannot draw back and that I and I alone am the one who must break off the affair. I have replied that I can do nothing, but that I would, with joy, approve a decision to do so on his part."[77]

William I increased his appeals to Karl Anton. He sent a special emissary, Colonel von Strantz, to Sigmaringen with a letter that said: "It is plain that, if Prince Anton should decide on the abandonment of the Spanish candidacy by the hereditary prince, the King [of Prussia] would, as head of the family, be at once in accord with him, as when he gave his assent to the acceptance several weeks before."[78] The letter, though not much more than a recitation of what had been said a dozen times before, is a reminder that William was committed to finding a peaceful outcome and that he was pushing his relatives in this direction. To the queen once more, he said: "God grant that the Sigmaringens have an understanding mind."[79]

It was a strange crisis, everyone waiting for some sort of revelation, William I waiting most anxiously of all. He was weighed down by troubles. The French were making menacing gestures; most of the courts and diplomats of Europe were now insisting that a voluntary renunciation of the throne by Leopold would be the first step toward peace. At Sigmaringen nothing would boil. William had intended to rely on the good offices of Strantz. His plan miscarried: on the evening of 11 July, Strantz missed his connection at Bruchsal and could not see Karl Anton until the morning of the 12th. For the next fourteen hours, there was stillness, no signs of life: William I received no information from Karl Anton, and Karl Anton received no advice from William I.

In the meantime, pressure built up from other sources. Ion Strat was the Rumanian envoy to Paris, most anxious over the effect that French hostility might have on the throne of Charles I of Rumania, Leopold's younger brother. For the last three years, Charles's position had been shaken by the difficulties that he experienced in governing his country. The Russians, in particular, viewed him with distaste and would have liked to displace him with someone more inclined to indulge their interests. Gramont shared their aversion and regarded him as an accomplice in the nefarious Hohenzollern designs that he saw springing up all over Europe. For the moment Napoleon overruled him. He let Strat know that if the latter could succeed in persuading Karl Anton to call off the candidacy, France was prepared to suspend against Charles any intrigues into which Gramont might have entered.[80]

Strat departed for Sigmaringen on the morning of 10 July, and he arrived there the next night. He found Karl Anton anxious and alarmed—doubly so when he placed in his hands a weighty communication, a letter of almost six pages from Olózaga, in which the latter (himself egged on by the more bellicose of the French ministers) poured out the full measure of his aroused feelings and opinions and described in the most lurid of terms the chamber of horrors that awaited Leopold in Madrid. Strat added that Olózaga's views were shared by others in Paris—that the French were and had been feeding secret and highly derogatory information about the king to his opponents—but that if Leopold were to step aside, Napoleon would lighten the weight of Charles's burden. This, coming from a mere envoy, was powerful stuff, and Karl Anton, fully sensitive to what was implied, did not take kindly to it. Nor was this surprising: Karl Anton was, as we have had occasion to note, an intensely ambitious man, wildly hostile to the French (even if he was more nearly connected by blood with Napoleon III than with the king of Prussia). The events of the winter and spring of 1870—the fact that he was approached by the Spaniards, was taken into confidence about Leopold's prospects, and was able to appear as the instrument through which the candidacy of the latter was born and established (and all this with Bismarck's encouragement and enthusiastic support)—induced in him a state of elation and self-importance so exalted as to unbalance to some degree his equanimity and good judgment. A serious attack of a nervous disorder at the time seems further to have affected his equilibrium.

Karl Anton therefore lost no time in taking up the challenge that Strat had hurled down. Stung to the quick by the threat against his son, he reacted explosively; the next few hours were taken up by angry exchanges. All the same, Strat's mission marked a significant turning point in Karl Anton's views and position. This is, at any rate, what he told Strantz when the latter, exhausted and breathless from the mishap over his travels, finally arrived from

Bruchsal on 12 July: "The thought of an imminent *casus belli* because of a family matter had become so unbearable that I had to rein in myself not to publish the decision yesterday. But I believed it my duty first to await Colonel von Strantz's arrival."[81] Shortly after nine o'clock in the morning on 12 July, Strantz wired Abeken at Ems: "Found everybody favorably prepared. My arrival turned the scales. Induced betrothed to renounce alliance. Returning tomorrow afternoon."[82]

Strantz's telegram was but the first step, however; the dramatic news would be conveyed to the other principals by a more circuitous route. In Paris, these were days of extreme tension and excitement. French policy was considered at a ministerial council on 12 July. The deadlock and silence brought to the highest intensity the varying views among the members of the government over what line of policy to adopt. Gramont said: "If immediate war against Prussia is not now at the head of our list of possibilities, no French policy is possible any longer. We have obtained nothing for our efforts. Absolutely nothing."[83] Despite this, the council did not resolve on war; it merely decided to reaffirm the French demands and to see what would happen. But everyone was anxious. Ollivier and Gramont, in particular, had developed a feeling that the entire French attitude toward the negotiations, if not the future of France herself, was at stake. Both men experienced a frantic sense of urgency for some gesture of support and of understanding from the European governments. It must not be forgotten that this was the darkest and most crucial hour of the crisis, when anxieties and the sense of personal frustration were at their highest pitch, nerves and energies drawn to the utmost level of endurance.

Still, all was not lost. At quarter to one in the afternoon on 12 July, Gramont telegraphed to Benedetti: "Our object has never been to provoke a conflict but to protect the legitimate interests of France in a question that we did not explode. . . . We cannot refuse the king of Prussia the delay he asks for, but trust that this delay will not exceed a day. We approve the language that you used in your last message."[84] Here was a gleam of light in the darkness. Despite the deep-seated suspicion with which Gramont had regarded all previous communications from William I, his dispatch to Benedetti was a genuine, if belated, gesture of conciliation that had been absent before. The tension, though not extinguished, seemed slightly to relax.

This first telegram was followed by another, dispatched at 1:40: "Very confidential. Use all your skill, I would say your subtlety, to establish that the renunciation of Prince Leopold of Hohenzollern is *announced, transmitted,* or communicated to you by the king of Prussia or by his government. This is of the utmost importance to us. The king's participation must, *at any price,* be consented to by him or result from what has occurred."[85] Gramont's telegram was prompted by sensational news he had learned only an hour before, the news that Strantz had already conveyed to Abeken, the news of Karl Anton's decision to renounce his son's acceptance of the throne. After Strantz's initial message that morning, the telegraphs at Sigmaringen had tapped out the necessary messages to others—one to Marshall Prim in Madrid, the second to Olózaga. The latter telegram read:

> To the Spanish ambassador, Paris. I deem it my duty to inform you, Sir, as Spanish minister at Paris, that I have now sent Marshall Prim in Madrid the following telegram: "In view of the complications that the candidacy of my son, Leopold, for the throne of Spain seems to have encountered, and of the painful impression that recent events have created for the Spanish nation by placing it in a dilemma in which it can take counsel only of its sentiment of independence; and persuaded that, in such circumstances, its choice would not have the sincerity and spontaneity upon which my son counted when he accepted the candidacy, I hereby withdraw it in his name.—Prince of Hohenzollern"[86]

Foreshortening the intended route of transmission, the French interior ministry intercepted a copy of the dispatch, bringing the unexpected news to Paris.

Gramont made out later that there was a powerful case against accepting this news at face value, and so there was. Assuming that the renunciation was genuine, was it not odd that it came not from the candidate but from his father? Was it not possible that Leopold would shut his eyes to the promise of the latter and declare that he could not be bound by it? Could he not steal off in disguise only to turn up at Madrid later on? Had not this been the path followed by King Charles of Rumania in 1866? Such were the concerns that prompted Gramont's second telegram to Benedetti that day.

The news of Leopold's renunciation had the reverse effect on Ollivier. He was mesmerized by the apparent victory. He wrote later: "I believed that the whole situation was saved, and so great was my joy at having peace within our grasp, so great was my dread of losing it again, that the combative disposition that I had displayed on the 11th melted away. . . . There was no further occasion to appear stiff and unyielding but rather accommodating and pliant; to make more secure the result arrived at, lest it become endangered by some untoward action on our part. The incident was certainly at an end if we were guilty of no imprudence, and I was so overjoyed at times as not to believe it."[87] All the same, Ollivier and his colleagues still had vulnerable points. On the one hand, they could not be sure of the genuineness of the renunciation, which still had not been confirmed in any official way; on the other, even the telegram that they had was not intended for them; it had been acquired through somewhat underhanded (if perfectly common) means. In a flash of legality, Ollivier wanted somehow to demonstrate that this telegram was authentic.

At ten minutes after two, he went to the chamber to reassure the government's critics—and to calm the doubts of its supporters. He found the members disturbed and unhappy. One of them said: "What's the news?" Ollivier sang small and replied only: "Nothing as yet." There was a bizarre interruption: Olózaga, sweating and gasping for breath, appeared in the lobby and burst through a throng. Pulling Ollivier into a corner, he shoved into his hand the telegram that he had received from Prim. Ollivier could not restrain himself and read it out to a crowd of deputies.[88] The French victory seemed complete.

Or was it? Duvernois, leader of the right, was not so sure: "We ask to interpolate the cabinet concerning the guarantees that it has stipulated, or that it ought to stipulate, in order to avoid a recurrence of complications with Prussia."[89] Ollivier attempted to answer this question. Before he could do so, an adjutant passed him a message that Napoleon wanted a consultation. Ollivier left the chamber, and Duvernois's great question hung fire.

Irreparable damage had been done all the same. Albert Sorel has argued that the telegram from Karl Anton "in no way represented the satisfaction of the demands that the French government had been pressing upon Prussia," and one can see what he means.[90] But clearly this is the impression that

Ollivier, by blurting out the news in the chamber of deputies, managed to give. Ollivier conducted himself with a lack of discretion remarkable even at a time when old-style diplomacy was everywhere breaking down. The temper of the times demanded exactly the opposite approach. Regarding the candidacy as an intrigue of Prussia against France, the government was unshakably convinced—or allowed itself to be convinced by French opinion—that the renunciation was useless unless King William's name were associated with it. Gramont's telegram to Benedetti was intended as the means by which this object could be realized: William would acquiesce, however indirectly, in Leopold's withdrawal, he would communicate this news to Benedetti the minute it came through, and Benedetti would pass the word along to Paris. But none of this had yet happened, and the French government needed to hush up the question until it did.

The French were trapped. They had not yet done enough to satisfy public opinion, still less to alarm those who had launched the intrigue. Instead, they were caught up in the objections that slowly gathered strength in the wake of the uncertain news. Ollivier himself heard the first mutterings of the storm as he left the chamber. One member said: "Prussia is making fun of you." Faced by assurances from Ollivier that all would be well, the member replied: "That's fine! But make no mistake, you are a ruined man!"[91] The chauvinists in the press were no less vocal; returning to their offices over the next two hours, they learned of the strong current of feeling that was running against the announcement—particularly, it was said, in the city of Paris.[92] No doubt the reaction was made all the stronger by the suddenness with which the news was sprung on the public by Ollivier—a point later made much of by Gramont. A little less talkativeness may well have tipped the scales the other way. French policy now cast about for assurances that the renunciation of the Hohenzollern candidacy was genuine—for guarantees, that is, that it would never be renewed.

5

The French Declaration of War

Ollivier arrived at the Tuileries at three o'clock. He found Napoleon III in an antechamber, surrounded by officers and chatting amicably with them. Napoleon III had good reason to relax; he had found himself faced by a crisis as grave as any he had ever seen, and he liked the news that he had just received. He said to a confidant: "What has happened is a vast relief to me. A war is always a very great risk."[1]

This was, no doubt, the reaction of the diplomatic community in Paris as well. Most of the ambassadors, exhausted from the exertions of the past few days, were again getting ready to abandon the French capital, glad to have a respite from delicate and intensive diplomacy and believing that quiet would descend for a time on the political scene. Lyons insisted that the French had achieved everything they had asked for,[2] and Beust wired to Metternich along much the same lines.[3] Nigra was equally enthusiastic; the entire frenzy, he told Napoleon, was out of the way, and the chauvinists (both organizations and individuals) who had been extensively instrumental in creating it could now rest content in the belief that it was over.[4]

But strong and unsatisfied impulses still gnawed at the various actors on the French side of the drama. William I, as the French understood it, still had not associated his name with Leopold's withdrawal, and the French ministers had further to examine the circumstances in which it had been delivered. They had received the news from Olózaga, who had launched himself—in a manner which, considering that he had no instructions along this line from either Prim or the provisional government, can only be called astounding—on a discussion of this most delicate of questions. Napoleon III knew that—for the chamber of deputies, in any case—Olózaga's assurances would not be enough; therefore, there could be no thought of saying anything on the subject to its members. Moreover, if—as everyone assumed—Olózaga was acting on his own authority, who could tell what was in the minds of his superiors in Madrid? Olózaga was the ambassador of Spain; he had no official connections with Karl Anton or with Prussia. Therefore, Napoleon and Ollivier agreed that nothing should be done before the council could meet at St. Cloud the next morning.[5] Behind it all, the government wanted to do nothing that would run the risk of a scathing response from Bismarck that could reopen this Pandora's box.

All the same, Napoleon III, reviewing all that had happened on that frantic and incredible afternoon of 12 July, had reason to be satisfied. Such was the overriding impression of almost all the authoritative sources in Paris. In a telegram to King Victor Emmanuel, Nigra quoted the emperor as saying: "It is peace, and I have invited you to come to me so that you can telegraph this to your government. . . . I know that some elements of public opinion in France would have preferred . . . war, but I see in the renunciation a satisfactory solution that deprives us of any pretext for it."[6]

A few hours earlier, William I had expressed much the same feelings to Queen Augusta: "A stone has been lifted from my heart." But he added more ominously: "Take care to keep silent."[7] There was, after all, no sense in revealing anything to the French until he had something to reveal—until, that is, he had in hand the renunciation that Karl Anton had drawn up. The decision had come to him only by telegrams from the latter and from Colonel von Strantz. For this reason, he determined to avoid official discussion with Benedetti. Yet his fertile mind had no trouble in grasping the full import of Karl Anton's decision. Like Napoleon III, he was satisfied, happy that Leopold's withdrawal meant that the crisis was at an end. Who could have known that in a matter of hours, the situation was to undergo so drastic and fatal an alteration?

So convinced was William I the affair was now behind him that he took an extraordinary step. On 12 July he invited Benedetti to dinner and talked openly and amicably, and their exchange had a salutary effect on the battered self-esteem of the French ambassador. More important, he revealed, almost in a casual aside, that an answer from Sigmaringen was expected at Ems the next morning. The affair seemed over at last, peace now secured. Benedetti telegraphed to Paris: "The king has just said to me that he has received a telegram stating that an answer from Karl Anton will arrive here tomorrow morning and that he will make its contents known to me the minute it is placed in his hands." And he added: "Bismarck is arriving tomorrow at Ems."[8]

Bismarck had not liked the way that William I had handled the negotiations with Benedetti. From the moment Leopold's candidacy became known, Bismarck had recognized the dangerous ground that he was on. Had he intended to provoke war with France, he would have hurried off to join the king at Ems; instead, he remained at Varzin, on the margin of events. He was indignant when he learned that William had listened to Benedetti's complaints, but there was nothing he could do about it. Things could not have gone worse for Bismarck—he knew it, and so did everyone else in the Prussian government.

On 12 July Bismarck at last left Varzin. When he reached Berlin, he learned of Leopold's renunciation and of William's hope that the affair was at an end. His first thought was to resign; he soon went one better and proposed to demand the summoning of the North German parliament under the threat of resignation if the king turned him down. It was a masterly stroke. Bismarck could pose as the defender of German honor either by surrendering his office or by delivering a flaming, though belated, blast at France from the tribune of parliament. William I would appear as the muddling spokesman for an antique dynasticism. These devices showed rather less regard for the king's policies than perfect loyalty would require, but this was not the first time—nor, one might add, the last—that Bismarck was ready to undercut his master when his own fate was on the line.

At all events, Bismarck had good reason to be angry. He was depressed that Prussia had missed a great chance. She could have asserted herself by answering sternly; instead the king had let her down; William I had surrendered to French dictation and to French obstruction. Bismarck's concern was now to divert attention from the mistakes that William I had made in his dealings with Benedetti and to rescue Prussian prestige from the muddle into which it had fallen. In practice, these aims worked themselves out as a belated attempt to limit the extent of the French success. At ten minutes to six, he dramatically announced that he would go to Ems and take over direction of affairs.[9] Half an hour later he consulted Roon, the minister of war, and Eulenburg, minister of finance, over a great feast of beef, hams, champagne, and wine. They talked, obviously, about William I.

The decision to go to Ems was an example of the unreasoning haste that characterized the whole of Bismarck's behavior on the evening of 12 July. At the dinner with Eulenburg and Roon, that decision was abruptly canceled. Moltke, who attended the meeting also, was crestfallen and dejected at the turn of events. In his later accounts of these momentous days, Bismarck liked to stress the fact that Moltke always looked ten years younger or older as the chance for war became better or worse. He remarked to Moritz Busch on 4 October 1870, "I remember that, when the Spanish business became especially hot, Moltke at once looked ten years younger. Then, when I told him that the Hohenzollern prince had reneged, he at once became quite aged and weary."[10] Moltke expressed grave concern over the military situation, and he complained bitterly about this to Bismarck. Moltke's spirits recovered markedly, however, when Bismarck told him of the series of new initiatives that he was planning to launch. The chances of war, it seemed, had not evaporated after all.

In fact, the new strokes of policy that Bismarck discussed with his guests that night had little to do with Moltke. They were an attempt to distance himself from William I; perhaps he even despaired of victory so late in the day and sought to load onto the king's shoulders responsibility for further failures. The decision not to go to Ems was telegraphed to Abeken at 7:37 in the evening. In further telegrams, Bismarck sought to challenge William's policy with every display of offended honor, and he recited the dangers that would arise if William I again received Benedetti: "A decision to see the French ambassador again would give the impression in Germany and elsewhere that we have humiliated ourselves before the abuses of France." He added: "The king should say only that Prince Leopold will communicate his decision directly to the Spanish government and that he will do so as soon as possible."[11] In view of the French threats, any concession—any explanation—on the part of the king would offend German opinion beyond description. William had already stretched conciliation to the limit in receiving Benedetti after Gramont's bluster. At all events, the renunciation must be made to appear to end as it had begun—that is, as a family matter concerning only the members of the house of Hohenzollern.[12]

There was one striking element in Bismarck's approach. Most of his complaints had been unfolded behind the scenes; the campaign of public propaganda into which he would be encouraged by the military chiefs was still one full day into the future. It is true that there had been attempts as early as 8 July to drum up support in the press, but this had been an answer to Gramont's provocation two days earlier and, in any case, the effect of these efforts did not come up to what had occurred on the French side of the line. Bismarck was still waiting on events—developments at Ems, news from Paris, information from Madrid. His threats, however wild they may appear to the later reader, were all made in private conversations.[13] Bismarck's behavior at the time was far from his later claims to a far-sighted policy. On 15 July, when war was certain, he read a sentence of Luther's and underlined it in his family Bible: "In this affair no sword can advise or help. God alone must create here without human effort."

In the meantime, new alarms came tumbling in from Paris. Gramont had grown increasingly impatient over the delay in the negotiations at Ems. At three o'clock in the afternoon he called in Werther, who had returned to Paris that morning. Gramont complained: "The resignation of the prince of Hohenzollern has taken place without any advice from the king of Prussia."[14] In the middle of the interview, a development occurred that seemed to confirm Gramont's worst fears: he received from Olózaga official confirmation of what was in Karl Anton's telegram. This was meant as a friendly gesture—a sign that a tame ending to the crisis had come at last. With Gramont, however, it produced the opposite effect. He had been brooding gloomily over how he was to present the renunciation to French opinion; the telegram from Olózaga implied that by her demands, France had wished to strike a blow at the independence of a lesser power. Gramont commented: "Far

from advancing our position, Karl Anton's telegram made it more difficult. . . . There was still not a word for France; the whole thing was between
the prince of Hohenzollern and Spain."[15]

The divergence of outlook among the members of the French cabinet,
always present beneath the surface, now blazed into the open. In Ollivier's
words,

> Gramont did not welcome the renunciation with a delight equal to mine. I was
> concerned simply to see the vanishing of the candidacy, caring but little for the
> manner of its vanishing. Gramont was particularly impressed by the form, and
> in the notification by Prince Karl Anton to Prim he detected a purpose to dodge
> the king's indirect participation. From that moment, the complete agreement
> that had hitherto existed between us came to an end: he continued to attach
> greater importance to this participation by the king, which was in my eyes a
> secondary matter.[16]

Gramont had a fresh resource. William I had made out—and Werther
had made out even more strongly—that the candidacy had never been intended to give offense to France; then let William I say as much in a letter
to Napoleon III. The letter would have as its object the calming of French
opinion. It would say that in authorizing Leopold to accept the throne, William had not meant to estrange the goodwill of Napoleon III; that he associated himself with Leopold's renunciation; and that good relations with France
were and remained a central object of Prussian policy.

Werther duly gave way. He agreed to convey this new proposal to William
I in the belief that otherwise the French ministers would order Benedetti to
do so. Nor was this all. Werther was on close terms with Gramont; he had,
from the start, showed himself resolute in his opposition to the candidacy,
and he continued to believe that France could be swung away from war if
his own acts were bold enough. But he left Gramont under no illusion: "Such
a letter would be extremely difficult after the declaration given by the duke
on the 6th of July. That declaration had in it sentiments of hostility to the
king that have produced the most painful of impressions."[17]

After this hectic conversation, Werther went back to the Prussian embassy,
and Gramont departed also. Ollivier, who had joined the two during the last
hour, returned to his offices with the assurance—so he made out later—that

no additional steps would be taken until the council met the next morning. He still believed that he was advocating compromise, and he was not discouraged by Gramont's proposal. But he was himself exhausted. The day had been one of extreme tension and excitement: he had been to the Tuileries, to the chancellery, to the Corps législatif; he had twice held meetings with the Spanish ambassador; he had thrown himself into Gramont's interview with Werther. For Ollivier, in short, as for so many others, 12 July had been a day of measureless frenzy. All he wanted now was to sleep.[18]

At four o'clock Gramont went to see Napoleon III at St. Cloud, ostensibly to summarize the events of that great day. No other member of the cabinet was present. At seven in the evening, he returned to Paris. A few minutes later, he telegraphed to Benedetti:

> We have received, by the hand of the Spanish ambassador, the withdrawal by Prince Karl Anton, in the name of his son, Leopold, of the latter's candidacy for the throne of Spain. In order that the withdrawal by Prince Karl Anton may have its full effect, it is necessary that the King of Prussia associate himself with it and give an assurance that he will not again sanction that candidacy. You will go at once to the king to request from him a declaration to that effect, which he cannot refuse if he is, in truth, actuated by no secret motive. Despite the withdrawal, which is now known to all, the public excitement here is so great that we do not know whether we shall succeed in controlling it. Make a paraphrase of this dispatch, which you can communicate to the king. Reply as quickly as possible.[19]

What motivated Gramont and Napoleon III? Were they taken aback by the storm over *Père Antoine*? Did they suppose that a fresh display of resolution would shake William I? Did they shrink from confrontation with the chamber of deputies until the king had been more forthcoming? Motives are, of course, almost never wholly scrutable, and the full spectrum of the two men's calculations can never be fully recovered, but there are certain suggestive circumstances that might be worth noting.

At the root of the problem lay the form of the renunciation and the way

it had been presented to the French government. Karl Anton had telegraphed to Olózaga that his son had given up the throne of Spain, and Olózaga had duly informed Napoleon III and Ollivier. Karl Anton had telegraphed the same news to William I at Ems and to his daughter, the countess
of Flanders. In the first flush of excitement that had followed the telegram,
Napoleon forgot the origins of the dispute, and Gramont unhesitatingly re-
minded him of them. Beyond that, the telegram was curiously worded; it
seemed to imply that by her demands, France had infringed the independence of Spain. How would Spanish pride react to so gratuitous an affront?
Would it revolt and proclaim Leopold—who had, most unaccountably, got
lost somewhere in the Austrian Alps—king of Spain in spite of the withdrawal that the father had issued in his son's name?

There was a secondary consideration, which gradually moved up to first
place: French opinion had been hardening, and it professed to see the resignation as a cover for the real issue—the intrigues of Prussia. Even though
the news of the withdrawal of Leopold's candidacy was too recent to have
evoked much public response, Gramont, like many of his colleagues, was
aware of the early symptoms of dissatisfied opinion not only in Paris but also
in the provinces and anticipated a fuller expression of opinion along the same
lines. It is, of course, true that—as with the declaration of 6 July—Gramont
once again was racing ahead of the evidence, going beyond popular clamor,
and taking the very steps that would unleash the flood of chauvinism that he
later lamented he could not control. Still, the central element in his calculations was, by and large, accurate: there was little satisfaction to be derived
from the renunciation so long as the Prussian government refused to acknowledge that it was responsible for the candidacy and to stamp upon Leopold's withdrawal its official approval.[20] Indeed, in this connection it might
be noted that Gramont's demand was actually somewhat more moderate
than the dizzying cries for satisfaction now being sent up even in the official
organs of the French press—most outstandingly, in the *Moniteur*, the morning edition of which was now demanding that the Prussians, as a gesture of
good faith, be called upon to evacuate, unconditionally and immediately, the
great fortress of Mainz on the Rhine. There was also a deep-seated institutional flaw. Though the Second Empire had ministerial responsibility, there
was no clear division of authority. Had there been, it is difficult to see how

either Gramont or Napoleon III could have made their decisions: they would have had to secure the approval of the cabinet or at least its leading ministers. But here the constitution was a muddle, as Ollivier bore witness when he later wrote: "I wished that the prime minister, which I was in name, had become and remained more responsible. As it turned out, I had no responsibility, only a title."[21]

Therein lay the essence of the situation. Despite ministerial responsibility and the introduction of a parliamentary system, Napoleon III continued to pursue his own policies behind the backs of his ministers. He continued to dominate foreign affairs. To be sure, by this time (and not unnaturally) he had come close to the limit of his own physical powers and was unable to play the role that he once would have in the debates. His energy, his sensitivity to outside events, and his liveliness of reaction were all beginning to fade. From a constitutional point of view, however, he still very much had the upper hand. When Napoleon III received Gramont at St. Cloud, he still supposed—and it suited Gramont's book to suppose with him—that the direction of French affairs remained firmly under imperial control.

For the moment, these considerations were stilled. Shortly after eleven o'clock, Ollivier appeared at the foreign ministry to inquire after developments at Ems, and Gramont received him. The latter immediately produced a copy of the telegram that he had sent to Benedetti. Ollivier could not believe his eyes. He later wrote:

> However high one may have tried to raise one's spirit above vulgar remonstrance, it was impossible not to feel frustration of a certain sort. To have agreed with the emperor at three o'clock that no decision should be made until the council met the next day, and then to learn at eleven o'clock at night, by mere chance, that a momentous decision had been reached and put in execution without one's being consulted or even notified, to find oneself confronted by an accomplished fact of very great importance—therein was abundant justification for an explosion of harsh words.[22]

Ollivier was furious when he learned of the demand for guarantees and was wholly unreceptive to it. Under no circumstances, he said, must one even think of approaching William with such a demand. None of Gramont's proposals, he said, would have been accepted had they been put forward

146

when French policy was under discussion on the afternoon of 12 July. Why couldn't Gramont have let him know before sending the telegram?[23] The truth was, as Ollivier was soon to learn, that he and Gramont had not dual but dueling agendas.

Ollivier's first impulse was to rush to St. Cloud in the hope of persuading Napoleon III to withdraw the new demand. Then he reflected: "It's too late."[24] Back at his office shortly after midnight (as he later recounted), he encountered Robert Mitchell, the editor of the *Constitutionnel*. The dark hour before the storm produced a fresh display of independent resolve. Mitchell asked: "How shall we present the renunciation?" Ollivier said nothing of the demand for guarantees that had been presented five hours before and replied only: "Say it's over and we're satisfied."[25]

Ollivier was trapped. He had been ignored by Napoleon III and by Gramont. His government was facing parliamentary attack; his personal prestige, running ever faster downhill. There was no escape. Ollivier was reduced to solitary brooding: "Left alone I debated with myself during a sleepless night the line of conduct I should pursue and passed in review all the happenings of the day. My first thought was to resign ... I was conscious of being ill-served, humiliated, betrayed on all sides; it was absolutely essential to purge the personnel of the ministry, but I had not the hardness of heart to do it."[26]

What would have happened had Ollivier quit? Would not a resignation by him at so crucial a time have been a shot in arm to the opponents of a hard line? Not according to Ollivier: "Immediately upon my resignation, a war ministry, which was already waiting in the wings, would succeed me, and would meet the king's refusal with overwhelming insistence from which war would inevitably result. On the other hand, by remaining in the government, I might hope to secure the abandonment of the demand of guarantees and persuade the council and emperor himself to accept the king's refusal and not prolong the crisis by fruitless indiscretion."[27]

This was an explanation of sorts, but at best only a partial one. A personal factor was more decisive. At every turn in the drama, Ollivier had shown himself hesitant, inadequate, and insecure. In a word, he was not a fighter, the kind of robust man of will who follows his own objectives without scruple or distraction. His natural diffidence disarmed him when confronted by arro-

147

gance and self-confidence, and when push came to shove he was always over-come by fatalism. Moreover, had he himself not indulged in the same line of conduct for which he now reproached Gramont? Had he not, contrary to what had been decided at the council of 12 July, joined the latter in the suggestion to Werther of a letter from King William to Napoleon III? In the wake of the excitement of the recent days, an abrupt and unexpected resignation would rob French policy of the continuity that it so badly needed and might even, he feared, provoke the Prussians into launching the very attack against which he had been guarding all along. More probably, Ollivier had run out of steam. In his own words, "Such a retreat seemed reprehensi-bly selfish. It would have been to go over to the enemy in the heart of battle, to offer myself as a witness against my country's cause." Some years later he wrote: "What do you do when your country is in danger? You remain, and I remained."[28]

Things were moving too fast for Ollivier and, for that matter, for everyone else. Shortly after eight o'clock in the morning on 13 July Benedetti, stung into action by the peremptory orders that he had received from Gramont the night before, placed himself in the path of the king on the Brunnen-promenade, the long stretch of street where William I was accustomed to taking his morning walks and where gardens and parks filled with onlookers were never far away. The famous conversation that followed is too familiar to require a lengthy retelling or reinterpreting. The central fact emerging from all the developments of that extraordinary morning was the failure of Benedetti to win William for a statement of guarantees that Gramont could read to the French chamber. The incident touched and offended a powerful emotional nerve in William I. He could not understand what was being asked of him. The French were now demanding that he underwrite Leopold's withdrawal and promise that it would never be renewed; otherwise, they could not regard the affair as over. William I was adamant. Benedetti wired Gramont: "The king categorically refused to authorize me to transmit to you such a declaration."[29] To the queen William wrote: "Instead of being satisfied, Benedetti came up to me on the promenade and asked me to bind myself for the future. This I naturally refused. I said to the ambassador: 'Who can guarantee that the emperor might not someday find that the prince of Hohenzollern is not the best candidate for the throne of Spain?'"[30]

Though the episode left a bad taste in William's mouth, it was by no means the end of the affair. Indeed, for our purposes, it was not even the central part of it. What happened was this. At one o'clock a copy of Karl Anton's letter at last reached Ems. Benedetti hoped to use this letter to make one more appeal to the king. The hope was disappointed. William I took soundings from Eulenburg, who had by this time arrived at Ems in Bismarck's stead; accepting Eulenburg's advice, he determined he would not see Benedetti again. Instead an emissary was dispatched to Benedetti's hotel with a copy of Karl Anton's letter.[31]

This would not do for Benedetti. Once more he appealed to William I; once more he asked for an interview; once more he was disappointed. The inordinate nature of these new demands was utterly beyond William's comprehension. Had he not sent to Benedetti a copy of the morning newspapers that brought word of Leopold's withdrawal? Had he not congratulated the ambassador on his good fortune? What more could the French want? All the same, William I determined not to show any resentment toward his luckless respondent; whatever happened, he wished to keep up appearances—to remain conciliatory, sensitive, and high-minded. A second message was therefore drawn up. Benedetti reported to Gramont: "The king has authorized me to telegraph to you in his name that he gives his approval *entière et sans reserve* to the resignation of the prince of Hohenzollern; he is unable to do more."[32]

Here was a concession, and a significant one at that. It was made known to Paris by Benedetti in his telegram of seven o'clock on 13 July. Its meaning was clear and straightforward. William could not accept guarantees for the future; he gave his unconditional approval to the resignation all the same. Moreover, he answered with a conciseness that left nothing to be desired: he had communicated the withdrawal of the candidacy to the French government, declaring that he had approved it—precisely what Gramont had been after from the beginning, as his instructions to Benedetti of 7 July (described previously) attest. Had Gramont been intent on ending the crisis, the message should have satisfied him. But Gramont had no such intentions. He belittled William's concession as a triviality and preferred to remain the provocative and irresponsible critic. He complained to Ollivier: "The king has communicated the Hohenzollern letter to us, and says he has approved, but what does it amount to?"[33]

In the meantime, reports from Berlin brought sensational news. Opinion in Germany was becoming offended. The Prussian generals, and some politicians also, were eager for war. Officers and leading figures in the government were returning to the capital. Moltke, the chief of staff, laid down: "Nothing could be more welcome to us than to have *now* the war that we must have."[34] Nor was this all. According to French military officials, the Prussians could have 100,000 men in the Saar within eighteen or twenty days—so an attaché warned Paris, adding: "We should not forget that our enemies are in the highest degree audacious, enterprising, and unscrupulous."[35]

Bismarck, too, found himself in difficulties. Leopold's withdrawal and William's hope that the crisis was over seemed to him a humiliation worse than that of Olmütz in 1850, and one for which he could not escape responsibility. In reality, the picture was not as black as Bismarck supposed; by one in the afternoon on 13 July the tables had been turned. William determined that he would do what Bismarck had advised via telegram the previous evening: no more interviews with Benedetti. The latter, on his side, duly reported this to Paris, and he added: "Bismarck will not be coming here. I have observed only the arrival of Eulenburg"[36] And there was more. Sometime between two and three o'clock, King William of Prussia, surprised and annoyed by the astonishing turn of events that morning, authorized Abeken to telegraph to Bismarck in Berlin an account of the events of that day. The telegram contained a significant rider: according to the king, Bismarck could, if he saw fit, inform both the press and the Prussian ambassadors abroad of the French demand—and of the firmness with which it had been refused.

By three o'clock Abeken was ready. The Ems telegram summarized the events of 13 July in three parts. The first part was but a recapitulation, taken

from a message sent by the king to Abeken that morning, of what had occurred on the promenade. The second part—agonizingly drawn up with
much editing and rewriting—described the arrival of Karl Anton's letter, the
king's decision to break off further talks with Benedetti, and the note to that
effect that was delivered to the latter. The third and final part of the telegram
was the most important: the authorization to make the news public.[37]

At 3:10 in the afternoon on 13 July, Abeken dispatched his telegram to
Bismarck. It arrived at 6:09 and was certainly deciphered by eight o'clock.
The manipulation of the Ems telegram was one of the great set pieces of
which Bismarck and his family would never weary, and Bismarck's recollection of what happened improved with each telling. The story is quickly told.
Brooding over dinner with his two guests, Roon and Moltke, a light dawned
on Bismarck as he went over Abeken's telegram. In a flash of insight, he cut
out the conciliatory passages, leaving only (in his words) "the head and the
tail," and instead of merely reporting the recitation of the demand, he concluded his release with an explosive statement: "His Majesty the King thereupon decided not to receive the French ambassador and sent an aide-de-
camp to tell him that His Majesty had nothing further to communicate." This
wonderful sleight of hand provided the tonic of relief for his disgruntled
guests. Moltke commented: "Now the telegram has a different ring. Before
it sounded like parlay; now it is in the nature of fanfare, a response to a
challenge."[38]

Later, Bismarck would present himself not as the man who had been mastered by events but rather as the creator of Germany. Against all his previous
statements, he would make the war appear necessary and inevitable, long
planned by the master statesman. Bucher was not long in calling the candidacy of Leopold "a trap for France," and Bismarck claimed to have provoked
the war with the Ems telegram. However, almost every word of Bismarck's
explanation can be progressively and comprehensively disproved. We now
know, for example, that the picture that Bismarck would draw of himself did
not reflect long planning but rather specific events—namely, those of 12
July, the day of frustration, depression, and boiling anger during his dinner
with Roon and Eulenburg. There was, as noted above, the riveting surprise
of Leopold's renunciation; the overpowering sense of betrayal and humiliation; the contemplation of resignation; the rebukes of Roon followed by the

reproaches of Moltke; the resentment and depression of the military chiefs as they saw the prospect of war slipping through their fingers; the poring over of the telegrams that were coming in; the birth of a new idea to recall the crisis to life; the recovery of nerve on the part of the generals; and finally, the launching of a new initiative.

Even before the day was out, Bismarck's spirits had revived because of information that he had gleaned from the Italian minister, Edoardo de Launay, who happened to be in Berlin just at the time that Bismarck was returning to the capital from Varzin. Launay was an active man—high-powered in manner and a glib if long-winded talker, capable (when it suited his purposes) of displaying a rather fancy adroitness. He was not well liked by his staff or, a more important point, by his boss, Visconti-Venosta, who suspected him of dipping his hand too frequently into the embassy till. But he was at the least an experienced diplomat. It should be added that Launay, whether by his close ties to leading figures at the Prussian court or by virtue of some innate anti-Gallicism, seems to have been strongly committed to the idea of intimate Italo-Prussian relations, and this was especially the case now. He was burning to find out all that he could about the reported withdrawal of the Hohenzollern candidacy. Aware from his sources in the Berlin cabinet that Bismarck was planning to pay a courtesy call at nine o'clock that evening on Gorchakov (who happened to be visiting the capital at the time), Launay took pains to station himself at a point which he knew Bismarck would have to pass en route to the Russian embassy. Thereupon he intercepted him and began what can only be described as a most curious conversation.

Launay began by revealing to Bismarck that he had a deep personal interest in keeping Italy out of a Franco-Prussian war, and let him know that this flowed from the fact that he wished to shape Italo-Prussian relations during his period of ambassadorship in such a way that they would require no further development when (as he confidently expected) someone with views opposite to those of Visconti-Venosta would take the latter's place as foreign minister. Moreover, the conversation had not continued for a few minutes before Launay, by way of vindicating the suspicions Visconti-Venosta had long held about him, muddied the waters by introducing into it at the last minute a new assurance, which (on all evidence available) represented nothing more than his own idea and for the advancing of which he had no authority at all from his own government. This assurance would have required the Italians to bind themselves, in the event of a Franco-Prussian war, to a policy of the strictest neutrality.[39] Launay eventually backed down, let the proposal fall to the ground, and agreed, after being severely reproved by Visconti-Venosta, to talk no more of it. But this whole performance, obviously conceived by him in the hope of demonstrating to Bismarck that the latter had succeeded in obtaining for the Prussians more than Italy was, in fact, willing to give, was grist for Bismarck's mill. Between 12 and 15 July, when Berlin learned of France's intention to declare war, Launay did not see Bismarck, and during this interval, as the latter recovered his nerve, the conversation of 12 July remained the sole basis of his evaluation of Italy's intentions.[40]

In this context, a mid-afternoon visit by Gorchakov to Bismarck on 13 July, following on the latter's call upon the Russian the night before, proved of the utmost importance. Gorchakov did what he could to soothe Prussian feelings over the political fireworks of Benedetti's demand for guarantees, and he made a particular effort to persuade Bismarck how impressed was the tsar with William I's effort to bring the crisis to an end. But Bismarck had bigger fish to fry. According to Gorchakov's report to the tsar, "Bismarck has telegraphed to Werther: The Hohenzollern incident being settled, he is to demand of Gramont guarantees on the present intention of France and to tell him that if the replies are not satisfactory, the Reichsrat [sic] would be convoked a week hence to vote the funds necessary for the mobilization of the entire army." This, said Bismarck, would mean war, but "in the uncertainty in which France has kept us, we would have no other recourse."[41] With this assertion Gorchakov could but concur, for he was, as we have seen, convinced that the French meant to have war with Prussia and that it was William I who, more than anyone else, had done his best to avert it.

Indeed, he at once made available to Bismarck a telegram from Okunev, the Russian chargé in Paris, reporting that Gramont was dissatisfied with the renunciation, had said as much to Werther, and, in connection with these remarks, had referred to the remaining *mauvais procédé*.[42] Bismarck soon became the recipient of a flurry of alarmed warnings from the Russian chancellor that things were quite different than he understood them to be and that more information was urgently needed. At 4:10 in the afternoon, Bismarck telegraphed to Werther inquiring as to the facts, and an hour later he repeated his inquiry with added urgency. Always suspicious, and fearing that Werther's messages were intercepted, he wired London, requesting that the British ambassador be instructed to inquire of Werther when the latter had last telegraphed to Berlin.[43]

It is now time to sort out Bismarck's views with respect to the dinner of 13 July with Roon and Moltke, and perhaps the best place to begin is with his assertion that he was at this time on the point of resignation. That he should have been thinking in this way is, considering what had just happened, nothing short of preposterous, doubly so because he knew that William I would not again see Benedetti prior to Eulenburg's arrival. As for the staggering effect of the Abeken telegram, this is, by any stretch of the imagination, again positively incomprehensible. The telegram contained what for all of the guests was good news. The French had made certain demands under the threat of war, and these demands had been rejected. Having promised Benedetti on two earlier occasions that he would convey the news of Leopold's withdrawal when he received word of it, the king had sent an adjutant to say that this news had been received and that he had nothing further to say to the ambassador. Eulenburg (who enjoyed Bismarck's full confidence) had arrived at Ems and had dissuaded William from personally communicating the news that the emissary had conveyed. Bismarck had every reason to be pleased; the telegram, which for the first time provided reliable information as to what the French were up to, should have brought elation, not dejection. Faced with convincing evidence of the virulent anti-Germanism of the French; faced with the superb opportunity now presented to him of making a war for the aggrandizement of Prussia look like a war of national defense against French hostility; faced with the choice between continuing to acquiesce, for the first time, in public humiliation of Prussia or of transforming humiliation into a once-and-for-all triumph, he took the only course such a man might be expected to take. In view of what has been said, one can see what William L. Langer—to whose brilliant, but obscure, work on this subject one may turn for a wealth on information—means when he writes: "In view of what is known about the general situation, it is hard to escape the conclusion that Bismarck's account of the impact of the telegram from Ems is entirely fictitious."[44]

At Ems there was activity to the last minute. Shortly after Bismarck had released his version of the Ems telegram, a second dispatch from William reached him: "The French ambassador has asked for another audience in reply to which I informed him through my adjutant that if what he had to say concerned the Spanish candidacy, I have nothing further to say to him."[45] On the morning of 14 July, Benedetti read the telegram in the *Gazette de Cologne*, but his dispatch to Paris of that day made only a passing reference to it and—a more important point—did not prevent him from soliciting an audience with the king. He continued to believe that his difficulties could be overcome if he could only see William one more time, and he was not disappointed when he learned that William had decided to admit him to an antechamber outside the railroad station where he would board a train for Berlin. At three o'clock, the two men saw each other for the last time. Benedetti reported: "The king confined himself to saying that he had nothing further to say to me, but he added that negotiations might still be continued with his government."[46] This was something that one would not normally expect to hear from a man who believed that the guns were about to go off; William I still thought he had made a fine stroke for peace at Ems. Only when he read Bismarck's version of the Ems telegram did he understand what had really happened, and soon he was railing against the French insults that he had not noticed at the time.

Feeling against France was now irresistible throughout Germany. The present rulers of the south German states were Bismarck's opponents, men of a conservative political bent who had always been sensitive to any attempt to force their hand through the pressure of public opinion, but this was precisely the effect that Gramont's flamboyant formulations were already beginning to have. This was apparent as early as 7 July, when news of the Gramont declaration first flashed across Munich. It created a sensation, as the French ambassador Cadore, wiser than his superiors at home, was not slow to appreciate: "Count Bray [the foreign minister of Bavaria] has let me know that he is very disturbed by the proceedings and wonders why we have expressed ourselves in so strident a form on a question as delicate as this."[47]

Cadore, a man deeply concerned for the successful progress of France's relations with the south Germanies, scarcely needed to be told of Bray's reasons for wishing some sort of *détente;* he knew those reasons only too well and shared the views on which they were based. In further dispatches he described the deteriorating effect that Gramont's demands were having on opinion south of the Main. The rulers in Munich were now beginning to realize what had been their worst fear—that the French were bent on seeking a war of revenge against Prussia into which all Germany would soon be dragged. Cadore, finding himself under the necessity of guarding his fences in Paris, took care not to associate himself too deeply with this view of the political situation, but there is no doubt that he shared it. He even elaborated on it by pointing out that the states of south Germany (it was, of course, mainly Bavaria that he had in mind) had certain ties with Prussia—ties that, though they had become frayed over the years, were now fast being cemented as a result of Gramont's bluster. And he went on to observe that in these circumstances "no one should be surprised if Bray is driven against his will into the arms of Prussia for his own safety."[48] He drove this last point home even more bluntly in a report of 12 July: Bray must "have sound reasons for seeking to moderate our language and our actions, which could have an effect highly unfortunate for our goals and objectives." Anyone in Bavaria, he wrote, was apparently free to press with impunity for war and to encourage her rulers to resort to it. A hatred of France was being fostered that in a few days, if things continued this way, would be beyond the Bavarian government's power of control. It was, moreover, a contagious hatred, and it would not fail, sooner or later, to become general and sweep over Germany.[49] In light of these passages in Cadore's reports, it is impossible to say that the French government was not fairly warned that persistence in too strong a line could well start a process leading to a Bavarian-Prussian reconciliation. The message from St. Vallier, minister at Stuttgart, was even stronger and—more significant still—was written before news of the Ems telegram had come out. Its hard core read: "Any new demands on our part to the cabinet of Berlin will now be looked upon here as proof that we are now bent on war."[50] The messages of d'Astorg at Karlsruhe said much the same thing.[51]

Thus, the opportunity for France to defend her vital interests in south Germany arose in 1870, but Gramont's policy made it impossible. At no time did Gramont consider the possibility of using the crisis over the candidacy as a means of strengthening the states of south Germany against Prussia—the key to driving them into France's arms. His policy toward Bavaria and south Germany, insofar as he had a policy, was to point to the precedents of 1831 and 1862, when the Great Powers had collectively imposed kings upon the peoples of Belgium and Greece. Lacking utterly was the hint of the danger—the mortal danger—that lay in store for the four south German states if they became involved in a war over what were purely Prussian dynastic interests rather than German national ones. This omission was even more startling after 12 July 1870, when, having won Leopold's renunciation, Gramont embarked upon his campaign to play up the magnitude of his good fortune and to demand guarantees. What better time could there have been to remind the south German states how close they had come to war and to emphasize that they owed their escape from it only to French skill and persistence? Indeed, such a ploy would have been even more effective in view of Bismarck's elaborate pretense that the candidacy was a purely Hohenzollern matter with which the Prussian government had nothing to do.

This is not guesswork; it was precisely the policy that was being urged upon Gramont by Beust and by Bray.[52] Gramont waved their advice aside. Instead, he based his policy on the assumption that the candidacy was a matter of indifference to the states of south Germany, thereby overreaching himself and tumbling his nation into disaster. Gramont's bluster, his declaration of 6 July, and his more extreme demands six days later (the demands that led to the Ems telegram)—all of these threatened south Germany far more than they did Prussia, no matter what Bismarck might argue, with an effect doubled by the probability that they would make more likely a Franco-German war. Bray said: "If Prussia is defeated we will most certainly lose the Palatinate; more we cannot now foresee. If France wins, we are probably safe in assuming that she will respect the independence of the middle states. A Prussian victory is something else altogether. In that case, God help us! We can expect to suffer the fate of Hanover."[53] Gramont, in other words, cut the ground out from under the feet of the very men who had fought union with Prussia and who had the most to lose from it. Hence the bankruptcy of his policy. As Paul W. Schroeder has pointed out, one can only note the determination with which the rulers of Bavaria and of Württemberg struggled to maintain their independence between 1820 and 1821 and the speed with which this determination melted away in the heat of July 1870.[54]

In view of what has already been said about the degree to which Gramont and his supporters in Napoleon III's government were determined to seek guarantees from Prussia, it should come as no surprise that the decision for peace or war lay, in the last resort, in their laps. Bismarck, speaking of the Ems telegram in his memoirs, plumes himself as having goaded the French into war and quotes himself as saying, "If I not only publish this text . . . at once in the newspapers, but also transmit it by telegram to our embassies, it will become known in Paris before midnight and, not only because of its contents but because of its mode of publication, will have the effect of a red flag on the Gallic bull."[55]

What Bismarck said was true only in part, and it was by no means the whole story. The Ems telegram and other developments to be recounted here took place within a ramshackle structure of communication, which included a break at the joint between the offices of the senior personalities of the French government. No one is ever likely to find out what actually happened, because of the paucity and defectiveness of the materials needed for such a study. The most detailed account we have is the extended apologia of Ollivier; there is also the confused and often circumstantial evidence presented in the memoirs of Gramont, along with sketchy bits of material given by newspaper editors and other informants to the historian Pierre de la Gorce and published by him in his classic history of the Second Empire. More important, it is obvious that 14 July 1870, the crucial day on which the question of peace or war hung in the balance, marked but the culmination of a storm that had been brewing at least since 3 July—and even, in some sense, since the Prussian victory at Königgrätz four years before.

That the France of July 1870 was tormented and in an overwrought psychic state is beyond question, and this was so because she stood in the shadow of several developments that were destined to destroy the foundations of imperial rule and that posed an immediate threat to its stability. The candidacy of Leopold, the endless volume of rumor and speculation that flowed from Ems, the dubious renunciation—all of this coming on top of the frantic sessions in the chamber of deputies—produced, by mid-July 1870, a state of excitement, anxiety, and panic in the French population that defies description. The result was a hysteria, a bombast, an orgy of self-admiration and of breast-beating indignation—almost all of which was, as events were soon to show, preposterous, bizarre, and monstrously self-defeating. Seldom, surely, has France been exposed to so much oratory—or to oratory more strained, more empty, more defensive, more virulent. All was righteousness and hatred. Under these circumstances the government could count on a large body of opinion to support a hard line—to insist, that is, that the name of the king of Prussia be associated unequivocally with the renunciation. It has already been seen that the declaration of 6 July, though it clearly involved for Prussia a humiliating retreat or acceptance of war, evoked widespread approval all over France.

Some historians of French opinion have argued that Gramont, in drawing up the demand for guarantees on 12 July, was again racing ahead of the evidence, for the news of Leopold's withdrawal was too fresh and could not have spread from Paris to the provinces. But as Lynn Case has pointed out, there can be no doubt that Gramont was right to believe that given the aroused state of opinion at the time, his demand would carry popular support—even though his rivals and enemies within the cabinet viewed it as a daring scheme that should be watered down and delayed in its execution, if not rejected outright.[56] Such concerns were of little moment to Gramont. He believed that the fabric of the Second Empire could not withstand the strain of a further international rebuff, and he was by no means alone in this view. The Paris press, it should be noted, had developed a sense of grievance against Prussia—and against Bismarck in particular—that came to match, in intensity and bitterness, the reactions evoked over the disaster experienced at Königgrätz. There was a sense of national humiliation at foreign hands—and this in an age of almost pathological intensity of national feeling.

What needs to be stressed here is that the Ems telegram, first published in the *Norddeutsche Allgemeine Zeitung* around ten o'clock at night on 13 July, was of negligible impact and thus of no significant influence on the deliberations of the French ministers that took place the following day. Paris did not, as Bismarck had intended, learn of the telegram until midnight of 13 July; word of it reached the capital only on the morning of 14 July and then in ragged, indeed almost incomprehensible form. The *Correspondance du Nord-Est* printed a version that reflected, albeit sketchily and haltingly, what had appeared in the Berlin paper; on the other hand, Havas, the most prestigious agency of the day, made it appear that the telegram, though dated from Berlin, was nothing more than a report from a regular correspondent at Ems. More seriously, it ended with a paragraph proclaiming that France had won a dramatic victory: the king had officially approved the renunciation, all grounds for conflict had been eliminated, and the crisis was at an end. The two paragraphs stood in flagrant contradiction one to the other, and readers were left to speculate in the void. Not until six-thirty in the evening on 14 July did five Paris papers pick up this article, and only at seven-thirty did the *Soir*, a sensationalist and flamboyant organ, print it, with the comment that the French ambassador had been roundly abused by the king of Prussia. Even then no proper inquiry was made into its authenticity. The examination by the leading authorities of the press and of the government was hasty and conducted in circumstances not conducive to the elucidation of the full facts. The mystery surrounding the question how Benedetti had really been treated continued, one may add, right down to midday on 15 July, when the legislature took up the question. A prominent politician was not wide of the mark when he observed: "Certain papers, instead of reporting what happened, are resorting to guesses and assumptions, deviating from objectivity, and placing themselves in contradiction to the facts."[57]

It is thus clear that the Ems telegram had no significant impact on the deliberations of the French ministers or even on French opinion, which was, to be sure, in an inflamed and highly excitable state by 14 July and more than ever insistent upon receiving from Prussia the guarantees for future good conduct that Gramont had demanded. Both Gramont and Ollivier roundly declare that the white heat of public opinion made itself intensely felt not only on members of the cabinet, already alarmed and greatly shaken, but also on the emperor himself, and there is certainly nothing in the record to contradict them. On 14 July Lyons addressed a letter to Granville summarizing the situation: "Though the . . . article in the *North German Gazette* had not become generally or officially known, the public excitement was so great, and so much irritation existed in the army, that it became doubtful whether the government could withstand the cry for war, even if it were to announce a decided diplomatic success. It was felt that when the Prussian article appeared in the evening papers, it would be very difficult to restrain the anger of the people, and . . . that the government would feel bound to appease the public impatience by formally declaring its intention to resent the conduct of Prussia."[58] He spoke truly. In a word, the leading figures of the imperial council deliberated on 14 July amid a mounting crescendo of public excitement and felt themselves under enormous pressure to declare war.

All the same, some outstanding figures of the cabinet still favored a moderate course, wishing to draw back and to arrange a peaceful settlement of affairs. This was the unmistakable impression when the council of ministers met in the presence of the emperor on the morning of 13 July and learned for the first time of the demand for guarantees. Several of its members had built up frustration over Gramont's failure to consult them before making so drastic and dangerous a decision and resented their exclusion from it. Ollivier, in particular, was disturbed. He resolved to arrest the run toward war by arguing that the government should content itself with the withdrawal of the candidacy and, in the event that the requirement of guarantees was turned down, should abstain from making an issue of the king's refusal. The more important of the ministers—Louvet, Segris, Parieu, Plichon, Chevandeier de Valdrôme—concurred, recognizing as they did the implications of a refusal of Gramont's demand on the king's part.

Moreover, Le Boeuf was again up in arms. As early as 11 July, before the renunciation of the candidacy had taken place, there had been serious talk of mobilization, but that pressure—to the realization of which the powers of Europe (Great Britain and Russia most of all) would have violently objected—was successfully resisted by Gramont's opponents, whose dreams ran in the first instance to the simple defeat of the candidacy. Now it appeared to Le Boeuf that more tension was on the horizon. He therefore demanded that the reserves be called up at once, arguing that every day lost would place the country in mortal peril. Ollivier would have none of this; he knew only too well that the calling up of the reserves would be next door to a declaration of war. After fierce bickering, the ministers by a vote of eight to four agreed to this proposal, but as it was impossible for them to announce and justify their decision, it was decided to move in the chamber for a postponement of the debate to 15 July.[59]

Despite the stormy session, Ollivier returned to his home stimulated and well satisfied by this renewal of his personal diplomatic initiative. He felt that he had poured oil on troubled waters, that he had corrected to some extent the overdramatic excesses aroused in Gramont and Napoleon III the day before, and that he had succeeded in recovering firmly into his hands the vital Franco-Prussian exchanges concerning a possible solution. His satisfaction over these achievements was heightened by the fact that rumors of his success had reached the moderate politicians even prior to his return, so that he found himself being congratulated on what he had achieved. But Napoleon III, to whom he had directed his energies, had no word of appreciation. In place of it he wrote Ollivier a note that said merely: "There remains much to be done." "Very kind of him," observed Ollivier dryly in his journal the next morning.[60]

In the meantime, there occurred an event that was destined, as it happened, to complicate immeasurably the discussions over French policy: Napoleon had again fallen seriously ill from an acute attack of bladder trouble. The full seriousness of the illness was not initially apparent, as it was diagnosed only as a minor kidney inflammation—an ailment that, however serious, normally could have been surmounted with the proper drugs in the space of a few days. But actually this was only the beginning. Twenty-two years at the helm of French politics, added to the normal ravages of age, had taken their toll on this venerable statesman. What would be left for the remaining two and a half years of life was a physically helpless figure, mentally quite alert but racked with a succession of illnesses, often and for long periods dazed, never able to assume the full burden of his duties, yet also (so long as the generals and the empress had anything to say) never able to question the demands to which he was constantly being subjected by the most inflammatory figures in his own entourage. Napoleon's condition was now such that he was often—in fact usually—unavailable to those who most needed to see him. Yet such was the secrecy of imperial style that there was no one else in the whole of the French government who knew what was going on. For ambassadors and members of the government alike this presented a dreadful situation. To ask for a special audience would not only risk a rebuff but, in case the request was granted, invite public attention to the audience and stimulate press speculation about its purpose.[61]

Napoleon III was, in fact, pulled two ways. Anxious to avoid war, yet quite unable to withstand the pressure of the war party, he put off decisions to a more opportune future. Gramont, on the other hand—ever the flamboyant figure with formidable powers of persuasion and sensing the national humiliation that would result from accepting the renunciation in its present form—pressed for a hard line. From the afternoon of 13 July onward, telegrams poured in from Benedetti at Ems repeating what Gramont already knew—namely, that King William, while approving the renunciation *entière et sans reserve,* steadfastly refused to give assurances about the future. Gramont remained unmoved. He continued to view Benedetti as an excessively timid figure in his relations with William I and fancied that a bolder and stronger voice, coming from a more high-powered and motivated person, could alter the monarch's disposition.[62]

According to the decision of the council that very morning, Gramont should have contented himself with the king's approval of the renunciation. Nothing of the kind happened. At seven that night he wired Benedetti: "Make one last effort with the king. Tell him that we require only that he forbid the prince of Hohenzollern to reconsider his withdrawal. Let him say to you. 'I will forbid it,' and let him authorize you to write us to that effect." Otherwise, said Gramont, there would be no alternative to war. And he added: "I have every reason to believe that the Great Powers of Europe will consider our efforts measured and just."[63] Gramont's demand was, one may add, repeated later the same evening in conversations with Lyons and Okunev.[64] The king's approval of the renunciation seemed to him pretty small beer (*c'est une bagatelle*), and before leaving for St. Cloud to bring the emperor up to date on the various developments, he wrote a note to this effect to Ollivier. Ollivier, quite naturally, objected and replied that he was saddened and uneasy, but as Gramont did not receive this message before he left Paris, the communication fell upon deaf ears. Greatly disturbed and in full anxiety over the fate his own position, Ollivier retired for the night. In the meantime, returning from St. Cloud, Gramont recounted his discussions with Napoleon and his advisers: "Great indecision. First, war. Then doubts on account of the king's approval. The dispatch from Spain [accepting the renunciation] might tip the scales towards peace."[65]

What it all boiled down to was this: By the morning of 14 July, Gramont's position had become shaky in the extreme. His determination to wring from William I assurances of good behavior on the part of Prussia had led to the formulation of the demand for guarantees. It was known all over Europe that the Great Powers and all four of the south German states had become gloomily apprehensive, regarding his demand as ludicrous and needlessly inflammatory and beginning to suspect that it was but a pretext for war. Furthermore, it had become obvious that William would not, under any circumstances, proffer assurances for the future. Finally, reports from the French ministers described the rapidly mounting excitement not only in Berlin but, more ominously, throughout Germany. The French military attaché replied to Le Boeuf's request for information that the Prussian generals and officers were on their way back to the capital.[66] The staff of the Prussian embassy in Paris reported similar information to Berlin.

Le Boeuf's actions during this time, in particular, stand as a revealing measure of the extent to which French policy in the crisis with Prussia was now influenced by military considerations. His messages to Gramont over the next two days suggest a mind dominated by three impressions: (1) that a Prussian attack was, if not actually imminent, likely to occur in the very near future; (2) that the Prussians, with a view to placing the French in a position where they would not be able to call upon their allies for assistance, were demanding that the states of south Germany now honor their military obligations under the treaties of 1866 and place their armies under Prussian command; and (3) that if war did develop between Prussia and France, the latter, in the absence of a head start in mobilization, was likely to meet disaster, and this at the hands of an enemy who would stop at nothing to destroy everything she held dear—her civilization, her culture, her way of life.[67]

These communications struck the foreign minister with the force of a thunderbolt. Yet what could he do? Were his hands not tied by the council's decision of 13 July? By no means. He felt himself obliged to disregard the decision and now cast about furiously for some device that would tell against William I. The Ems telegram, abrupt and unexpected, dropped into his lap to satisfy this felt want. The article in the *Norddeutsche Allgemeine Zeitung* reached Paris through the offices of the French chargé in Berlin at 3:45 in the morning. As communicated, it was terse and sharp and was, of course, intended by Bismarck to be so. It is easy to believe that a man like Gramont, fighter par excellence that he was, would have exerted himself vigorously and immediately to avenge the insult. Ollivier tells us that as he was in the throes of drafting a pacifying message to the legislature, Gramont confronted him. Arriving unannounced at the door of the prime minister's office, Gramont was greeted by Ollivier's astounded secretaries, themselves busy refining Ollivier's message. Ollivier, to whom Gramont's presence was, of course, at once reported, invited him in. "My dear fellow," Ollivier later quoted Gramont as saying, "you see before you a man who has just been slapped in the face." Gramont gave the impression of a man gravely shocked and outraged. It did not take long before Ollivier was overcome by similar emotions. To Gramont he said: "We must not delude ourselves any further; they mean to drive us into war."[68] Ollivier immediately summoned several of his colleagues (which ones we cannot tell), who requested that Napoleon convene a full session of the imperial council that afternoon. Gramont relates that at least some of the ministers (he says *"le gouvernement"*) shrank from using a newspaper article, no matter how invidious its tone or content, as a pretext for taking France into war and wished to concentrate their attention on the task at hand. He quoted uneasily an urgent message that he had received from Lyons imploring the ministers not to take any precipitous step before more information had come to light: "We were uneasy, but resolved not to commit ourselves until we had full information."[69]

The Ems telegram stimulated in Ollivier a new order of anxieties and a new order of visions. National honor, as he had repeated times without number, required that France not be trifled with, and he began to think—though not without doubts and hesitations—that war between France and Prussia could now no longer be averted. This, one may be sure, did not frighten him from the standpoint of the prospective bloodshed involved; like many others of his time, he still had a romantic conception of warfare as a test of national virtue, an exercise in which were exhibited the qualities of valor, heroism, and devotion to the national cause and in which the braver and more inspired could (granted anything resembling equality of forces and armaments) be expected to win. Dovetailing beautifully with Ollivier's change of heart was, one must note, another development of the first order. Behind the scenes, the wheels of the two great competitive military establishments, the French and the Prussian, had begun to gather speed—grinding along in the manner of such establishments, impervious to any hopeful political possibilities, accepting (if only for the hypotheses of military planning) the inevitability of a war that was otherwise, even at this stage, not at all inevitable, and thereby creating a virtual inevitability that, but for their own efforts, would not necessarily have existed at all. The nationalistic hysteria on both sides of the Rhine provided a moral justification for those visions of an all-out military effort and of total military victory that unavoidably commanded the imagination, and shaped the efforts, of the military planners. And between the two of them—between the hysteria of the population and the planning of the strategists—they now began to obliterate, in the minds of Ollivier and his supporters, all consciousness of any solution to the crisis.

At half past noon on 14 July, the council of ministers met at the Tuileries. Napoleon III presided. Outside, French opinion stirred, with angry mobs surging about the ministry and the chamber. There was another reason for this, apart from Ems: Quatorze Juillet had special significance. In 1789, the Bastille had fallen on that day. More generally, the date had become enshrined in memory as the date when a new France had been born—the France that had been created by the great revolution after the old order had been destroyed, the France that cared for Liberty and the Rights of Man. Did the celebration of France's national day embolden the council of ministers? It is difficult to see how it could not. Certainly it did nothing to weaken the arguments of Gramont and the military chiefs who insisted that the French nation had to confront the Prussian danger.

The atmosphere of the palace grew heavy with intolerable suspense. When the session opened, Gramont's self-control deserted him. He walked into the room, flung his briefcase furiously on the table, and announced: "After what has happened, a minister of foreign affairs who would not make up his mind for war would not be worthy of his office."[70] Other ministers refused to be hurried. The old arguments in favor of negotiating and against precipitous action reappeared in the mouths of the more moderate faction. They had solid evidence to which they could point: William clearly had approved of the withdrawal of the candidacy, a fact borne out by Benedetti's latest telegrams, which displayed William's intentions as honorable and utterly devoid of discourtesy. There was a renewed discussion of the state of alliances. On everyone's mind also was the publication in the *Norddeutsche Allgemeine Zeitung* of what had transpired between Benedetti and William I. Le Boeuf, appalled and intensely angered that there could be any doubt, again stressed the urgency of the situation and demanded the immediate calling up of the reserves.

But on this occasion, as on others, the moderate faction gained the upper hand. There could be no burking the fact that William had agreed *entière et sans reserve* to the renunciation and that indeed Benedetti's telegrams contained no hint of monarchical disrespect or disapproval. That the realization of Gramont's goal was wholly unacceptable to the king was clear to Ollivier and the moderates, and under these circumstances William's refusal to see Benedetti was, in their eyes, by no means unnatural. In Ollivier's words, "He had done so in courteous terms; no one had been insulted."[71] On the other hand, it was hard to treat the Ems telegram as an ordinary newspaper article. It was demonstrably an official communication of the Prussian government, a grievous offense against the honor of France that deserved to be protested, denounced, condemned. Still, the hazards of war were not to be taken lightly.

The ministers wore themselves down. No one could carry the council. This did not matter. All shared to the full the general feeling of the educated French public that the successful development of the French armed forces, to a point where they were now (at least statistically and on paper) much superior to those that faced them on the other side of the Rhine, gave France a new lease on life and placed her in a position where she could well afford to pursue a more self-confident and aggressive stance than had been possible in 1866. But Le Boeuf insisted that she must strike while the iron was hot; she must get her blow in first: she had a two-week head start in mobilization but would throw away this advantage if there were further delay. At four o'clock, the council "almost unanimously" accepted Le Boeuf's proposal to call up the reserves, and even those who made the decision knew that it was as good as a declaration of war.[72]

Le Boeuf left the council to confer with the military leaders. Shortly before five-thirty in the evening a new telegram came in from Benedetti. It recounted, accurately enough, the events of 14 July—that is, the willingness of the king to see him again at the railway station prior to William's departure for Koblentz that afternoon.[73] The immediate effect of this communication was to knock yet another card out of Gramont's hand, underlying as it did the futility of further bargaining over the guarantees. There were new reports, whose accuracy could not be verified, that the Ems telegram owed its origin to highly placed figures in the king's cabinet. Even more puzzling was the report of the Berlin correspondent of the London *Times,* who wondered out loud whether such disrespectful treatment on the part of a seasoned diplomat like Benedetti had not been carried out on the explicit instructions of Gramont. It was said that Benedetti had received instructions to be brusque with the king and that, after William had turned his back upon him in the public promenade, within sight of many bystanders, Benedetti had chased him to his quarters and was stopped only when William asked an adjutant to throw him out.[74] News of this came through shortly before six. What on earth had happened?

More wrangling followed. Some ministers demanded immediate action; others pleaded for delay. In the middle of it, someone hit on a way out: a congress convened for the purpose of settling every grievance that existed between France and Prussia. There were some attractive features about this wonderful plan. It would meet the French need as to assurances over the future and yet reaffirm the principle that the thrones of Europe would be barred from the reigning houses of the Great Powers without previous agreement. Who was behind this idea? According to Ollivier, it was Gramont, and in his memoirs (published in 1872), Gramont does not dispute him. Yet Gramont is an unlikely candidate for such a role. The idea of appealing to others to obtain satisfaction for his country was not in keeping with his character, still less with the aims that he had developed during the crisis. At the same time, a congress would bring diplomatic advantage to Gramont. On more than one occasion he had asserted his belief that France could draw on the fund of goodwill that, over the course of the years in which

Napoleon III was emperor, she had accumulated from the other powers.[75] Maybe he believed that a congress would end in the isolation of Prussia or that its very suggestion would be enough to consign it to oblivion. In any case, it is not easy to trace the origins and development of the congress proposal that swept over the council in the late afternoon of 14 July 1870. But this much is clear: Napoleon III seized on the idea and pushed it hard. Ill and in pain through much of the afternoon, on heavy doses of analgesic drugs prescribed by the imperial physician, he had taken no part in the discussions, but may indeed have shared the belief of his more moderate ministers that using the Ems telegram as a reason to break the peace would be a confession of helplessness and despair. A congress to discuss every topic under the sun had been on his mind ever since he took power; hence his enthusiasm for the idea now. There was, in any case, no doubt on the latter score in the minds of the politicians close to him. The ministers—"almost without exception," says Ollivier—embraced the suggestion without debate.[76] A running start was made on drafting a statement for the Corps législatif.

A strange interruption followed. Napoleon broke off the discussion and sent for Prince Metternich, his old confidant, to whom he had always spoken with frankness and with earnestness. What the emperor said on this occasion is not certain, but it is not unlikely that he related in detail what had just happened. Twice before the interview Metternich had reported that opinion in Paris was such that a declaration of war could be expected any minute; with France seemingly locked in mortal combat with Prussia, the imminence of the congress proposal must have astonished the minister. But Napoleon insisted that it was indeed at the top of his agenda and showed Metternich the proposed declaration: "Despite Prussia's rejection of our legitimate demand, we do not consider conflict on the horizon. However, we feel obliged to call up our forces. We are prepared to accept a congress at which all questions at issue would be decisively solved in the interest of the general peace."[77]

Napoleon returned to the council and, with tears in his eyes, read out the declaration. He said to Ollivier: "Go into my study and put into writing what has just been said." Ollivier thereupon withdrew only to reappear a few minutes later with a new ending stuck on.[78] The ministers went home, agreeing to meet the next morning. The inescapable conclusion was this: the council regarded the Ems telegram as an affront, an intolerable challenge to French greatness; it must be rejected categorically. The demand for guarantees had been refused, but France could still pull out of the scrape with her prestige intact if the Great Powers went along with the congress.

Within three hours, however, the tables had turned. What happened?

Briefly, this: Ollivier, deep down, had doubts about the congress idea; he regarded it as cowardly and as unworthy of his government and of France. Not many minutes had elapsed before his beautiful declaration began to burn a hole in his pocket. When he got home, he tried out the proposal on his family—namely, on his wife and daughters—and found them appalled and astounded by what he proposed.[79] Exactly the same thing happened to Napoleon III. Back at St. Cloud shortly after seven in the evening, he encountered Empress Eugénie and Marshall Le Boeuf. They pointed out the difference between the call for a congress and the decision to call up the reserves. Le Boeuf had consulted the French generals and reported that they were already sending out orders to the relevant commanders. Ollivier would have us believe that Le Boeuf was not averse to the congress proposal—a reaction that, incidentally, drew upon his head a stinging reprimand from the empress—and that he, Le Boeuf, pressed only for a decision one way or the other. In any case, Napoleon gave way. Badgered by Le Boeuf, he sent word at eight o'clock to Ollivier that a second council would convene at St. Cloud later that evening.[80] It was this council that would take France into the war of 1870–71.

The huge show of martial fervor that dominated the foregoing discussions, together with everything else that had happened in the preceding eight days, obviously had told heavily on the nerves of those concerned with the conduct of diplomacy. The long exertion was now taking its psychic toll. Tempers were frayed, sensibilities chafed and tender. There was in some quarters a loss of elasticity. The decisions taken throughout the remainder of the evening of 14 July were those of harried, overworked men, operating in the vortex of tremendous pressures, military and otherwise, which today we find difficult to imagine. Relationships between the members of the government, never good, were strained and unsatisfactory, torn this way and that by a never-ending succession of resentments, suspicions, misunderstandings, and political maneuvers. Despite all formal and institutional devices, real unity of decision was not fully achieved.

When Ollivier arrived at St. Cloud at nine o'clock, he found Napoleon III in a different frame of mind than earlier—he was now out of sympathy with the congress proposal. This new line was music in Ollivier's ears: "Sire, I agree. If we take this proposal to the chamber, people will hurl mud at our carriages and hoot us." Napoleon III replied: "You see in what a situation a government can sometimes find itself—even if we should have no available cause for war, we should still be obliged to decide on it for the good of the country."[81] These words were clear enough. The way was being paved to overturn the decision taken earlier. Eugénie and Le Boeuf had, it appeared, intervened with devastating effect.

At ten o'clock the ministers assembled once more. Sentiment was not all one way. Some members favored keeping the congress proposal alive and were anxious to suspend military maneuvers; others dissented. Chevandier de Valdrôme, minister of the interior, wavered. Shortly before eleven-thirty, Gramont, armed with fresh evidence, tackled him. Just before coming to St. Cloud, he had seen Werther, who was about to depart for Berlin and go on an extended leave, having been rebuked by Bismarck and William I for being party to the transaction of 12 July. Werther left no doubt as to the reason for his departure—confirmation, as if further were needed, of King William's refusal to meet the French demands. Nor was this the only problem. Gramont came to the council bearing with him telegrams from Le Sourd at Berlin and from Benedetti at Ems; the first stressed the discontent with French behavior and the rising temperament throughout Germany; the second reported that William was returning to the capital. Yet a third, from Bern, spoke of a telegram from Bismarck to the president of the federal council of Switzerland that announced that William I had broken off further discussions with Benedetti. Finally, and most significant, there was a telegram from Cadore that arrived while the ministers were in the middle of their deliberations. It created a sensation. Gramont read it out: "M. de Bismarck goes so far as to accuse Benedetti of having been discourteous in approaching the king during his walk on the promenade and, in an effort to give the situation a new twist, he describes it as wounding the honor of the German sovereign and believes that this account will evoke the liveliest sentiment in Bavaria."[82]

Here was unmistakable proof that Bismarck was treating the Ems telegram in an official manner—that he had transmitted to foreign governments the French demand for guarantees and William's refusal to accept it. The supplement to Cadore's report added insult to injury, suggesting as it did that the French ambassador had placed himself in the king's path on the promenade and virtually forced himself on the latter's presence—itself a grievous offense against established protocol. Ollivier, who claims that there had been no doubt whatsoever in the minds of any of the ministers from the start, would have us believe that these telegrams were nothing more than secondary considerations brought in to justify what had already been decided—that is, to meet the Prussian challenge at once by confirming the orders for mobilization. He vigorously and unambiguously disputes Gramont's contention that above and beyond the humiliation involved in Bismarck's machinations, the overriding anxiety was fear of Prussian mobilization:[83] "Everything was being decided on the other side of the Rhine as if war had already been declared. Our backs were against the wall. It was no longer a question of negotiation; we had to defend ourselves."[84] To which Ollivier lamely replies: "It would have been impossible to conceal the mobilization of a great army and the council was without any report of mobilization on 14 July."[85] But this is not much more than empty wordplay. The council had been warned from the beginning by Le Boeuf that the key French advantage would be squandered if the Prussians were allowed to steal a march in any matters having to do with military operations. For some days he had busied himself with the question what the French should do about the reports of mobilization that were coming out of Prussia (most of which, in fact, were either exaggerated or downright false). But Cadore's report, referred to above, reached Paris at 7:15 on 14 July and, one supposes, could easily have found its way into the hands of the council and have given Le Boeuf a winning card to play in the game of competition that he was waging against the more moderate faction.

One is led irresistibly, by a long chain of circumstantial evidence, toward the conclusion that the Ems telegram and the uses to which it was put by Bismarck were considerations that Ollivier, in the heat of the moment, exaggerated so that he could emphasize, ex post facto and to the exclusion of all else, the question of honor. In order to recognize the force of this suspicion, one need only compare the accounts offered of the 14 July meeting by Ollivier and Gramont respectively. The former argues tendentiously (and thoroughly implausibly) that there was only loose and tentative discussion and that sentiment ran from the start against the congress and in favor of military action.[86] Gramont is nearer the mark in stressing military considerations, and here is he supported strongly by evidence from Le Boeuf, who in testimony three years later before a legislative commission asserted that with respect to mobilization, the council swung first one way then the other until "a certain telegram" was received during its deliberations, thus turning the tables.[87] The great French scholar Pierre de la Gorce, in his work on the history of the Second Empire, makes the interesting statement that there was one particular document that clinched the decision;[88] he does not say whence he derived his knowledge of this source, but he had more extensive access to the records of Napoleon III's ministers than many contemporary historians have, and it is not to be assumed that he pulled it out of thin air. The suggestion finds a most powerful—and to this day undisputed—confirmation in the memoirs of Malmesbury, former prime minister of Great Britain and a close friend of Gramont, with whom he had been exchanging messages throughout the crisis and from whom he had received a lengthy recounting of the meeting of 14 July almost immediately after it had ended. Malmesbury claims that the empress used a telegram brought by Le Boeuf to intervene with brutal effect and to argue that unless the French were to allow the Germans to continue to play around irresponsibly with the purpose of throwing sand in their eyes, there could now be no question, no thought, of turning back. Supported by Le Boeuf, she carried the day for mobilization.[89] By eleven o'clock the die had been cast, and the ministers voted that the chamber should be informed on the following day.[90]

This brings to an end the incredible tale of the events that shaped the critical decision of the French council of 14 July 1870. This is not the proper point for a full appraisal of the significance of the result, but there are a few features of the final action that might well be noted before we leave the subject entirely.

1. There is no evidence that Gramont ever really had any faith in the negotiations between the French government and Prussia. He was only too aware from the reports that he received from Ems and elsewhere that Benedetti had not really been insulted by William I. What weighed with him, however, was not a mere newspaper article but the fact that Bismarck had notified

foreign governments of what had taken place. Even then, the ministers were not prepared to make the issue a cause for war with Prussia. There is powerful evidence of this. On 15 July Gramont met with Metternich and Vitzthum (confidant of Francis Joseph and his special representative to Paris), on which occasion he indulged in one of the melodramatic and inflammatory forensic outbursts to which he was temperamentally given. Pacing about his office, his body shaking, his finger jabbing the air, his voice rumbling with fury, his face red and dripping with sweat, his shirt wet through, swearing and shouting almost to the point of incoherence, Gramont declared that as late as the evening of 14 July, the idea of a European congress still carried so much weight with Napoleon III that he had been brought to the point of resignation in order to persuade his master to give it up.[91]

2. This almost fantastic display of misguided behavior on the part of Gramont over the congress idea seems to have arisen because of the strong attachment to that idea on the part of Napoleon III—an attachment that apparently continued well after the evening session had broken up, despite what Ollivier alleges he was told by the emperor when the conference opened. This, at any rate, is the overriding impression given in the report of a meeting with Napoleon written by Vitzthum on 15 July.[92] Napoleon took the step, unusual for him, of rebuking Ollivier for his conduct during the whole of the crisis. The congress idea was a dead dog, but Napoleon III was genuinely delighted when Vitzthum raised it again, maybe in the belief (belied in the event) that it would carry favor with Francis Joseph, on whose military support he was continuing to count in the coming war with Prussia. But once the order for mobilization had been given, there could be no turning back.

3. Ollivier's claim that no decision for war was taken at the meeting on the night of 14 July is one that may be taken with a large pinch of salt. True, no formal vote was taken because of the absence of some of the ministers, but no one could mistake or doubt the obvious meaning of the ominous decision to call up the reserves. This decision (in addition to those already described), occurring in the relations between two highly armed Great Powers, was the familiar sign, the unfailing sign, of a decision for war—that and nothing else. The episode may stand, in fact, as a revealing instance of the rather desperate, pathetic, and wholly unsuccessful efforts of Ollivier to influence policy

during the whole of the July crisis. Napoleon III seems not to have cared for him, if only because he symbolized the new parliamentary regime and therefore consistently ignored his advice. As for Ollivier himself, he felt out of his depth in foreign affairs, tended to rely heavily on Gramont, and in general showed himself (as Henry Salomon once noted) overbearing, long-winded, and rather pretentious.[93]

Events now were much in the nature of an epilogue. At nine o'clock in the morning on 15 July, a full council was convened at St. Cloud. Gramont read out the declaration of war that he had worked out with Ollivier. The declaration was no call to action; it merely ascribed the decision for war to William's refusal to receive Benedetti and to the communication of this refusal to the governments of Europe. When Gramont ended, Napoleon III clapped his hands. Chavandier said: "When anyone strikes me without considering whether or not I am . . . able to fight, I return the blow."[94] Benedetti, who had traveled overnight from Ems, saw Gramont and Ollivier just after this cabinet meeting; he gave his account of what had actually happened on the promenade and ended by describing how the king had shaken his hand as he had left the station at Ems, murmuring: *"Au révoir à Berlin."* Gramont and Ollivier remained unmoved. Prussia, in their view, was unshakably bent on war.

When, on 15 July, Gramont and Ollivier addressed the senate and the Corps législatif to demand a vote of war credits, the voice of opposition broke through. Thiers, in particular, was provoked. Having always been a man of considerable ability, and one whose support for the ministers had been unshakable until the withdrawal of the Hohenzollern candidacy, he followed Ollivier to the rostrum and attacked the demand for war credits: "Do you want all Europe to say that although the substance of the quarrel was settled, you have decided to pour out torrents of blood over a matter of form?"[95]

A coalition of the left supported Thiers, but faced by the solidarity of the right and center, he could make no headway. Guyot-Montpayroux, another deputy, expostulated: "Prussia has forgotten the France of Jena and we must remind her!"[96] Ollivier, replying to Thiers, had to argue that the government's decision was not based on the offensive terms of the Ems telegram but on its intentional publication and its communication to foreign powers. He added that he accepted the heavy responsibility for war "with a light heart" (*d'un coeur léger*), a phrase that he immediately qualified: "I mean with a heart not weighted down by remorse, a confident heart, and a clear conscience."[97]

There was much debate on whether the government should be required to submit key documents. Two deputies, Bouffet and Fauvre, demanded to see the Prussian dispatch to foreign courts, but the motion lost by a vote of 159 to 84. Instead, a commission was appointed to hear evidence in support of the request for credits. Its deliberations produced a curious turn of events. Gramont had made much of the objectionable telegram that Bismarck had sent abroad, but in fact he did not have a copy of it; when examined by the commission, he was reduced to arguing that it was not important—the fact was that King William had refused to see the French ambassador, had refused to continue with him the discussion of the question at issue, and it was plain to all the world that France could not tolerate these enormities. Pressed on the question whether France had any allies upon whom she could rely, he rubbed his hands and replied: "If I have kept the commission waiting, it was because I had with me at the foreign ministry the Austrian ambassador and the Italian minister."[98] His reply was of little moment. In a flash of legality, the commission wished to show that somehow the French resort to war was justified. It therefore botched together a report that supported the government's case. The chamber as a whole was bent on war and made a great stir in order to drown out the cries of the opposition. Late on the evening of 15 July the war credits were voted 245 to 10. Outside the crowds roared.

There was a last sputter of diplomatic alarm. Benedetti's demand for guarantees alarmed Visconti-Venosta even more than it did the British and the Austrians. France's action, coming so soon after Leopold's withdrawal, seemed to him "insane." If, as was to be expected, William I refused to comply, war was certain to follow, and the danger of Italian involvement would have to be wrestled with all over again.[99] Visconti-Venosta thought he saw a way out. He turned to Beust for support. Beust evaded him; he insisted from the first that the crisis had nothing to do with Austria-Hungary. The French had started it without consulting him; they were provoking German opinion instead of isolating Prussia from Germany, as he had always advised; they would not even tell him their military plans. Like the Russians, like everyone else in Europe, he expected a French victory, but he intended to exploit this victory, not to aid it. His immediate object was to keep French favor without alienating either side. Those who argue that Beust was bent on revenge against Prussia (and there are plenty of them) ignore the many things he did that worked in the other direction. To read his correspondence—particularly with Metternich but also with Austria's representatives in the south German states—is to understand how thoroughly out of step with European opinion he believed the French to be, especially after Gramont's declaration of 6 July.[100] In his view, France was bent on provoking a crisis rather than trying to find a way out; she was demanding a role in the European system to which she was not entitled. Beust complained to Metternich and to the Italian representative in Vienna: "When I look at what is, I ask myself whether I have become an imbecile."[101]

Visconti-Venosta attempted a last let-out. The Aosta candidacy had been put on the shelf since 12 July; now Visconti-Venosta proposed to recall it to life. In his own words, "No more positive guarantee against the return of the Hohenzollern candidacy could be found than that which would result from the election of another prince to the throne of Spain."[102] Consequently, the Spanish government "should immediately be urged to proclaim the duke of Aosta and to summon the Cortes to ratify the choice."[103] Once again Visconti-Venosta pressed this solution on the British; on 15 July he called in Paget. Paget was in agreement and immediately telegraphed to London for instructions. Paget also suggested that Italy could win the other powers for this scheme if she would guarantee the duke's acceptance. Visconti-Venosta at once agreed, though he now feared that "things had gone too far" and that Gramont's demand for guarantees would mean the end of further negotiations. Paget left Visconti-Venosta, went home and sobbed, and telegraphed to London: "I don't think anybody could behave better than Visconti-Venosta has done and is doing."[104]

Visconti-Venosta defined his views on the point in a letter to Nigra on 12 July:

> It is our duty to point out earnestly to the French government the responsibility it would assume and the embarrassment it would cause its best friends if it precipitated complications and refused to allow time for a solution to mature in London, Madrid, and Florence. That we believe such a solution is possible is most true. I beg you to communicate this without delay to the government of the emperor. We count on its friendship for a proper understanding of a step that is being forced upon us by the obligation, which we share with everyone, of doing whatever possible we can for the maintenance of the peace. Let us hope that the government abides by the advice of its well-wishers and does not allow the excitement and bellicosity of mobs to impel it into a catastrophe the likes of which we are not likely to witness ever again.[105]

These observations lend to the pattern of Visconti-Venosta's hopes and strivings in July 1870 a dignity that does not flow from the bare record of his dealings with the European rulers. It is comforting to note that the qualities that brought Visconti-Venosta (albeit through grievous thoughts and many illusions) to perceptions of this order have not escaped the notice of statesmen and historians and have not failed to influence, by and large favorably, their judgment of at least a portion of the actions he undertook.[106] And this is only as it should be. Anyone who observed him at all sympathetically during those brief but crowded days could reasonably have concluded that he was teetering on the edge of a major personal tragedy from the effects of which—one suspects—he was never fully to recover. All his efforts to mobilize support for the Aosta candidacy had failed—his strenuous, at times frantic appeals to France to defuse the crisis before the guns went off and the lives of tens of thousands sank in blood. On a portion of the press, it is true, and on some of diplomatic community in Florence, Visconti-Venosta had some palpable influence.[107] But his counsel was simply brushed off by Paris; the fateful decisions on the Hohenzollern question were made either in total disregard or in direct defiance of his stated views, and it is no exaggeration to say that no serious effort was ever made by Gramont or by Ollivier to hear and to weigh on their merits the details of the case that he sought to present.

The heavy measure of frustration and disappointment that Visconti-Venosta faced was, in part, of his own making, for it is doubtful that he ever fully understood the depth and power of the forces arrayed against him—not only in France but at home as well. Politically weak to the point of debility; physically weak to the point of exhaustion; supported only by a dwindling band of cabinet ministers and journalists less thoughtful, less knowledgeable, less moderate than he; reviled, harassed, undercut by his own king—he yet continued to believe that somehow the great French ship of state would right itself and that he would realize the object of his exalted hopes. And then came Gramont's fiery speech to the French chamber on 15 July, which meant for him world's end.

But it would be wrong to end the story at this point. Here, as so often, it was the totality of the human personality rather than its partial manifestations that was of the greatest importance. In light of his apprecations, Visconti-Venosta cannot be permitted to depart of stage of Europe 1870 without a word of recognition for the efforts that he put forth, with such unique dedication, to end the Franco-Prussian crisis at its apogee; nor can he be denied posthumously a pang of sympathy for the unfeeling rejection to which those efforts were subjected by those who, had events taken a different turn, would surely not have been averse to sharing the credit for his achievement. Among the tragedies that attended the period of July 1870, there was none (aside from that of William I and Benedetti) that bore so great a poignancy and dignity as his.

The actual declaration of war drawn up by the French foreign office was presented in Berlin on 19 July 1870. Three of the southern German states, those that would take the brunt of the French attack, were already on a war footing. Nobody knew, nobody had the least premonition, that the French were preparing to march to their own destruction, so universally was it taken for granted that the French army was still the finest fighting machine in the world. At the very least, everyone expected a deep penetration into German territory, with the Germans, their backs to the wall, hard put to contain the attack. Moreover, it seemed likely that Austria and Italy in the south and Denmark in the north would seek to avenge their own past humiliations by joining hands with a triumphant France. By contrast, Gorchakov, the Russian minister, was at pains to emphasize that Prussia had nothing to fear from Russia. English sympathies were almost wholly with their former ally at Waterloo: here was the third Napoleon following in the footsteps of the first.

The third Napoleon could not disillusion them. He was still in acute pain, almost past endurance, suffering from stone. He could not think, indeed had no heart for war, but was driven on by Eugénie and the war party, sick with apprehension for the consequences if he failed to assert the honor and glory of France after so many rebuffs from Berlin. But even Napoleon, in his agony, took it for granted that his armies would soon be in Germany. His wish was to see France mighty, and to see her feared, admired, and respected for this might and for all that it would reflect in the way of superiority of the French spirit, of strength and virtue and cleverness on the part of France's people and of her leaders. The Order of the Day that he issued when he arrived to take command of the armies on 28 July underscored the depth of his conviction: "Whatever the road we may take beyond our frontiers, we shall come across the glorious tracks of our fathers. We shall prove worthy of them. All France follows you with her fervent prayers, and the eyes of the world are upon you. On you hinges the fate of liberty and civilization."[108]

Moltke, too, fully expected a deep initial penetration into enemy territory, whereas King William (as commander-in-chief) thought it unnecessary yet to think of issuing maps of France.[109] As for Bismarck, not even he understood the forces that had been at work to strengthen Germany and to weaken France. Germany had no reason for a war with France, and the gains she won from it proved a perpetual embarrassment. France had more reasons for attempting to prevent German unification, and if the war had gone well for France, no French statesmen would have been averse to claiming credit. In truth, the French rulers blundered into a war that was not unwelcome to them, and Bismarck, though taken by surprise, turned their blunder to his advantage.

180

Notes
Bibliographical Essay
Index

Notes

CHAPTER 1. A BIT ABOUT PERSONALITIES

1. Cowley to Stanley (prime minister), 10 August 1866, quoted in *Conversations with Napoleon III during the Second Empire,* Victor Wellesley and Robert Sencourt, eds. (London, 1934), 303–4.

2. Amedée Achard, *Souvenirs personnels d'émeutes et de révolutions* (Paris, 1872), 266.

3. *Kaiser Wilhelms des Grossen Briefe, Reden, und Schriften,* ed. Ernst Berner, 2 vols. (Berlin, 1906), 1:230.

4. Erich Marcks, *Kaiser Wilhelm I* (Leipzig, 1897), 101–2.

5. *Bismarck: Die gesammelten Werke,* ed. Herman Petersdorff et al., 15 vols. (Berlin, 1924–35), 15:194–95 (hereafter cited as *GW*).

6. Frederick William to Bunsen (his confidant), 27 March 1849, *Aus dem Brief-wechsel Friedrich Wilhelms IV. mit Bunsen,* ed. Leopold von Ranke (Leipzig, 1874), 160.

7. Ludwig Bamberger, *Count Bismarck: A Political Biography,* trans. Charles Lee Lewes (London, 1869), 113.

8. Gordon A. Craig, *The Politics of the Prussian Army 1640–1945* (New York, 1955), 138–48.

9. Albrecht Graf von Roon, *Denkwürdigkeiten,* 5. Aufl., 3 vols. (Berlin, 1905), 1:346.

10. Erich Marcks, *Männer und Zeiten,* 2 vols. (Leipzig, 1912), 1:303–4.

11. Roon, *Denkwürdigkeiten,* 2:514.

12. A. J. P. Taylor, *Bismarck: The Man and the Statesman* (New York, 1955), 9–31; Otto Pflanze, *Bismarck and the Development of Germany,* 3 vols. (Princeton, 1990), 1:85–88.

13. Quoted in Eduard von Wertheimer, *Bismarck im politischen Kampf* (Berlin, 1930), 9–10.

14. Quoted in Gordon A. Craig, *From Bismarck to Adenauer: Aspects of German Statecraft* (Baltimore, 1958), 7. The whole tenor of my remarks on Bismarck is based

on this most incisive piece. See also *Fürst Bismarcks Briefe an seine Braut und Gattin,* ed. Fürst Herbert Bismarck (Stuttgart, 1900), 281.

15. *GW,* 2:142.

16. Ibid., 6:44; 6a:40–42, 284–86, 321; 6b:163, 217, 260.

17. Quoted in Siegfried von Kardoff, *Wilhelm von Kardorff* (Berlin, 1909), 120; Craig, *From Bismarck,* 19.

18. *GW,* 14, pt.1:533.

19. *Bismarcks Briefe,* 269; Craig, *From Bismarck,* 23.

20. Quoted in Otto Vossler, "Bismarcks Ethos," *Historische Zeitschrift* 131 (1951): 274; Craig, *From Bismarck,* 21.

21. Bismarck to Hans von Kleist-Retzow, 4 July 1851, quoted in Joachim von Muralt, *Bismarcks Verantwortlichkeit* (Göttingen, 1955), 89–90.

22. Quoted in Sir Walter Richmond, "Bismarck at Home: Personal Impressions," *Daily News* (London), 2 August 1898, 5.

23. *GW,* 14, pt. 1:534.

24. Ibid., 14, pt. 2:778.

25. Craig, *From Bismarck,* 13.

26. *GW,* 6b:1.

27. A statement of Bismarck's at the beginning of December 1869, cited by Robert von Keudell, *Fürst und Fürstin Bismarck* (Berlin and Stuttgart, 1901), 419.

28. *GW,* 9:45; Craig, *From Bismarck,* 13.

29. Quoted in Pierre Renouvin, *Histoire des relations internationales,* vol. 5, *Le XIXeme Siècle, 1: De 1815 à 1875* (Paris, 1954), 270.

30. A. J. P. Taylor, "The Men of 1862," *From Napoleon to the Second International* (London, 1993), 274–83.

31. Memorandum by Queen Victoria, 2 May 1855, *Letters of Queen Victoria,* ed. Arthur Christopher Benson and Viscount Esher, 2d series, 3 vols. (London, 1907), 1:155.

32. Napoleon III to Walewski (later foreign minister), 28 May 1852, Papiers Walewski, Mèmoirs et documents, Archives du minister des affaires étrangères, Paris.

33. *GW,* 14, pt. 1:413.

34. Memorandum by Eugénie, on the Nile, 27 October 1869, *Papiers et correspondance de la famile impériale,* 2 vols. (Paris, 1871), 1:220.

35. Hermann Oncken, *Die Rheinpolitik Kaiser Napoleons III,* 3 vols. (Berlin and Leipzig, 1926), 1:103.

36. *Papiers et correspondance,* 2:23.

37. Ludovic Halévy, *Carnets,* 2 vols. (Paris, 1935), 2:36–37.

38. Quoted in Maurice Paléologue, *The Tragic Empress: Conversations of the Empress Eugénie, 1910–1919* (New York, 1928), 126.

39. Quoted in I. Tchernoff, *Le Parti républican au coup d'état et sous le Second*

Empire (Paris, 1902), 274; see also Theodore Zeldin, *The Political System of Napoleon III* (London, 1958), 62, 122–23.

40. A. J. Toynbee, *A Study of History,* 10 vols. (London, 1951), 3:287.

41. Émile Ollivier, *L'Empire libéral,* 18 vols. (Paris, 1895–1918), 1:178.

42. *Les Origines diplomatiques de la guerre de 1870–71,* 29 vols. (Paris, 1910–32), 29:501–2 (hereafter cited as *OD*).

43. Émile Ollivier, *Journal, 1846–1869,* ed. Theodore Zeldin and Ann Troisier de Diaz, 2 vols. (Paris, 1961), 1:362; Ollivier, speech of 15 March 1867, pub. as *Démocratie et liberté* (Paris, 1867); Lyons to Clarendon, 30 January 1870, C. 474, Clarendon Papers, Bodleian Library, Oxford (hereafter cited as Clar. dep.).

44. Ollivier, *Journal,* 2:87.

45. Quoted in Oncken, *Rheinpolitik,* 1:103.

46. Lyons to Clarendon, 30 January 1870, C. 474, Clar. dep.

47. Ollivier, brown notebook, n.d. (probably from 1872), Ollivier Papers, privately held, La Moutte and Paris (hereafter cited as OP).

48. Hübner to Buol (prime minister), 13 May 1857, quoted in Lynn M. Case, *French Opinion on War and Diplomacy during the Second Empire* (Philadelphia, 1954), 6.

49. Mosbourg to Ollivier, 24 April 1870, *OD,* 27:221.

50. Quoted in a letter from Beust (prime minister, Austria-Hungary) to Metternich (Paris), 31 May 1870, Oncken, *Rheinpolitik,* 3:371.

51. Gordon A. Craig, *Germany 1866–1945* (New York, 1978), 55.

52. Gramont to Escudier (a close friend), 17 January 1870, Gramont Papers, 45 Archives privées, Archives nationales, Paris (hereafter cited as GP).

53. *GW,* 6b:321.

54. Lothar Gall, *Bismarck: The White Revolutionary,* English trans., 2 vols. (London, 1980), 1:354.

55. Costantin de Grunwald, *Le Duc de Gramont: Gentihomme et diplomat* (Paris, 1950), 182.

56. *OD,* 27:296.

57. *Constantino Nigra: Poesie originalli e tradotti,* ed. Alessandro d'Ancona (Florence, 1914), 87.

58. Henry Salomon, "Une Expérience politique en 1870 and ses conséquences," *Revue de synthèse historique* 32 (1921): 90.

59. C. H. Pouthas, "Les Ministères de Louis Philippe," *Revue d'histoire moderne et contemporaine* 1 (1954): 102–30.

CHAPTER 2. NAPOLEON III AND THE SPANISH REVOLUTION OF 1868

1. Eric Christiansen, *The Origins of Military Power in Spain, 1800–1854* (London, 1967), 105–6.

2. Bismarck to von der Heydt (vice-president of the Prussian ministry of state), 27 September 1868, *GW*, 14, pt. 2:741.

3. Bismarck to the Foreign Office, 15 October 1868, *GW*, 6a:392–93.

4. Pierre de la Gorce, *Histoire du Second Empire*, 6 vols. (Paris, 1894–1905), 5:301–3.

5. See, for example, Lyons to Clarendon, 20 December 1868, 27/1748, no. 162, Public Record Office–Foreign Office, London (hereafter cited as PRO-FO).

6. Friedrich Frahm, "Frankreich und die Hohenzollernkandidatur bis zum Frühjahr 1869," *Historische Vierteljahrschrift* 29 (1935): 342–70; Marcel Emerit, "L'Opinion de Napoléon III sur la question du thrône d'Espagne en 1869," *Revue d'histoire moderne et contemporaraine* 16 (1969): 431–38.

7. Pierre de Luz, *Los Españoles en busca de un Rey (1868–1871)* (Barcelona, 1948), 67–88.

8. Quoted in Émile Ollivier, *L'Empire liberal*, 18 vols. (Paris, 1895–1912), 11:63.

9. R. Olivar Bertrand, *El Caballero Prim: Vida política y revolucionaria*, 2 vols. (Barcelona, 1952), 2:235–60.

10. See, for example, Hoyos (Madrid) to Beust (Vienna), 8 October 1866, quoted in Hermann Oncken, *Die Rheinpolitik Kaiser Napoleons III*, 3 vols. (Berlin and Leipzig, 1926), 3:38.

11. See, for example, the reports of Dubsky (Madrid) to Beust, 9, 16, 22 February 1869, XXVI, Haus-, Hof- und Staatsarchiv–Politisches Archiv, Vienna (hereafter cited as HHSA-PA).

12. La Valette to Bartholdi (Madrid), 17 April 1869, Espagne 872, Correspondance politique, Archives du minister des affaires étrangères (hereafter cited as AMAE-CP); Oskar Meding, *Memoiren zur Zeitgeschichte*, 3 vols. (Leipzig, 1884), 3:440–42.

13. Bismarck to Reuss, 9 March 1869, *GW*, 6b:11.

14. Mercier to Tour d'Auvergne (political director, foreign ministry), 15 October 1869, Espagne 874, AMAE-CP.

15. The duke of Seville was Isabella's first cousin and her husband's brother, as well as Montpensier's brother-in-law. He had the reputation of aspiring to the role of Philippe Égalité of the September 1868 revolution, and he might have succeeded if he had carried more weight in Spanish politics.

16. Quoted in Ildefonso Antonio Bermejo, *Historia de la interinidad y guerra civil in España desde 1868,* 3 vols. (Madrid, 1875–77), 1:60; Wilhelm Lauser, *Geschichte Spaniens von dem Sturz Isabellas bis zur Thronbesteigung Alfonsos*, 3 vols. (Leipzig, 1871), 1:28.

17. Metternich to Beust, 3 July 1868, Oncken, *Rheinpolitik*, 3:10.

18. Moustier to Mercier, 5 November 1868, Espagne 870, AMAE-CP; Ollivier, *L'Empire*, 11:63, 65.

19. See, for example, Saurma (Madrid) to Bismarck, 20 October 1869, *Die aus-*

wärtige Politik Preussens, 1858–1871, ed. Erich Brandenburg et al., 10 vols. (Berlin, 1932–39), 10:232 (hereafter cited as *APP*).

20. Banneville (Vatican) to Moustier, 29 January 1869, Ollivier, *L'Empire,* 11:573; Enrique Vera y González, *Pi y Margall y la política contemporánea,* 2 vols. (Barcelona, 1886), 2:118; Eduardo María Vilarrasa and José Ildefonso y Gatell, *Historia de la revolución de setiembre,* 2 vols. (Barcelona, 1875), 2:369–70.

21. Clarendon to Layard, 8 November 1869, 72/1206, no. 2, PRO-FO.

22. Mercier to Gramont, 10 June 1870, *OD,* 27:365–66.

23. Frahm, "Frankreich und die Hohenzollernkandidatur," 355.

24. Jesús Pabón, *España y la cuestión romana* (Madrid, 1972), 78.

25. Angel Fernandez de Los Rios, *Ma mission en Portugal* (Paris, 1877), 347.

26. Javier Rubio, *España y la guerra de 1870,* 3 vols. (Madrid, 1989), 3:764–66.

27. Reported by La Valette to Montholon, 20 December 1868, Portugal 202, AMAE-CP; Jerónimo Bécker, *Historia de las relaciones exteriores de España durante el siglo XIX,* 3 vols. (Madrid, 1924–26), 3:48–50.

28. Mercier to La Valette, 7 February 1869, Espagne 873, AMAE-CP.

29. See La Valette to Mercier, 24 April 1869, Espagne 873, AMAE-CP. This account was given by the foreign ministry more than a month after the events that it recounted took place, but the evidence is confirmed in Ollivier, *L'Empire,* 11:55, and in two leading Spanish sources for the period: Antonio Pirala, *Historia contemporaña,* 6 vols. (Madrid, 1875–80), 3:185–87, and Conde de Carnota, *Memoirs of Field-Marshal the Duke of Saldanha,* 2 vols. (London, 1880), 2:375.

30. See La Valette to Bartholdi, 13 April 1869, Espagne 873, AMAE-CP.

31. Quoted in Vincent Benedetti, *Ma mission en Prusse* (Paris, 1871), 307.

32. Bermejo, *Historia,* 1:563–65; Carnota, *Memoirs,* 2:386–404; Pirala, *Historia contemporaña,* 3:552–53.

33. Ollivier, *L'Empire,* 13:425–27.

34. For the full text of the letter, see Fernandez de los Rios, *Ma mission,* 357.

35. Federico Chabod, *Storia della politica estera italiana dal 1870 al 1896* (Bari, 1962).

36. Pabón, *España,* 3–25.

37. See Ollivier, *L'Empire,* 11:70–71. For Berlin's reaction to the reports in the French press, see Thile to the Prussian representatives at Paris, London, and St. Petersburg, 5 and 9 October 1868, *APP,* 10:209n, 214–15.

38. Tour d'Auvergne to Mercier, 8 November 1869, Espagne 873, AMAE-CP.

39. Paget to Clarendon, 18 December 1869, 45/145, PRO-FO.

40. Mercier to Ollivier, 17 May 1870, *OD,* 27:292.

41. Mercier to Gramont, 25 June 1870, *OD,* 27:423.

CHAPTER 3. BISMARCK AND THE HOHENZOLLERN CANDIDACY

1. *Letters of Queen Victoria,* ed. Arthur Christopher Benson and Viscount Esher, 2d series, 3 vols. (London, 1907), 2:10–11.

2. Norman Rich, "Bismarck and the Origins of the War of 1870," unpublished paper (Brown University, 1963). I am grateful to Professor Rich for sharing this paper with me.

3. The most extensive and best-documented statement appears in Josef Becker, "Zum Problem der Bismarckschen Politik in der spanischen Thronfrage," *Historische Zeitschrift* 212 (1971): 529–607. Becker has also produced three other articles that have influenced the discourse on the subject: "Der Krieg mit Frankreich als Problem der kleindeutschen Einigungspolitik Bismarcks 1866–1871," in *Das kaiserliche Deutschland, 1870–1919,* ed. Michael Stürmer (Düsseldorf, 1970), 75–88; "Bismarck, Prim, die Sigmaringer Hohenzollern und die spanische Thronfrage," *Francia* 9 (1981): 436–71; and "Von Bismarcks ‚spanischer Diversion' zur ‚Emser Legende' des Reichsgründers," in *Lange und Kurze Wege in den Krieg,* ed. Johannes Burckhardt (Augsburg, 1995), 87–113. His views are contested effectively in Hans-Otto Kleinmann, "Die spanische Thronfrage in der internationalen Politik vor Ausbruch des deutsch-französischen Krieges," in *Europa vor dem Krieg von 1870,* ed. Eberhard Kolb (Munich, 1987), 125–49. An elegant statement of Becker's position is also to be found in Otto Pflanze, *Bismarck and the Development of Germany,* 3 vols. (Princeton, 1990), 1:451–62.

4. *GW,* 6b:1–2.

5. Ibid. There is a good analysis of this correspondence in Hajo Holborn, "Bismarck und Werthern," *Archiv für Politik und Geschichte* 5 (1925): 469–71.

6. Adam Wandruszka, "Zwischen Nikolsburg und Bad Ems," in *Reichsgründung 1870/71: Tatsachen, Kontroversen, Interpretationen,* eds. Ernst Deuerlein and Theodor Schieder (Stuttgart, 1970), 56.

7. Bismarck to Fleming (Karlsruhe), 28 February 1870, *GW,* 6b:261–62.

8. Rich, "Bismarck," 5.

9. Moritz Busch, *Tagebuchblätter,* 3 vols. (Leipzig, 1899), 1:22.

10. Pflanze, *Bismarck,* 1:451.

11. Lothar Gall, "Bismarcks Süddeutschlandpolitik, 1866–1870," in *Europa vor dem Krieg von 1870,* 26–28; Klaus Erich Pollman, *Parlamentarismus im Norddeutschen Bund, 1867–1870* (Düsseldorf, 1985), 1–47; Eberhard Kolb, "Mächtepolitik und Kriegsrisiko am Vorabend des Krieges von 1870," in *Europa vor dem Krieg von 1870,* 206–7.

12. *GW,* 6b:166–67.

13. James J. Sheehan, *German History, 1770–1866* (New York, 1989), 261.

14. Quoted in Hans Rall, *König Ludwig II. und Bismarcks Ringen um Bayern 1870/71* (Munich, 1973), 77.

15. Busch, *Tagebuchblätter,* 1:371.

16. Jonathan Sperber, *Popular Catholicism in Nineteenth-Century Germany* (Princeton, 1984), 212.

17. Rich, "Bismarck," 6.

18. *GW,* 6a:xxx.

19. Heinrich Abeken, *Ein schlichtes Leben in bewegter Zeit,* 4. Aufl. (Berlin, 1910), 363.

20. *GW,* 6a:413.

21. Bismarck to Thile, *GW,* 6a:413–14.

22. *GW,* 6a:413–14.

23. Lawrence D. Steefel, *Bismarck, the Hohenzollern Candidacy and the Origins of the Franco-Prussian War* (Cambridge, Mass., 1962), 22–24.

24. Jochen Dittrich, *Bismarck, Frankreich und die spanische Thronkandidatur der Hohenzollern* (Munich, 1962), 351; *GW,* 6b:267.

25. *GW,* 6b:268–71.

26. Ibid., 270.

27. Ibid., 271–74.

28. Ibid., 273.

29. Gordon A. Craig, *Germany 1866–1945* (New York, 1978), 22.

30. *GW,* 6b:273.

31. For a summary, see Dittrich, *Frankreich,* 366–68.

32. *GW,* 14, pt. 2:776.

33. Georges Bonnin, ed., *Bismarck and the Hohenzollern Candidature for the Spanish Throne* (London, 1957), 372–73; Dittrich, *Frankreich,* 366–68; *GW,* 6b:321–24.

34. Pflanze, *Bismarck,* 1:419–24; Craig, *Germany,* 23.

35. *GW,* 6b:328.

36. Quoted in Pierre Renouvin, *Histoire des relations internationales,* vol. 5, *Le XIXeme Siècle, 1: De 1815 à 1875* (Paris, 1954), 378–79.

37. All quotations from ibid., 379.

38. Ibid.

39. Bonnin, *Candidature,* 131–33.

40. Karl Anton to Charles I of Rumania, *Aus dem Leben König Karls von Rumänien,* 4 vols. (Stuttgart, 1894–1900), 2:85.

41. See the comments of William I to Karl Anton, 12 May 1870, quoted in Karl Theodor Zingeler, *Karl Anton Fürst von Hohenzollern* (Leipzig, 1911), 243; Richard Fester, *Briefe, Aktenstücke, und Regesten zur Geschichte der Hohenzollernschen Thronkandidatur in Spanien,* 2 vols. (Berlin and Leipzig, 1913), 1:77–78.

42. *GW,* 6b:324–25.

43. Bonnin, *Candidature,* 162; Dittrich, *Frankreich,* 391.

44. Dittrich, *Frankreich,* 394.

45. Versen, diary, quoted in Bonnin, *Candidature,* 269–70.

46. *GW,* 6b:330–31; Rich, "Bismarck," 13.

47. *GW,* 6b:315–16.

48. Quoted in Fritz Stern, *Gold and Iron: Bismarck, Bleichröder, and the Building of the German Reich* (New York, 1977), 127.

49. *GW,* 6b:331.

50. Dittrich, *Frankreich,* 388–97; Bonnin, *Candidature,* 190–91.

51. Bonnin, *Candidature,* 197.

52. *GW,* 6b:335.

53. Bonnin, *Candidature,* 233–34.

54. Rich, "Bismarck," app. 1–2.

55. Javier Rubio, *España y la guerra de 1870,* 3 vols. (Madrid, 1989).

56. Rich, "Bismarck," app. 1–2.

57. *OD,* 28:23–27.

58. Lawrence D. Steefel, "Bismarck and Bucher: The 'Letter of Instructions' of June 1870," in *Studies in Diplomatic History and Historiography,* ed. A. O. Sarkissian (London, 1961), 217–24.

59. Becker, "Bismarck, Prim, die Sigmaringer Hohenzollern und die spanische Thronfrage."

60. Quoted in Steefel, "Bismarck and Bucher," 218.

61. Pflanze, *Bismarck,* 1:459.

62. *GW,* 6c:63.

63. I am grateful to Professor Paul W. Schroeder for pointing this out to me.

64. Dittrich, *Frankreich,* 36–83.

65. Versen, diary, quoted in Bonnin, *Candidature,* 278.

CHAPTER 4. THE NEGOTIATIONS AT EMS

1. Antoine Agénor, duc de Gramont, *La France et la Prusse avant la guerre* (Paris, 1872), 14; see also Émile Ollivier, *L'Empire libéral,* 18 vols. (Paris, 1895–1918), 14:20; Richard Fester, *Briefe, Aktenstücke, und Regesten zur Geschichte der Hohenzollernschen Thronkandidatur in Spanien,* 2 vols. (Berlin and Leipzig, 1913), 1:116.

2. Ollivier, *L'Empire,* 14:20–21.

3. Mercier to Gramont, 3 July 1870, *OD,* 28:19.

4. Lynn M. Case, *French Opinion on War and Diplomacy during the Second Empire* (Philadelphia, 1954), 241.

5. For Napoleon's reaction, see *OD,* 28:21n. 3.

6. Gramont to Mercier, 3 July 1870, *OD,* 28:21–22.

7. Gramont to Le Sourd, 3 July 1870, *OD,* 28:22.

8. Gramont to La Valette (London), 3 July 1870; to Fleury (St. Petersburg), 5 July 1870; to Cazaux (Vienna), 6 July 1870; *OD,* 28:39, 41–44, 65–66.

9. Ollivier, *L'Empire,* 14:21–29.

10. Case, *French Opinion,* 242.

11. Albert Sorel, *Histoire diplomatique de la guerre franco-allemande,* 2 vols. (Paris, 1875), 1:71–72.

12. R. H. Lord, *The Origins of the War of 1870* (Cambridge, Mass., 1924), 32–33. Lord remains the best account of the meeting—an impressive scholarly achievement, especially given Lord's sources and time.

13. Le Sourd to Gramont, 4 July 1870, *OD,* 28:31.

14. Gramont to Mercier, 6 July 1870, *OD,* 28:61.

15. Gordon A. Craig, *Germany 1866–1945* (New York, 1978), 24.

16. *GW,* 15:282.

17. *GW,* 6b:339.

18. Ibid., 339–40.

19. Ibid., 342.

20. Georges Bonnin, ed., *Bismarck and the Hohenzollern Candidature for the Spanish Throne* (London, 1957), 222–24.

21. Lord, *Origins,* 129–32.

22. Quoted in Ollivier, *L'Empire,* 107–8; Pierre de la Gorce, *Histoire du Second Empire,* 6 vols. (Paris, 1894–1905), 6:227–28.

23. Ollivier, *L'Empire,* 14:568–73.

24. Gramont, *France,* 38.

25. Pierre Lehautcourt, *Les Origines de la guerre 1870: La Candidature Hohenzollern 1868–1870* (Paris and Nancy, 1912), 247–53.

26. Ibid., 258.

27. Reported by La Valette to Gramont, 17 July 1870, *OD,* 28:102.

28. Fleury to Gramont, 8 July 1870, *OD,* 28:118–19.

29. Fleury to Gramont, 11 July 1870, *OD,* 28:221.

30. Gramont to Benedetti, 7 July 1870, *OD,* 28:89.

31. Gramont to Benedetti, 7 July 1870, *OD,* 28:91.

32. Ibid.

33. Sorel, *Histoire diplomatique,* 1:78.

34. Theodor Fontane, *Der Krieg gegen Frankreich 1870–1871,* 2 vols. (Berlin, 1872), 1:3–4.

35. Reported by Abeken to Bismarck, 6 July 1870, Lord, *Origins,* 134.

36. Benedetti to Gramont, 9 July 1870, *OD,* 28:151–52.

37. Ibid.

38. Gramont to Ollivier, 9 July 1870, GP. Ollivier also refers to this comment in an undated note to Chavandier de Valdrôme, the minister of the interior; see Ollivier's brown notebook, OP.

39. Gramont to Benedetti, 10 July 1870, *OD,* 28:184.

40. Vincent Benedetti, *Ma mission en Prusse* (Paris, 1871), 322.

41. Benedetti to Gramont, 10 July 1870, *OD*, 28:188–89.

42. Gramont to Benedetti, 10 July 1870, *OD*, 28:190.

43. Benedetti to Gramont, 11 July 1870, *OD*, 28:218–19.

44. Ibid., 219.

45. Benedetti to Gramont, 11 July 1870, *OD*, 28:223.

46. Benedetti to Gramont, 11 July 1870, *OD*, 28:234.

47. See for example, La Valette to Gramont, 10 July 1870, *OD*, 28:202; Fleury to Gramont, 12 July 1870, *OD*, 28:266.

48. Lehautcourt, *Origines*, 343.

49. Ibid., 344; Gramont, *France*, 80–83.

50. Metternich to Beust, 11 July 1870, quoted in Hermann Oncken, *Die Rheinpolitik Kaiser Napoleons III*, 3 vols. (Berlin and Leipzig, 1926), 3:427.

51. Reported by Lyons to Granville, 7 July 1870, Fester, *Briefe*, 2:5.

52. Ollivier, *L'Empire*, 14:191.

53. Ollivier, brown notebook, n.d. (but probably 12 July 1870), OP.

54. Gramont, *France*, 98–99.

55. Gramont to Benedetti, 10 July 1870, *OD*, 28:190.

56. Gramont to Benedetti, 11 July 1870, *OD*, 28:222.

57. Benedetti, *Ma mission*, 302.

58. William I to Queen Augusta, 7 July 1870, Fester, *Briefe*, 2:11.

59. William I to Queen Augusta, 11 July 1870, Fester, *Briefe*, 2:76.

60. Benedetti to Gramont, 11 July 1870, *OD*, 28:229–33.

61. Gramont to Napoleon III, 12 July 1870, Gramont, *France*, 102; Ollivier, *L'Empire*, 14:198–201.

62. S. William Halperin, *Diplomat under Stress: Visconti-Venosta and the Crisis of July 1870* (Chicago, 1963), 2.

63. Malaret to Gramont, 8 July 1870, *OD*, 28:117.

64. Granville to Layard, 7 July 1870, 72/1231, no. 3, PRO-FO.

65. Layard to Granville, 10 July 1870, 72/1231, no. 9, PRO-FO.

66. Malaret to Gramont, 16 July 1870, *OD*, 29:21.

67. Quoted in E. Mayor des Planches, "Re Vittorio Emanuele II alla vigilia della guerra settanta," *Nouva antologia* 1 (1920): 351–52. See also the most revealing note from Visconti-Venosta to Caraccilo (St. Petersburg), 9 July 1870, no. 1179, Telegrammi spediti, Archivo storico, Ministero degli affari esteri., Rome (hereafter cited as MAE, AS, TS).

68. Paget to Granville, 9 July 1870, 391/23, no. 3, PRO-FO.

69. Vimercati to Victor Emmanuel, 10 July 1870, quoted in Halperin, *Diplomat*, 92.

70. Granville to Paget, 9 July 1870, 45/160, no. 4, PRO-FO.

71. Ibid.; see also S. William Halperin, "Visconti-Venosta and the Crisis of July 1870," *Journal of Modern History* 21 (December 1959): 301.

72. Vimercati to Victor Emmanuel, 10 July 1870, quoted in Halperin, "Visconti-Venosta," 301.

73. Halperin, *Diplomat*, 28–29.

74. Halperin, "Visconti-Venosta," 307–8.

75. Lord, *Origins*, 64–65.

76. Abeken to Bismarck, 10 July 1870, quoted in Lord, *Origins*, 171; William to Karl Anton, 10 July 1870, Fester, *Briefe*, 2:64–65.

77. William I to Queen Augusta, 11 July 1870, Fester, *Briefe*, 2:76.

78. William I to Karl Anton, 10 July 1870, Fester, *Briefe*, 2:64–65.

79. William I to Queen Augusta, 11 July 1870, Fester, *Briefe*, 2:76.

80. Lord, *Origins*, 61; Ollivier, *L'Empire*, 14:139–41, 206–20.

81. Karl Anton to William I, 12 July 1870, Bonnin, *Candidature*, 250.

82. Strantz to Abeken, 12 July 1870, Bonnin, *Candidature*, 248.

83. Gramont to Escudier, 12 July 1870, GP; summary of the meeting in Ollivier, *L'Empire*, 14:227–28.

84. Gramont to Benedetti, 12 July 1870, *OD*, 28:250.

85. Gramont to Benedetti, 12 July 1870, *OD*, 28:251.

86. Karl Anton to William I, 12 July 1870 (enclosing copies of telegrams), Bonnin, *Candidature*, 251–52.

87. Ollivier, *L'Empire*, 14:229.

88. Ibid., 230–32.

89. Ibid., 235–36.

90. Sorel, *Histoire diplomatique*, 1:128.

91. Ollivier, *L'Empire*, 14:233, 235.

92. Case, *French Opinion*, 254.

CHAPTER 5. THE FRENCH DECLARATION OF WAR

1. Nigra, "Souvenirs diplomatiques 1870," *Bibliothèque universelle et revue suisse* 65 (1895): 454–55.

2. Lyons to Granville, 12 July 1870, Fester, *Briefe, Aktenstücke, und Regesten zur Geschichte der Hohenzollernschen Thronkandidatur in Spanien*, 2 vols. (Berlin and Leipzig, 1913), 2:109.

3. Beust to Metternich, 12 and 13 July 1870, Hermann Oncken, *Die Rheinpolitik Kaiser Napoleons III*, 3 vols. (Berlin and Leipzig, 1926), 3:433–34.

4. Nigra, "Souvenirs," 454.

5. Émile Ollivier, *L'Empire libéral*, 18 vols. (Paris, 1895–1918), 14:239–41.

6. Nigra, "Souvenirs," 455.

7. William I to Queen Augusta, 12 July 1870, Fester, *Briefe*, 2:93.

8. Benedetti to Gramont, 12 July 1870, *OD*, 28:256.

9. Bismarck to Abeken, 12 July 1870, R. H. Lord, *The Origins of the War of 1870* (Cambridge, Mass., 1924), 202.

10. Busch, *Tagebuchblätter,* 1:258–59.

11. Bismarck to Abeken, 12 July 1870, Lord, *Origins,* 203–4.

12. Ibid., 204.

13. Eberhard Kolb, *Der Kriegsausbruch: 1870* (Göttingen, 1970), 100–101.

14. Antoine Agénor, Duc de Gramont, *La France et la Prusse avant la guerre* (Paris, 1872), 114.

15. Quoted in Pierre Lehautcourt, *Les Origines de la guerre 1870: La Candidature Hohenzollern 1868–1870* (Paris and Nancy, 1912), 382–83.

16. Ollivier, *L'Empire,* 14:243.

17. Werther to William I, 12 July 1870, Lord, *Origins,* 208.

18. Ollivier, brown notebook, n.d. (but almost certainly 12 July 1870), OP.

19. Gramont to Benedetti, 12 July 1870, *OD,* 18:255. Gramont, one must note, did not take the trouble to explain to Benedetti what had happened with Werther.

20. Lynn M. Case, *French Opinion on War and Diplomacy during the Second Empire* (Philadelphia, 1954), 263–64.

21. Émile Ollivier, *Le Ministère du 2 janvier: Mes discours* (Paris, 1875), 120.

22. Ollivier, *L'Empire,* 14:268–69.

23. Ibid., 272.

24. Lehautcourt, *Origines,* 427.

25. Ollivier, *L'Empire,* 14:272.

26. Ibid., 273.

27. Ibid., 273–74.

28. Ollivier, brown notebook, n.d. (but probably 12 July 1870), OP.

29. Benedetti to Gramont, 12 July 1870, *OD,* 28:318.

30. William I to Queen Augusta, 13 July 1870, Fester, *Briefe,* 2:118–19.

31. Benedetti to Gramont, 13 July 1870, *OD,* 28:306.

32. Benedetti to Gramont, 13 July 1870, *OD,* 28:307.

33. Gramont to Ollivier, 13 July 1870, *OD,* 28:309.

34. *GW,* 6b:357; Lord, *Origins,* 100.

35. Le Sourd to Gramont, 14 July 1870, *OD,* 28:336.

36. Benedetti to Gramont, 13 July 1870, *OD,* 28:307.

37. Abeken to Bismarck, 12 July 1870, *OD,* 28:220–21; Lawrence D. Steefel, *Bismarck, the Hohenzollern Candidacy and the Origins of the Franco-Prussian War* (Cambridge, Mass., 1962), 183–84.

38. *GW,* 15:310.

39. S. William Halperin, "Bismarck and the Italian Envoy in Berlin on the Eve of the Franco-Prussian War," *Journal of Modern History* 33 (1959): 36–37.

40. Ibid., 38.

41. Quoted in Chester W. Clark, "Bismarck, Russia, and the War of 1870," *Journal of Modern History* 14 (1942): 200–201.

42. Ibid., 202.

43. Lord, *Origins*, 222, 224.

44. William L. Langer, "Bismarck as a Dramatist," in *Studies in Diplomatic History and Historiography*, ed. A. O. Sarkissian (London, 1961), 209.

45. Lord, *Origins*, 218.

46. Benedetti to Gramont, 14 July 1870, *OD*, 28:342.

47. Cadore to Gramont, 7 July 1870, *OD*, 28:137.

48. Ibid.

49. Cadore to Gramont, 12 July 1870, *OD*, 28:255–56.

50. St. Vallier to Gramont, 10 July 1870, *OD*, 28:209.

51. See, for example, d'Astorg to Gramont, 11 July 1870, *OD*, 28:237–38.

52. See, for example, Beust to Metternich, 11 July 1870, Oncken, *Rheinpolitik*, 3:214–15.

53. Bray to Lerchenfeld (private secretary), n.d. (but probably 14 July 1870), quoted in Hans Rall, *König Ludwig II. und Bismarcks Ringen um Bayern 1870/71* (Munich, 1973), 129.

54. Paul W. Schroeder, "The Lost Intermediaries," *International History Review* 6 (1984): 21.

55. *GW*, 15:310.

56. Case, *French Opinion*, 254; see also Jean Stengers, "Aux origines de la guerre de 1870: Gouvernement et opinion public," *Revue belge de philologie et histoire* 34 (1956): 701–47.

57. Quoted in Lehautcourt, *Origines*, 501.

58. Lyons to Granville, 13 July 1870, 27/1801, no. 162, PRO-FO.

59. Pierre Muret, "Ollivier et Gramont les 12 et 13 juillet 1870," *Revue d'histoire moderne et contemporaine* 13 (1909–10): 310–20.

60. Ollivier, brown notebook, 14 July 1870, OP.

61. Roger L. Williams, *The Mortal Napoleon III* (Princeton, 1971), 139–45.

62. Gramont, *France*, 160–61.

63. Gramont to Benedetti, 13 July 1870, *OD*, 28:298–99.

64. See, for example, Lyons to Granville, 14 July 1870, 27/1806, no. 16, PRO-FO.

65. Ollivier, *L'Empire*, 14:351.

66. Le Sourd to Gramont, 14 July 1870, *OD*, 28:336.

67. Lehautcourt, *Origines*, 499–500.

68. Ollivier, *L'Empire*, 14:355.

69. Quoted in ibid., 357.

70. Lehautcourt, *Origines*, 497–98.

71. Ollivier, *L'Empire*, 14:360.

72. Pierre de la Gorce, *Histoire du Second Empire,* 6 vols. (Paris, 1894–1905), 6:289, provides the most convincing evidence, based upon the papers of Louvet, minister of agriculture.

73. Benedetti to Gramont, 14 July 1870, *OD,* 28:340–41.

74. Karl Abel, *Letters on International Relations before and during the War of 1870,* 2 vols. (London, 1871), 2:138.

75. Gramont, *France,* 197–201.

76. Ollivier, *L'Empire,* 14:365.

77. Reported by Metternich to Beust, 14 July 1870, Oncken, *Rheinpolitik,* 3:439–40.

78. La Gorce, *Histoire,* 6:292–93.

79. Ollivier, *L'Empire,* 14:369–70.

80. Ibid., 370–71.

81. Ibid., 373.

82. Cadore to Gramont, 14 July 1870, *OD,* 28:345.

83. Ollivier, *L'Empire,* 14:618–19.

84. Gramont, *France,* 233.

85. Ollivier, *L'Empire,* 14:619.

86. Ibid., 619–20.

87. Gramont, *France,* 233.

88. La Gorce, *Histoire,* 6:297.

89. Malmesbury, *Memoirs of an Ex-Minister,* 2 vols. (London, 1884), 2:665.

90. Lehautcourt, *Origines,* 527–28.

91. See the reports of Metternich to Beust, 31 July 1870, and of Vitzthum to Andrassay, 16 January 1873, Oncken, *Rheinpolitik,* 3:491, 440–43.

92. Vitzthum to Andrassay, 16 January 1873, Oncken, *Rheinpolitik,* 3:440–43.

93. Henry Salomon, *L'Incident Hohenzollern: L'Événement, les hommes, les responsabilités* (Paris, 1922), 265.

94. Lehautcourt, *Origines,* 527.

95. Ibid., 581.

96. Ibid.

97. Ollivier, *L'Empire,* 14:422.

98. Ibid., 451.

99. Visconti-Venosta to Nigra, 13 July 1870, quoted in S. William Halperin, *Diplomat under Stress: Visconti-Venosta and the Crisis of July 1870* (Chicago, 1963), 134–35.

100. See especially Beust to Walterskirchen (Stuttgart), 8, 9, and 11 July 1870, VI 32, HHSA-PA.

101. Beust to Metternich, 11 July 1870, Oncken, *Rheinpolitik,* 3:424.

102. Reported by Paget to Granville, 18 July 1870, 45/165, no. 4, PRO-FO.

103. Ibid.

104. Paget to Hammond (a friend), 16 July 1870, 391/23, PRO-FO.

105. Visconti-Venosta to Nigra, 12 July 1870, no. 1197, MAE, AS, TS.

106. See, for example, Federico Chabod, *Storia della politica estera italiana dal 1870 al 1896* (Bari, 1962), 563–99; Halperin, *Diplomat*, 1–18, 148–169.

107. Malaret (Florence) to Gramont, 12 July 1870, *OD*, 28:323–24.

108. Napoleon III's Order of the Day, 28 July 1870, quoted in Michael Howard, *The Franco-Prussian War* (London, 1961), 78.

109. Howard, *Franco-Prussian War*, 77.

Bibliographical Essay

ABBREVIATIONS AND PURPOSE

AHR	*American Historical Review*
APG	*Archiv für Politik und Geschichte*
BURS	*Bibliothèque universelle et revue suisse*
CRL	Center for Research Libraries, Chicago, Illinois
DR	*Deutsche Revue*
EHR	*English Historical Review*
EK	*Europa vor dem Krieg von 1870*, ed. Eberhard Kolb (Munich, 1987)
ER	*Europa und die Reichsgründung*, ed. Eberhard Kolb (Munich, 1980)
F	*Francia*
H	*The Historian*
HG	*Der Historiker und die Geschichte*
HV	*Historische Vierteljahrschrift*
HZ	*Historische Zeitschrift*
IHR	*International History Review*
JBZ	*Jahresbibliographie. Bibliothek für Zeitgeschichte*
JMH	*Journal of Modern History*
KGGAv	*Korrespondenzblatt des Gesamtvereins und deutschen Geschichts- und Altertumsvereine*
NA	*Nuova antologia*
QuFiAB	*Quellen und Forschungen aus italienischen Archiven und Bibliotheken*
PJbb	*Preussische Jahrbücher*

RBPH	*Revue belge de philologie et d'histoire*
RG	*Revue de Genève*
RHMC	*Revue d'histoire moderne et contemporaine*
RV	*Rheinische Vierteljahrsblätter*
SMh	*Schweizer Monatsheft*
SZG	*Schweizerische Zeitschrift für Geschichte*
ZBLG	*Zeitschrift für bayerische Landesgeschichte*

I have designed this bibliography to serve two purposes: to record my intellectual debts and to state the reasons for my positions. This book, after all, takes up many themes and ideas, and again and again, I found myself obliged to choose among conflicting interpretations and to answer, as fairly as I could, questions over the character of a person or the meaning of a decision. Here I give the grounds for the stands I have taken. I need hardly add that this essay, like most others of its kind, is highly selective and arbitrary; covering as it does topics overlaid with controversy and passion, it could hardly be anything else. I have had many teachers, and this essay reflects (I hope with some accuracy) my countless debts.

Of course, the literature on the Franco-Prussian War and its multifaceted dimensions—military, diplomatic, domestic-political—is so enormous that it would be preposterous for me to supply a complete bibliography or to identify all of the works on which I have relied. I have, however, made a serious effort to list all of the sources and the most outstanding secondary material in the five great European languages (I do not read any other). I have included no book or article that I have not at least looked through; omission may mean that I have not run across the book or article, but it may also mean that I do not rate the book or article well enough to put it in. I have cited in the main books and articles that equipped me with facts or interpretations, gave me insights and ideas, or fired me to dissent, and I have appended evaluations—sometimes brief, sometimes extended—to most of the entries. In this respect, as in others, this is a highly personal composition.

Part 1 of my bibliography, the background, discusses works on the most important personalities of my story—William I, Bismarck, Napoleon III, and the latter's two principal ministers, Ollivier and Gramont—and the Spanish revolution of 1868 and the personalities associated with it. Part 2 deals with the primary sources on the origins of the Franco-Prussian War and is arranged in three sections. The first section describes the archives of the Great Powers and the relevant materials to be found therein. The second section surveys official publications of documentary materials. The third section gives the published private papers of individuals, themselves arranged as rulers, prime and foreign ministers, ambassadors and diplomats, and others. Each section lists materials by country, ordered—as becomes a work of diplomatic history—according to the French alphabet: that is, Germany (which includes Prussia), Austria-Hungary, France, Great Britain, Italy, and Russia. Part 3 gives secondary works on the origins of the war.

Of course, this arrangement is not watertight; many original sources, particularly biography, are also works of history, and most secondary works have some original material. This list of secondary works divides into four categories, the first of which is guides and sources. The second discusses books that deal mainly with one country or statesman. The third is confined strictly to histories of the origins of the Franco-Prussian War; having now produced a book on this subject I believe that I can review the ones I list with experience, though I hope without jealousy, by comparing their respective viewpoints to those I have advanced in the preceding pages. The fourth section lists a few works on military history. Where a book has been translated into English I usually give both the English and the foreign version.

PART 1. BACKGROUND
Personalities
Germany

There is no satisfactory biography of William I in English. The most recent life, a perceptive German study by Karl Heinz Börner (Cologne, 1987) is an altogether attractive portrait, no doubt the way that William would have preferred to be remembered; it includes forty-seven handsome illustrations. *Kaiser Wilhelm I* by Erich Marcks, which originally appeared in 1897 but has gone through many subsequent editions (including that edited by Karl Pagel, 9. Aufl. [Berlin, 1943]), is primarily a work of polemics, most useful for political affairs of the time. Günter Richter, "Kaiser Wilhelm I," in *Drei deutsche Kaiser,* ed. Wilhelm Treue (Freiburg, 1987), is a fine sketch; it is deplorable, however, that a work of such perception provides no references. *Wilhelm I: Kaiserfrage und Kölner Dom* by Karl Hampe (Stuttgart, 1936) illuminates its subject to some extent, giving scraps of his correspondence with the crown prince. *Der Regierungs-Anfang des Prinz-Regenten von Preussen und seine Gemahlin* by Ernst Berner (Berlin, 1902) is important for the origins of William's attitude on military matters.

The literature on Bismarck, of course, is too vast to list. The best approach is to go through the titles in the *Bismarck-Bibliographie* by Karl Erich Born (Cologne and Berlin, 1966), which, though tendentiously organized, is quite comprehensive. The work contains 6,138 titles. Of less value is the list, *Bismarck-Lexikon: Quellenverzeichnis zu den in seinen Akten, Briefen, Gesprächen und Reden enthaltenen Äusserungen Bismarcks* by Albrecht Graf zu Stolberg-Wernigerode (Stuttgart and Berlin, 1936), but it has information that is otherwise hard to come by. In addition to these two books, mention should be also made of a most admirable volume, *Das Bismarck-Problem in der Geschichtsschreibung nach 1945* by Lothar Gall (Cologne and Berlin, 1971). The author writes with wit and grace and provides an entertaining and enlightening analysis of the vast accumulation of Bismarckiana that has appeared in the period with which he deals. Four biographies also deserve mention. *Bismarck and the Development of Germany* by Otto Pflanze, 3 vols. (Princeton, 1990) is a magisterial work of detached scholarship based on comprehensive knowledge and informed by a magnificent synthetic sense. The first volume originally appeared in 1961, but the author has brought the notes up to date. Its sober style enables the reader to assess Bismarck in detail. Also important, especially for foreign policy, is *Bismarck: Der weisse Revolutionär* by Lothar Gall (Frankfurt am Main, 1980); the English translation by J. A. Underwood, 2 vols. (London, 1986) is choppy. *Bismarck: Urpreusse und Reichsgründer* by Ernst Engelberg (Berlin, 1985) is a Marxist account by a scholar of the former East Germany; it depicts Bismarck as the unwitting agent of an upper bourgeois revolution from above. Engelberg's second volume, *Bismarck: Das Reich in der Mitte Europas* (Berlin, 1990), carries the story to his fall from power. The most recent biography, *Bismarck: Dämon der Deutschen* by Johannes Willms (Munich, 1997), is a polemical work by a prominent German journalist; the thesis is in the title.

The older works are legion. The great German historians who wrote about

Bismarck—Erich Marcks (Berlin, 1909), Max Lenz (Berlin, 1913), and Erich Brandenburg (Leipzig, 1914, with an appendix volume in 1916)—all concentrate on the period of unification, and the same is true of the great French biography, *Bismarck et son temps* by Paul Matter, 3 vols. (Paris, 1905–8). *Bismarck: The Man and the Statesman* by A. J. P. Taylor (London, 1955) breaks this trend, as does the portrait by Gordon A. Craig in *From Bismarck to Adenauer: Aspects of German Statecraft* (Baltimore, 1958). Both are models of compression, the latter a miniature masterpiece. Joachim von Muralt, *Bismarcks Verantwortlichkeit* (Göttingen, 1955) is a work of great energy and scholarship, indispensable for an understanding of the role of religion in his life. *Bismarcks Ringen um Deutschlands Gestaltung* by Otto Becker, edited and supplemented by Alexander Scharff (Heidelberg, 1958), is an admirable book that is a straight essay in hero worship. *Bismarck* by Arnold Oskar Meyer (Leipzig, 1944) is an impassioned statement of faith in its hero during the Hitler era; the author described it as "my contribution to the national service during the war." *Bismarck: Leben und Werke* by Erich Eyck, 3 vols. (Zurich, 1941–44) is a book that still holds its own, written while the author was living in England during the Second World War; there is a reduced version in one volume for the English reader (London, 1950).

France

Napoleon III, like William I, would like a good life in English. The biography by Georges Bordonove (Paris, 1998) is a popular account exploring the whole of Napoleon's career; its handsome pages provide a great deal of uninteresting information. *Louis Napoléon le Grand* by Philippe Séguin (Paris, 1990) has value for the years after 1866 and for Bonapartist politics in the last days of the Second Empire. *Napoleon III* by W. H. C. Smith (London, 1972) combines biography and advocacy. Of the older lives, that by Robert Sencourt (London, 1933) has long enjoyed a great reputation. F. A. Simpson, *The Rise of Louis Napoleon III*, 3d ed. (London, 1950) and *Louis Napoleon and the Recovery of France*, 3d ed. (London, 1951) are both trailblazers. *Louis Napoleon and the Second Empire* by J. M. Thompson (London, 1955) combines arresting style and incorrigible subtlety. *Napoleon III in seiner Zeit* by Heinrich Euler (Würzburg, 1961) is an indispensable original study.

J. P. T. Bury, *Napoleon III and the Second Empire* (London, 1964) has a good bibliography. *The Mortal Napoleon III* by Roger L. Williams (Princeton, 1971) breaks fresh ground in short space. *The Fall of the Third Napoleon* by Theo Aronson (London, 1970) is a good popular account. On related matters, Theodore Zeldin, *The Political System of Napoleon III* (London, 1958) has much information on parties and on electoral management.

Eugénie is better provided for than is her husband. Robert Sencourt, *The Empress Eugénie* (New York, 1931) still has value, as does *The Tragic Empress* by Maurice Paléologue (New York, 1919), though both have been overtaken by *Distaff Diplomacy* by Nancy Nichols Barker (Austin, 1967). The life by Harold Kurtz (London, 1964) is an effective biography, well-written, sensible in judgment, and buttressed with some original research. *Napoleon III and Eugénie* by Jasper Ridley (New York, 1979) is readable but sloppy on details.

Émile Ollivier and the Liberal Empire of Napoleon III by Theodore Zeldin (Oxford, 1963) is an almost impeccable work of scholarship, urbanely tactful in its revelations. The life by Pierre Saint Marc (Paris, 1950) is less satisfactory.

Le Duc de Gramont by Constantin de Grunwald (Paris, 1950) is a brief portrait; there is a certain amount on foreign policy, little of importance otherwise. Gramont, like Ollivier, is in need of a good modern biographer.

The Spanish Revolution of 1868
Guides and Sources

There is a good deal of raw material in the older works. *Historia de las relaciones exteriores de España durante el siglo XIX* by Jerónimo Bécker, 3 vols. (Madrid, 1924–26) is a provocatively prejudiced account by a leading contemporary; it is distinguished by mastery of the sources, but the strict diplomatic history comes off very ragged. *Historia de la interinidad y guerra civil in España desde 1868,* 3 vols. (Madrid, 1875–77) by Ildefonso Antonio Bermejo is another potboiler, though essential as a work of reference. The same is true of *Historia de la revolución de setiembre* by Eduardo María Vilarrasa and José Ildefonso y Gatell, 2 vols. (Barcelona, 1875); it contains material that is otherwise hard to come by. By contrast, *Anales desde 1843 hasta la conclusión de la última guerra civil* by Antonio Pirala (Madrid, 1876) is magnificent on every count. Pirala was an archivist and a historian whose work has been enormously influential in the historiography of our subject. The second volume of his *Historia contemporánea. Segunda parte de la guerra civil* (Madrid, 1895) was the first source to print the "letter of instructions." *Pí y Margall y la política contemporánea* by Enrique Vera y González, 2 vols. (Barcelona, 1886) is a classic work on one of the great figures of the age.

Secondary Works

There are two good general accounts: *Spain, 1808–1975* by Raymond Carr, 2d ed. (Oxford, 1982), a work by a historian of almost faultless grasp who is also a beautiful writer; and *Toward the New Spain* by Joseph A. Brandt (Chicago, 1933), an agreeable if somewhat dusty survey.

Of works of detail, two books by Luis Álvarez Gutiérrez are important: *La revolución de 1868 ante la opinión pública alemana* (Madrid, 1976) and *La diplomacía bismarckiana ante la cuestión cubana, 1868–1874* (Madrid, 1988), both of which are models of art and charm. *Iglesia y revolución en España, 1868–1874* by Vicente Cárcel Ortí (Baraña-Pamplona, 1979) is a historical and political analysis of the first order, though it exaggerates some of the events that it recounts. *España y la cuestión romana* by Jesús Pabón (Madrid, 1972) is important for Prim's dealings with Victor Emmanuel. Prim's dealings with Prussia are in *España en la Europa de Bismarck* by Julio Salom Costa (Madrid, 1967); this is a brilliant narrative, though the reader may complain that one cannot see the forest for the trees. *Elecciones y partidos políticos de España (1868–1931)* by Miguel Martinez Cuadrado, 2 vols. (Madrid, 1969) ranges effectively over its subject. *Partidos y programas políticos, 1808–1936* by Miguel Artola, 2 vols. (Madrid, 1974–76) is more comprehensive, if less effective. An outstanding and reliable guide to the politics on the left is C. A. M. Hennessy, *The Federal Republic in Spain* (Oxford, 1962). Monarchist politics of the period appear in the marqués de Lema, *De la revolución a restauración,* 2 vols. (Madrid, 1927) and in an old, much-neglected, but brilliant book, *Les Origines de la restauration des Bourbons en Espagne* by A. Houghton (Paris, 1890). The best history of the Carlist campaign is Clara E. Lida and Iris M. y Zavala, *La revolución de 1868* (New York, 1970); it eclipses the older work by Francisco Hernando, *La campaña carlista (1872 a 1876)* (Barcelona, 1906). Willard A. Smith, "The Diplomatic Background of the Spanish Revolution of 1868," *AHR* 55 (July 1950) is a particularly valuable account of the subject in English, rich in detail but never losing sight of the general picture.

On personalities: *Isabella II* by Pierre de Luz (Paris, 1934; Spanish trans., Barcelona, 1962) is important for background, helping to explain why some Spaniards found Isabella attractive but also why she was a disaster as a queen. *Los españoles en busca de un rey (1868–1871)* by the same author (Barcelona, 1948) is helpful on the conflicts within the provisional government; this book is an excellent translation of the original French edition, which I have not seen. The lives by José Moreno (Barcelona, 1973) and Carmen Llorca (Alcoy, 1956) are useful, though not altogether reliable; the latter draws on records in the archives at Madrid. There are several good biographies of Prim: by far the best is that by R. Olivar Bertrand, 2 vols. (Barcelona, 1952), a distinguished work indeed, though with only one chapter on the Hohenzollern candidacy; the older life by Emeterio S. Santovenia (Madrid, 1933) is an exciting if rather overblown account; *Prim* by Henri Léonardon (Paris, 1901) is now out of date. *Amadeo de Saboya: El rey efímero* by conde de Romanones [Alvaro de Figueroa y Torres] (Madrid, 1935) is a biography of first-class quality. *El rey en Madrid y en provincias* by Antonio Pirala (Madrid, 1872) is an important statement by a highly placed contemporary. *Ma mission en Portugal* by Fernandez de los Rios (Paris, 1877), though old, is of value for Fernando's candidacy; the same is true of the *Memoirs of the Field-Marshal the Duke of Saldanha* by J. A. S., conde da Carnota, 2 vols. (London, 1880). Of the other works, *Geschichte Spaniens von dem Sturz Isabellas bis zur Thronbesteigung Alfonsos* by Wilhelm Lauser, which was originally published in Leipzig in 1877 but which I read on microfilm supplied to me by the CRL (MF-6370, reel 35), is a vivid account of the intrigues that chased the queen off her throne.

On the international aspects of the revolution, the best literature is in the learned journals and in edited collections of essays. Marcel Emerit, "L'Opinion de Napoléon III sur la question du trône d'Espagne en 1869," *RHMC* 16 (1969) is model of compression. Willard A. Smith, "The Diplomatic Background of the Spanish Revolution of 1868," *H* 13 (spring 1951) is a careful and scholarly account, but his piece on "Napoleon III and the Spanish Revolution of 1868," *JMH* 25 (September 1953) is better. Many of Smith's arguments are updated forcefully by Nancy Nicholas Barker, "Napoleon III and the Hohenzollern Candidacy for the Spanish Throne," *H* 29 (summer 1967). However, for matters both domestic and foreign we must rely on Hans-Otto Kleinmann's contribution to *EK*, "Die spanische Thronfrage in der internationalen Politik vor Ausbruch des deutsch-französischen Krieges," a work based on exhaustive and meticulous research and covering every phase of the problem with masterly authority. Bastiaan Schot, "Die Entstehung des Deutsch-Französischen Krieges und die Gründung des deutschen Reiches," in *Probleme der Reichsgründungszeit, 1848–1871*, ed. Helmut Böhme (Cologne, 1972) has fresh information on the subject in its opening pages. Richard Konetzke, "Spanien, die Vorgeschichte des Krieges von 1870 und die deutsche Reichsgründung," *HZ* 214 (1972) is a substantial and valuable contribution. "Lord Clarendon, the Foreign Office, and the Hohenzollern Candidature, 1868–1870" by C. J. Bartlett, *EHR* 75 (1960) plays old tunes with few enrichments.

On public opinion: *La revolución de 1868 y la prensa francesa* by María Victoria Alberola Fioravanti (Madrid, 1973) and Martin Winckler, "Die Rolle der Presse bei der Vorbereitung des deutsch-französischen Kriegs 1870/71," in *Presse und Geschichte,* ed. Elger Blühm (Munich, 1977) both cover the subject competently, clearly, perceptively, and judiciously. A doctoral dissertation by Luisa Ballestera Marcos, "La opinión pública ante la política exterior España" (Madrid, 1962), is a pioneering investigation that deserves to be better known in the English-speaking world. *España y la guerra de 1870* by Javier Rubio, 3 vols. (Madrid, 1989) is a work of outstanding scholarship and erudition; the final volume is enriched with much original documentary material from the Spanish archives, though not all of it is very readable.

PART 2. PRIMARY SOURCES ON THE ORIGINS
OF THE FRANCO-PRUSSIAN WAR
Archives

GERMANY (including PRUSSIA). Of great significance for the period in question are the documents of the German Foreign Office. Happily, these documents have all been microfilmed, and those who wish to learn more about this series may consult the American Historical Association, *A Catalogue of Files and Microfilms of the German Foreign Ministry Archives, 1867–1920* (Washington, 1959).

AUSTRIA-HUNGARY. The archival holdings of the former Austro-Hungarian Foreign Office are readily available to the serious scholar at the Haus-, Hof-, und Staatsarchiv in Vienna, in the entrance to which an elegant marble statue of the Empress Maria Theresa smiles down agreeably on the arriving visitor. Of outstanding value to this study were extensive reports on the south German press—particularly in Württemberg and in Bavaria—submitted at regular intervals by the ministers at those legations and housed in the Politisches Archiv section. The reports included (usually in clipping form) the texts—or excerpts thereof—of editorials and articles on diplomatic matters by leading south German figures of the day; given that the periodicals in question are today difficult if not impossible to find and for various reasons are not easy to use when found, this summary record of the pertinent contents is of exceptional historical value.

FRANCE. Comprehensive as is the published *Les Origines diplomatiques de la guerre de 1870–71* (discussed more fully below) for the purposes of the student of the general diplomacy of the period, there are many documents that the editors felt obliged to omit but which are nevertheless of interest from the standpoint of a more highly focused study such as the one presented here. The full archive may be found in the original files of communications from the French embassies at Berlin, Vienna, London, Florence, St. Petersburg, and especially Madrid and Lisbon, now available in the Correspondance politique section of the Archives du ministère des affaires étrangères (AMAE) at the Quai d'Orsay, Paris. Also of great interest to this study were the private papers of Gramont, housed in the Archives nationales (AN 45 AP). Here, of course, circumstances restricted my use of these materials to the clarification of specific questions, and the results did not always live up to my high expectations; very poorly arranged and indexed and neither copiously nor usefully annotated, the collection is not easy to use. Yvonnes Lanhers, "Les Archives de la maison de Gramont," *RH* 211 (1954) gives a brief and rather excessively laudatory description of these materials.

There are also a number of other personal papers that might well have a bearing on the events recounted in this volume; except for a brief glance at a small portion of the La Valette papers and Rouher papers also at the Archives nationales, and at the Walewski papers in the Mémoirs et documents section of the AMAE, I was unfortunately not in a position to explore these sources. I regret only my inability to remain longer in Paris to study a much larger part of this valuable material.

The most important papers are, as anyone who has gone through the notes to this book can see, those of Émile Ollivier. We owe to Professor Theodore Zeldin of Oxford University the valuable service of discovering, describing, and arranging for the publication of parts of this great collection. Ollivier's papers, widely dispersed in three family houses at La Moutte and Paris, may be divided (according to the scheme Professor Zeldin has devised) into three rough categories. (1) Correspondence: copies of the many letters sent by Ollivier, found in his diary before 1870 and for the period after in a series of bound volumes of carbon copies as well as in bundles of drafts of letters. (2) Diaries: a series of seven bound volumes, covering 1846–48, 1851–53, 1853–57, 1857–63, 1863–65, 1866–69, and 1870; loose sheets for 1853 and for 1874–76; and, most outstandingly for my purposes, small pocket notebooks from about 1870–73, few of which are dated. (3) Documents: for 1848, bound and unbound collections of speeches regarding his prefecture; for 1870, envelopes containing letters received during his ministry, miscellaneous notes, and drafts. Ollivier's papers are in no particular order because he used them to write his memoirs; documents on 1870, for example, are embedded in the proofs of his *L'Empire libéral*. Only after 1870 are they in a condition that approaches coherence; in other words, they are not thrown about and rearranged; on the other hand, a good number of the letters are printed either in the text or in the excellent appendices to his book. All in all these documents throw a vivid light on the activities of the French government and its entourage during the crisis of July 1870 and constitute a priceless addition to the available source material on the subject.

GREAT BRITAIN. The British Foreign Office correspondence for this particular period has unfortunately not been included in the excellent series of diplomatic documents that have been published for other periods of time

(*British Documents on the Origins of the War, 1898–1914,* published in London in various years by His Majesty's Stationery Office). However, the original files are available to scholars at the Public Record Office in Kew Gardens, not far from London. The manner in which they are catalogued and made available to the general public seems somewhat cumbersome in comparison with continental practices, but with patience and persistence most inquiries eventually yield their fruit. This was true of Foreign Office 64/688 Prussia, of 27/1789–1792 and 1797–1810 France, and 45/164 Italy—where one can find the correspondence of, respectively, Loftus, Lyons, and Paget with their superior in London. The most valuable of the private papers are unquestionably those of Clarendon at the Bodleian Library; of these, C. 477, "Private letters from the British Ambassador in Paris to the Foreign Secretary, January–June, 1870," and C. 474 (3), "Letters from Clarendon to Lyons," are the outstanding collections for the period in question.

ITALY. In addition to these outstanding collections, mention should also be made of Archivo storico del ministero degli affari esteri at Rome, in whose cramped but attractive rooms there repose the records (in sixty million documents, according to the official brochure) of the relations of other countries with the kingdom of Italy. These were transferred to that city when Italy's capital moved from Florence in 1871. A most important source is no. 586 (confidential), Seire Politica (1867–88), Prussia (1867–70), carton 1328, where one can examine the exchanges that took place between Launay, the Italian representative to Berlin, and his boss, the foreign minister Visconti-Venosta. Here, too, one can go through the correspondence in the private diaries of the members of the Lanza cabinet, which, while not primarily addressed to foreign affairs, throws an occasional light on the diplomatic practices of the day. In addition to this resource, the author had recourse to materials available elsewhere in Italy. The Archivo di stato in Florence, with its online database, and the elegant if less modern Archivi di stato in Venice and in Milan house the documents—particularly the private papers of newspaper editors—of those who either supported or opposed Visconti-Venosta's policy. I was able to consult these files on several occasions to clarify specific points of inquiry. On the focal point of my interest, however—the diplomatic relations of France and Prussia—many of the authors of these documents were not generally very well informed, and the picture conveyed in their correspondence and reports cannot compare in point of authority and detail to that which emanated from the dispatches of the foreign minister and his representatives at Paris and at Berlin. I used these materials in any case merely to supplement the official documents, most of which, it must be added, have been published and now appear in the magnificent *Documenti diplomatici italiani* discussed below.

RUSSIA. The comparable documents of the Russian foreign office are now being catalogued. But because of the difficulty and expense of visiting Moscow for the long period of time required for their study and because of the fact that the documents themselves have yet to be systematically catalogued, I was not able to avail myself of these no doubt most significant materials. I regret my inability to do so.

Official Publications

GERMANY (including PRUSSIA): *Preussens auswärtige Politik, 1850–1858,* ed. Heinrich von Poschinger, 2 vols. (Berlin, 1902) covers the period from the agreement at Olmütz (1850) to the time of William I's succession as regent of the kingdom in 1858. It gives mainly Manteuffel's dispatches, and while its arrangement and selections are a little tendentious, it cannot seriously be claimed that there was deliberate suppression. Poschinger was one of the earliest Bismarck scholars, and he also published the reports of his hero from Frankfurt as *Preussen im Bundestag, 1851–1859,* 4 vols. (Leipzig, 1882–84); this collection has largely been superseded by the relevant volumes of Bismarck's own works, though here one can still enjoy the earliest examples of Bismarck's literary genius.

Die auswärtige Politik Preussens, 1858–1871, ed. Erich Brandenburg et al., 10 vols. (Berlin, 1932–39) is a much grander affair, and in one quality it is unique: it reproduces, here and there, documents from the British and Russian archives. Though this provides a glimpse of material not otherwise available, it swells the volumes to enormous size, so that they cannot be held in the hand without muscular exhaustion. Its worst feature, however, is that Bismarck's correspondence is nowhere to be found, and the historian must shuffle back and forth from this source to his own collected works (discussed below).

AUSTRIA-HUNGARY. The Austrian material is less extensive than the German, though it is quite comprehensive for the period it covers. *Die Rheinpolitik Kaiser Napoleons III,* ed. Hermann Oncken, 3 vols. (Berlin and Leipzig, 1926) is a heavy selection from the archives; though it claims to start in 1863, it is most useful for our period—that is, after 1866. There is an aggressively anti-French introduction by the editor, which has been translated into English as *Napoleon III and the Rhine* (New York, 1928).

FRANCE. *Les Origines diplomatiques de la guerre de 1870–71,* 29 vols. (Paris, 1910–32) is the outstanding source for the period. The series is made up of a careful selection, from the standpoint of political and historical importance, of official communications—instructions, dispatches, and telegrams—exchanged between the Quai d'Orsay and the French diplomatic missions abroad; to which are added most usefully a not inconsiderable number of private letters (*lettres particulières*), usually addressed by the heads of these various missions to senior officials in the foreign office. Because this collection opened a new era in scholarship, it would be agreeable to discover clear, dramatic motives for its publication; unfortunately, this is not possible. An element of professional pride no doubt entered in: the French diplomatic service resented Ollivier's criticism of its predecessors and wished to show that the war had been caused by the "secret diplomacy" of Napoleon III and his unofficial advisors; in addition, republican politicians were provoked by the suggestion (which some Bonapartist apologists still make) that the opponents of the empire had caused the war. Diplomats, politicians, and professors alike appealed from polemics to the evidence. But whatever the background that led to its composition, we are forever in its debt. The series sets a model for scholarship, and it remains a mine of valuable information on the diplomatic undertakings of the day. It begins with Napoleon's call for a European congress in 1863 and continues to the outbreak of the war in 1870. The arrangement is chronological, with a summary of the documents (also chronological) at the beginning of each volume. Volume 28 (1931) and the last 63 pages of the appendix to volume 29 (1932) deal with the crisis of July

1870. There is one major fault: the individual editor of each volume is not named, and the reader is thus unable to allow for each editor's idiosyncrasies or special interests.

GREAT BRITAIN. The British government was dependent on parliament for support and, to get it, presented to it a selection from the official record in the form of Blue Books. Five of these cover the period leading up to the outbreak of the Franco-Prussian War. Blue Book no. 41 gives the reports of Lyons, the minister at Paris during the crisis of July; that of the 14th is the most famous and justly quoted. *Foundations of British Foreign Policy,* ed. H. W. V. Temperley and Lillian Penson (London, 1938), gives a random selection of documents from our period and can be used as a supplement to the Blue Books. *Bismarcks Reichsgründung im Urteil englischer Diplomaten* by Viet Valentin (Amsterdam, 1937) gives reports mainly of Loftus from Germany, unfortunately in German translations.

ITALY. A grandiose collection of documents from the founding of the kingdom of Italy to the armistice of September 1943 has now appeared: *Documenti diplomatici italiani,* 1st ser., vol. 13 (Rome, 1963) contains the correspondence dealing with the year 1870, and is most valuable for the candidacies of the dukes of Genoa and of Aosta. The selections are arranged chronologically, and the editing is meticulous.

RUSSIA. None of the Russian diplomatic correspondence for this period has been published by the tsarist Russian, Soviet, or former Soviet governments, but a number of official or semiofficial Russian documents have seen publication in Russian historical documentary series, particularly in the magazine *Krasny archiv* (the 1937 issue) as well as in some of the secondary treatises discussed below.

Published Private Papers
Rulers

GERMANY (including PRUSSIA). There are many collected volumes of the correspondence of William I, all uninteresting. The most substantial are his

Correspondence with Bismarck, ed. and trans. J. A. Ford, 2 vols. (New York, 1903); *Briefe an Politiker und Staatsmänner*, ed. Johannes Schultze, 2 vols. (Berlin, 1930); and *Kaiser Wilhelms des Grossen Briefe, Reden und Schriften*, ed. Ernst Berner, 2 vols. (Berlin, 1906). *Unser Heldenkaiser* by Wilhelm Oncken (Berlin, n.d. [1897?]) is written in an extravagant style; it gives the impression of being a work of fiction rather than a contribution to history. William's speeches to parliament from the throne in 1870 are to be found in volume 15 of *Das Staatsarchiv*, ed. Ludwig Aegidi and Alfred Klauhold, 21 vols. (Hamburg, 1861–1922). *Kaiser Wilhelm und die Begründung des Reiches*, ed. Ottokar Lorenz (Jena, 1902), gives his correspondence with his relatives and is not altogether uncritical of its subject.

Sir Frederick Ponsonby, *Letters of the Empress Frederick* (London, 1929), makes good use of the papers of the Prussian crown princess; Eduard von Wertheimer, "Kronprinz Friedrich Wilhelm und die spanische Hohenzollern Thronkandidatur," *PJbb* 205 (1926) does the same for the crown prince, though it is no substitute for the *Kriegstagebuch* of Emperor Friedrich III, ed. Heinrich Otto Meisner (Leipzig, 1926), which has some embarrassing if unconvincing material on Bismarck.

Grossherzog Friedrich I. von Baden und die deutsche Politik von 1854–1871, ed. Hermann von Oncken, 2 vols. (Stuttgart, 1927) is important for the relations of the south German states with Prussia; the work of Walther Peter Fuchs, 4 vols. (Stuttgart, 1968–80) takes up the story where Oncken leaves off.

Aus dem Leben des Königs Albert von Sachsen by Paul Hassel, 2 vols. (Berlin, 1898–1900) is useful as background. *Aus meinem Leben und aus meiner Zeit* by Ernst II of Saxe-Coburg-Gotha, 3 vols. (Berlin, 1887–89), though devoted to German affairs, has some curious material on Napoleon III. Its strong point is its forceful prose; though Ernst welcomed the coming to power of Napoleon III, he viewed with the liveliest suspicion the political situation in France and, as the years wore on, made no secret of his belief that Napoleon was aiming at nothing less than the destruction of Prussian hegemony north of the Main. The English translation, 4 vols. (London, 1888–90), is mediocre.

AUSTRIA-HUNGARY. The letters of Francis Joseph contain little either of personal or of political interest. *Franz Josef I. in seinen Briefen*, ed. Otto

Ernst (Vienna, 1924) may be supplemented by *Briefe Kaiser Franz Josefs I. an seine Mutter, 1838–1872,* ed. Franz Schnürer (Munich, 1930); the latter has a few important points. *Briefe Kaiser Franz Josefs an Kaiserin Elisabeth,* ed. Georg Nostitz-Rieneck, 2 vols. (Vienna, 1966) gives his correspondence with his wife; there is a gap between November 1869 and February 1874. *Briefe Kaiser Franz Josefs an Frau Katharina Schratt,* ed. Jean de Bourgoing (Vienna, 1949) gives the correspondence with his mistress.

FRANCE. No historical figure is more elusive than Napoleon III. He wrote few letters and fewer still survive. The only published scraps are in *Lettres inédites entre Napoléon III et le prince Napoléon,* ed. Ernest d'Hauterive (Paris, 1925). The empress Eugénie is better provided for. *Papiers et correspondance de la famille impériale,* 2 vols. (Paris, 1871) is rich in original material. *Lettres familières de l'impératrice Eugénie,* ed. the duke of Alba, 2 vols. (Paris, 1935) is a work of high scholarship, particularly valuable for developing the stories of the empress's loss of interest in her marriage and of the lively and flamboyant hostility with which her relations with members of the "liberal empire" came to be conducted. Maurice Comte Fleury, *Memoirs of Empress Eugénie,* 2 vols. (New York, 1920) makes a good showing with what material he has. *Les Entretiens de l'impératrice Eugénie* by Maurice Paléologue (Paris, 1928) is valuable as well, though it displays the selective memory of a politician and so must be used with care; there is a fine English translation, *The Tragic Empress* (New York, 1928). A good deal of material is also to be found in "Les Idées de l'impératrice Eugénie sur le redressement de la carte de l'Europe" by Count Egon Caesar Corti, *Revue des idées napoléoniennes* 19 (July–December 1922).

GREAT BRITAIN. *The Letters of Queen Victoria,* ed. Arthur Christopher Benson and Viscount Esher, are very important. The three volumes of the second series (London, 1926–28) cover 1861 to 1885, volume 2 giving the correspondence leading up to the crisis of July 1870. Of course, though the prime ministers and foreign secretaries were forever writing to the queen, they often did not reveal the workings of their minds.

ITALY. The official life of Vittorio Emanuele II by Giuseppe Massari, 2 vols. (Milan, 1878) has some original material. There is also much of value in *Pio IX e Vittorio Emanuele II dal loro carteggio privato*, ed. P. Pietro Pirri, 5 vols. (Rome, 1944–61) and in the *Lettere di Vittorio Emanuele II*, ed. Francesco Cognasso, 2 vols. (*Biblioteca storica italiana, nuova serie*) (Turin, 1966).

RUSSIA. The life of *Aleksandr II* by Sergei Spiridonovich Tatishchev, 2 vols. (St. Petersburg, 1903) has some points of interest.

OTHERS. The essential source for the Strat mission is *Aus dem Leben König Karls von Rumänien*, 4 vols. (Stuttgart, 1894–1900).

Prime and Foreign Ministers

GERMANY (including PRUSSIA). The essential source for Bismarck, as any reader of these pages by now knows, is the collection of his *Gesammelte Werke* (Berlin, 1924–33). The collection is arranged as follows:

Politische Schriften, vols. 1–6c: vol. 1 (1924): to 1854; vol. 2 (1924): 1 January 1855 to 1 March 1859; vol. 3 (1925): 1 March 1859 to September 1862; vol. 4 (1927): September 1862 to 1864; vol. 5 (1928): 1864 to June 1866; vol. 6 (1929): June 1866 to July 1867; vol. 6a (1930): June 1866 to July 1867; vol. 6b (1931): 1869–71, including virtually all of his correspondence during the period of July 1870; vol. 6c (1931): 1871–90. (Vols. 1–3 edited [meticulously] by Hermann von Petersdorff; 4–6b [also meticulously and with long introductions to the important pieces] by Friedrich Thimme; 6c [less successfully] by Werner Frauendienst.)

Gespräche, vols. 7–9: vol. 7 (1924): to the founding of the German Reich; vol. 8 (1926): to Bismarck's dismissal; vol. 9 (1926): to Bismarck's death. (All ed. Willy Andreas.)

Reden, vols. 10–13: vol. 10 (1928): 1847–69; vol. 11 (1929): 1869–78; vol. 12 (1929): 1878–85; vol. 13 (1930): 1885–97. (All ed. Wilhelm Schüssler.)

Briefe, vol. 14, pts. 1–2: pt. 1 (1933): 1822–61; pt. 2 (1933): 1862–98. (Both parts ed. Wolfgang Windelband and Werner Frauendienst).

The title of the collected works is misleading; though collected, Bismarck's works are not complete. His writings on foreign policy after 1871, for instance, must be sought in the first six volumes of *Die grosse Politik der europäischen Kabinette*, ed. Johannes Lepsius, Albrecht Mendelssohn-Bartholdy, and Friedrich Thimme, 39 vols. (Berlin, 1922–27). His speeches can be found in full only in the 14 volumes edited by Horst Kohl (Berlin, 1892–95). There are many collections of his letters, the most important of which are *Fürst Bismarcks Briefe an seine Braut und Gattin,* ed. Fürst Herbert von Bismarck (Stuttgart, 1900); those to William I, cited above in the latter's correspondence; those to his sister, Malvine von Arnim (Leipzig, 1915) (ed. Kohl); those to his son Wilhelm (Berlin, 1922) (ed. Wolfgang Windelband); those to Ludwig von Gerlach, 2 vols. (Stuttgart and Berlin, 1896) (ed. Kohl); and those to Schleinitz (Stuttgart and Berlin, 1905) (ed. Kohl).

The two volumes of Bismarck's *Gedanken und Erinnerungen* (Stuttgart, 1898) rank among the most remarkable political memoirs ever written, not least for his inaccuracy of detail; on the other hand, they are perhaps the only work of their kind that can be recommended as bedside reading for the layman. The edition in the *Gesammelte Werke* (1932) includes some curious scraps discarded from the original published version. *Die Parallel-Erzählungen Bismarcks zu seinen Gedanken und Erinnerungen* by Robert Pahncke (Halle am See, 1914) is the first critical (though not wholly successful) examination of them.

There is a vast accumulation of Bismarckiana of which I made use of bits and pieces. For example, there is *The Bismarck Calendar: A Quotation from the Writings and Sayings of Prince Bismarck for Every Day of the Year* (London, 1913). *Varzin: Persönliche Erinnerungen an Fürsten Otto von Bismarck* by Pauline Hahn (Berlin, 1909) is particularly valuable for atmospheric details that shed occasional minor flickers of light on the crisis of July 1870.

Of the other ministers, only the *Denkwürdigkeiten* of Hohenlohe, 2 vols. (Stuttgart, 1906) are important for the relations of Bavaria and Prussia in early 1870.

AUSTRIA-HUNGARY. Beust's memoirs, *Aus drei Viertel-Jahrhunderten,* 2 vols. (Stuttgart, 1887) are colorful though not always trustworthy recollections of the Austro-Hungarian chancellor. There is an English translation, 2 vols. (London, 1887), which is atrocious, and a French one, 2 vols. (Paris,

1888), which is superb. "Die deutsche Politik des Grafen Beust im Jahre 1870," a doctoral dissertation by Ernst Erichsen (Kiel, 1927), is a pedestrian account, competent but uninspiring. A full life has long been promised.

FRANCE. The recollections of Ollivier are in the *L'Empire libéral,* 18 vols. (Paris, 1895–1918). All in all, this work constitutes the most detailed history of the Second Empire ever written—over nine thousand pages, one and three-quarter million words, and surely one of the weightiest apologies in literary history. Ollivier's work takes the form of a general history of the Second Empire and of its intellectual and political antecedents; not the least of the motives that led to the composition of this elaborate book is a desire to recount the true causes of the war of 1870. The materials for Ollivier's defense of himself are the letters he exchanged with his colleagues in the cabinet of which he was prime minister, many of which were first embedded in the proofs and then finally are printed either in the text or in the appendices. An attack has been launched against them in *Emile Olliviers Memoiren und die Entstehung des Kriegs von 1870* by Siegfried Brase (Berlin, 1912)—a sillier book than any Ollivier ever wrote. Ollivier presented himself in his final miscellany, *Lettres de l' éxil, 1870–1874* (Paris, 1921) as defeated and embittered yet not without affection for Napoleon III. The book was published by his widow, Marie-Thérèse.

Gramont defended himself unconvincingly in *La France et la Prusse* (Paris, 1872), thin, inaccurate, and vague, yet with an odd penetration here and there.

GREAT BRITAIN. Lord Clarendon has a rather superficial life by Herbert Maxwell, 2 vols. (London, 1905); *A Vanished Victorian* by George Villiers (London, 1938) is an even less satisfactory account by an admiring grandson. On the other hand, his papers at the Bodleian Library are invaluable for the origins of Leopold's candidacy. Granville has a life by Edmond Fitzmaurice, 2 vols. (London, 1905), and his correspondence with Gladstone (prime minister, 1868–74) has been summarized and edited by Agatha Ramm (London, 1954); there is a supplemental essay by H. C. G. Matthew (London, 1995). Granville was a drab figure, the original stuffed shirt—starch outside, sawdust within. He is unworthy of all this attention.

ITALY. Italian memoirs are rather sporadic, but some are of first-rate importance. For example, there is a good deal of material on the foreign policy of Ricasoli (prime minister, 1861–62, 1866–67): *Lettere e documenti del barone Bettino Ricasoli*, ed. Marco Tabarrini and Aurelio Gotti, 10 vols. (Florence, 1887–95) and the last two volumes of *Carteggi di Bettino Ricasoli*, ed. Mario Nobili, Sergio Camerani, and Gaetano Arfè, 29 vols. (Milan, 1939–70). Marco Minghetti (prime minister, 1863–64) revealed something of the Roman question in *La convenzione di settembre: Un capitolo dei miei ricordi* (Rome, 1899). Alfonso Ferrero della La Marmora (prime minister, 1866) wrote a polemic against Bismarck: *Un po' più di luce sugli eventi politici e militari dell' anno 1866* (Rome, 1879). The last two volumes of the *Carte di Giovanni Lanza,* ed. Cesare Maria de Vecchi di Val Cismon, 11 vols. (Turin, 1935–43) are important for the negotiations for a triple alliance; less satisfactory, and now rather out of date, is *La vita e i tempi di Giovanni Lanza* by Enrico Tavallini, 2 vols. (Turin, 1887). *La politica estera di E. Visconti Venosta* by Francesco D. Cataluccio (Florence, 1940) is as sober as its subject, but extremely competent.

RUSSIA. The life of A. M. Gorchakov by Sergei Nickolaevich Semanov (Moscow, 1962) is a work of penetration, even though it is very long and occasionally presented in crabbed Marxist phraseology.

Diplomats

GERMANY (including PRUSSIA). Bismarck's account of his years at Frankfurt has been discussed above. The Prussian diplomats did not write much for the public. Schweinitz, ambassador at Vienna, gives important evidence for the July crisis in his *Denkwürdigkeiten,* 2 vols. (Berlin, 1927); they outrank his *Briefwechsel,* 3 vols. (Berlin, 1927–28). Bernstorff, ambassador to Great Britain, is partially though not deeply revealed in *Im Kampfe für Preussens Ehre* by Karl Ringhoffer (Berlin, 1906); it reached the presses only after the author's death and made a great stir when it did. There is an attractive English translation (New York, 1908). Hajo Holborn, *Aufzeichnungen und Erinnerungen aus dem Leben des Botschafters Josef Maria von Radowitz,* 2 vols. (Stuttgart, 1925) gives the impressions of the secretary of the Prussian legation at Munich in the prewar period; "Bismarck und Werthern," *APG* 5 (1925), by the same author, gives Werthern's dispatches to Bismarck, some not noted by the editors of the *Gesammelte Werke*.

AUSTRIA-HUNGARY. Henry Salomon, *L'Ambassade de Richard de Metternich* (Paris, 1931) does not go very deep.

FRANCE. Benedetti wrote a good deal in his own defense, much of it stimulating and effective: *Ma mission en Prusse* (Paris, 1871); *Essais diplomatiques* (Paris, 1895; English trans., New York, 1896); and *Trois ans en Allemagne* (Paris, 1900), a final miscellany. He also illuminated his difficulties as Gramont's ambassador in "Ma mission à Ems," *Revue de Paris* 5 (15 September 1895). *The Mission of Vincent Benedetti to Berlin* by Willard Fletcher (The Hague, 1964) is most valuable for its notes; it outranks the earlier life by Luise Schoeps (Halle, 1915), a crude doctoral thesis. There are suggestive and significant penetrations in *La France et la Russie en 1870* by Émil-Félix, Maurice Count Fleury (Paris, 1902). Fleury was an intimate friend of Napoleon III and, unlike his master, a prolific writer; letters, memoranda, and gossip poured from his untiring pen, making for interesting though not always reliable reading. Gustav Rothan, a shadowy Bonapartist diplomat, wrote five works—half recollection, half history—all published in Paris: *Souvenirs diplomatiques—l'affaire du Luxembourg* (1882); *La Politique française en 1866* (1884); *L'Allemagne et l'Italie, 1870–71* (1885); *L'Europe et l'avènement du Second Empire* (1890); and *La France et sa politique extérieure en 1867* (1893).

GREAT BRITAIN. Many of the British ambassadors have received biographies, most of little value. The papers of Cowley (Paris, 1850–68) are used unsuccessfully by F. A. Wellesley and R. Sencourt in *The Paris Embassy during the Second Empire* (London, 1928); the American edition, *Secrets of the Second Empire* (New York, 1929), is even less successful. Lyons is rather superficially treated by T. Newton, 2 vols. (London, 1913). The *Diplomatic Reminiscences*, 4 vols. (London, 1892–94), of Lord Augustus Loftus are fatuous.

ITALY. "Ricordi diplomatici (1870)," *NA* 160 (1895) gives the recollections of Nigra, Napoleon's Italian confidant, during the July crisis; they are exciting and dramatic but also impressionable and superficial. "Souvenirs diploma-tiques 1870," *BURS* 65 (1895) is the French translation.

RUSSIA. Not much here. The first pages of *The Saburov Memoirs* by J. Y. Simpson (London, 1929) have a certain amount of information on Franco-Russian relations before the war.

Other Witnesses

To be complete, this would include almost every figure in public life during the period. I have tried to cut it down to those who were primarily concerned with foreign affairs. These include journalists, soldiers, and politicians, with an occasional banker thrown in.

GERMANY (including PRUSSIA). Some important books here. *Lebenserin-nerungen* by Julius von Eckhardt (Leipzig, 1910) gives the impressions of a Saxon diplomat for the period 1866–70. Helmuth von Moltke, chief of the gen-eral staff, has left two prime sources of military strategy: *Gesammelte Schriften und Denkwürdigkeiten,* 8 vols. (Berlin, 1891–92) and *Die deutschen Auf-marschpläne,* ed. Ferdinand von Schmerfeld (Berlin, 1928), the latter espe-cially valuable for German strategy. The *Denkwürdigkeiten* of the North Ger-man military attaché Alfred Waldersee, ed. Heinrich Otto Meisner, 3 vols. (Stuttgart, 1922–23) supplies vital evidence of a similar kind and is important.
    Bismarck's aides had a great deal to say. For example, *Ein schlichtes Leben in bewegter Zeit* by Heinrich Abeken, 4th ed. (Berlin, 1910) is extremely useful for the negotiations at Ems; there is a rather unsatisfactory English translation, *Bismarck's Pen: The Life of Heinrich von Abeken, Edited from the Letters and Journals by his Wife* (London, 1911). The *Tagebuchblätter* of Moritz Busch, official of the North German foreign office for press relations (Leipzig, 1899) is packed with raw material and draws richly on his diaries; the English translation, *Bismarck: Some Secret Pages of His History,* 3 vols. (London, 1898) is crisp and clear. *Fürst und Fürstin Bismarck* by Robert von Keudell (Berlin and Stuttgart, 1901) is the most telling though also the rash-est defense of Bismarck's policy. *Bismarcks grosses Spiel: Die geheimen Ta-gebücher Ludwig Bambergers,* edited with an introduction by Ernst Feder

(Frankfurt am Main, 1932) gives trivial but interesting details from the diary of one of Bismarck's most articulate critics. Fürst Karl Anton has an official biography by Theodor Zingeler (Stuttgart, 1911) that uses his correspondence at Sigmaringen; it has been overtaken by the works of Jochen Dittrich, discussed below. Zingeler also produced two articles with some raw material: "Briefe des Fürsten Karl Anton von Hohenzollern an Grossherzog Friedrich I. von Baden," *DR* 37 (1912) and "Briefe des Fürsten Karl Anton von Hohenzollern an seine Gemahlin Josephine," *DR* 39 (1914). The private letters of Leopold and of other Sigmaringeners are used ineffectively by Zingeler in "Das fürstliche Haus Hohenzollern und die spanische Thronkandidatur," *DR* 37 (1912). *Aus dem Leben Theodor Bernhardis,* Achter Theil: *Zwischen zwei Kriegen: Tagebuchblätter aus den Jahren 1867 bis 1869* and Neunter Theil: *In Spanien und Portugal: Tagebuchblätter aus den Jahren 1869 bis 1871* (Leipzig, 1901, 1906) is the record of an eminent politician, an economist, and (according to Lord Acton) "the best military writer in Europe," who was close to Moltke and to the Prussian military staff; it is particularly important for the Spanish revolution, the overtures to Leopold by the provisional government, and the events that led Leopold to renounce the throne. Johann Sass, "Hermann von Thile und Bismarck," *PJbb* 217 (1929) gives some of the former's unpublished correspondence to his chief but presents it clumsily and heavily. The *Lebenslauf* of Julius Fröbel, 2 vols. (Stuttgart, 1890–91) is the work of a journalist that speaks for itself. *Die Bedeutung des preussischen Innenministers Friedrich Albrecht Graf zu Eulenburg für die Entwicklung Preussens zum Reichsstaat* by Gerhard Lange (Berlin, 1993) has much information, despite the author's propensity to use ten words when one would do. Of the remaining works none compares in importance to Oskar Meding, *Memoiren zur Zeitgeschichte,* 3 vols. (Lepzig, 1884). Meding was a Saxon diplomat (though Prussian-born) who was secretly sent to France by his master, George V, following the latter's downfall in the war against Prussia in 1866. A malicious busybody and snob, a master of the scurrilous, unnaturally excitable and neurotically oversensitive, he nonetheless managed to analyze with great refinement the complicated play of forces in French domestic political life, though the less familiar subtleties of international relations seem somewhat beyond his ken. His work reflects the many oddities of this most curious of men; it is anti-Prussian to the core, but because it also reflects the excellent connections that its author developed with the outstanding personalities of the various French governments between 1866 and 1870, it rewards respect and careful attention.

Aus dem Leben eines Glücklichen: Erinnerungen eines alten Beamten by Gustav von Diest (Berlin, 1904) has some information, particularly on constitutional and administrative matters, but is of something less than impeccable reliability.

AUSTRIA-HUNGARY. *Erinnerungen eines alten Österreichers* by Ludwig von Przibram, 2 vols. (Vienna, 1911–13) gives an account of the Austrian press bureau in the 1870s.

FRANCE. *Le Second Empire vu par un diplomate belge* by Napoléon-Eugène Beyens, 2 vols. (Lille, 1924–26) is more interesting for atmosphere than for facts. The author was the son of the Belgian minister to Paris, who began his career there in 1853 and died there in 1894 as minister plenipotentiary. The book is largely based upon and quoted from the private papers of the father, and it reveals the deep-seated Belgian anxieties over French expansion. His private papers may be examined in the archives of the Belgian Foreign Ministry in Brussels. Barthélemy Lebrun, *Souvenirs militaires, 1866–1876* (Paris, 1892) gives the Austro-French negotiations in 1869 and 1870. The first pages of Jules Simon, *Souvenirs du quatre septembre* (Paris, 1876) have scraps of information. *Le Ministre Pierre Magne, 1806–1879* by Joseph Durieux, 2 vols. (Paris, 1929) has some valuable quotations from a former minister who was a strident if ineffective critic of Gramont's policy. Dugué de la Fauconnerie, *Souvenirs d'un vieil homme (1866–1879)*, 4th ed. (Paris, 1912) does not go very deep. Marie-Thérèse Ollivier, "L'Épouse de l'empereur," *RG* (February and March 1921) gives Ollivier's second wife's recollections of Eugénie, and they are not very flattering. Jocelyn-Émile Ollivier, *La Dépêche d'Ems* (Paris, 1935), is a superficial polemic by an angry and embittered daughter. Comtesse Garets (née Marie de Larminet), *Souvenirs d'une demoiselle d'honneur auprès de l'impératrice Eugénie* (Paris, 1928) is an unusually perceptive diary by a young maid of honor at the court of Napoleon III. *Monsieur Thiers* by the duc de Castries (Paris, 1983) has some quotations from French sources.

GREAT BRITAIN. Malmesbury wrote *Memoirs of an Ex-Minister,* new ed., 2 vols. in 1, (London, 1885); they are weak and ineffective. On the other hand, the memoirs of Sir Robert Morrier, ed. Rosslyn Weymess, 2 vols. (London, 1911) are very important. Morrier was a British diplomat with excellent connections in Berlin, a close friend of the crown prince, and therefore in a position to know a good deal about the personal qualities of the leading figures of the country. *The War Correspondence of the Daily News,* 3d ed. (London and New York, 1871) has some valuable information in its opening pages.

ITALY. The *Memorie* (Rome, 1907) and *Scritti politici e militari,* 6 vols. (Bologna, 1932–37) of Giuseppe Garibaldi have some points of interest.

PART 3. SECONDARY WORKS
Guides and Sources

As an initial guide there is Widolf Wedlich, "Der deutsch-französische Krieg 1870/71: Literaturbericht und Auswahlbibliographie," in *JBZ* 42 (1970), a period piece written from the centenary of the Bismarckian Reich that gives the literature for the period 1870–1970. Though it analyzes only a handful of the works that it lists, it is indispensable for the student of the subject. Much of the more recent literature has been examined in *La Guerre de 1870/71 et ses conséquences,* ed. Philippe Levillain and Rainer Riemenschneider (Bonn, 1990), which reproduces papers from a series of conferences presented at the Centre de Recherches Adolphe Thiers on 10–12 October 1984 and 14–15 October 1985, though these have the defects as well as the virtues of such material. Most important of the earlier works are three books by Richard Fester: *Briefe, Aktenstücke, und Regesten zur Geschichte der Hohenzollernschen Thronkandidatur in Spanien,* 2 vols. (Leipzig and Berlin, 1913); *Neue Beiträge zur Geschichte der Hohenzollernschen Thronkandidatur in Spanien* (Leipzig, 1913); and the substantial volume of narrative to which these gave birth, *Die Genesis der Emser Depesche* (Berlin, 1915). Though the Fester series has occasionally been treated with severity by British and French historians, and also by some German writers of great distinction—of whom Jochen Dittrich is the most conspicuous, but by no means the only, example—I must say that I found those of the respective documents that deal with Franco-Prussian and Spanish-Prussian relations to be in no wise inferior in historical value to the ones published by the French or by Dittrich himself in the appendix to his book, and could discern no signs of tendentious editing or of any tendency to conceal significant portions of the record.

As to the record itself, it is possible for the interested scholar to follow the origins of it in *Drei psychologische Fragen zur Spanischen Thronkandidatur Leopolds von Hohenzollern* by Hermann Hesselbarth (Lepzig, 1913), the first book to publish the secret correspondence emanating from the principal Prussian figures—Bismarck, Thile, Bucher, Canitz—and in the main to correctly interpret it. The focus of Hesselbarth's curiosity concerned the identity of a certain M. de Gama, and three questions about him—(1) *Quel rang obentaint-il?* (2) *Est-il mort au service?* (3) *Descendait-il du célèbre Vasco?*—the answers to which he sought from the German ambassador in Spain. In these efforts he was singularly unsuccessful, and it is not hard to see why: M. de Gama was the cover name for Salazar y Mazarredo—a secret that historians had not yet pierced, and would not do so for another forty years. All in all, however, Hesselbarth's book elucidated many of the mysteries associated with the candidacy. These mysteries dissolve in light of the files published in *Bismarck and the Hohenzollern Candidature for the Spanish Throne,* ed. Georges Bonnin (London, 1957), which reproduces (unfortunately in English translation) the texts of documents from the German Foreign Ministry Archives that were kept secret since 1870. These documents were hardly the sensation that the editor made them out to be—see, for example, the mordantly witty and cutting review of the volume by A. J. P. Taylor, "Taylor's Law Confirmed," *Observer,* 19 January 1958, 16, and some had already been revealed in the documentary appendix to *The Origins of the War of 1870* by R. H. Lord (Cambridge, Mass., 1924), a work of outstanding scholarship and erudition—but taken together, the materials in the Bonnin volume were a not inconsiderable achievement, and they make subsequent compilations such as the *Emser Depesche,* ed. Ernst Walder (Bern, 1959) seem pretty small beer.

On the French side, *Foreign Policy of the Second Empire: A Bibliography* by William E. Echard (New York, 1988) is a competent and clear outline.

Countries

GERMANY (including PRUSSIA). *The Founding of the German Empire* by Heinrich von Sybel, 7 vols. (New York, 1890–97) is the official history. It is centered too much on Bismarck and tends to accept his version of events, but it must be cited if only for general reasons having to do with historiographical purposes. There were many attempts to deal with the hundredth anniversary of the founding of the Bismarckian Reich, of which *Reichsgründung 1870/1871: Tatsachen, Kontroversen, Interpretationen*, ed. Ernst Deuerlein and Theodor Schieder (Stuttgart, 1970) is the most competent; it contains a series of telling pieces, all written in an unassuming style and replete with copious documentation and sound bibliographies. "Zwischen Nikolsburg und Bad Ems" by Adam Wandruszka is easily the most outstanding essay in the collection, a work of almost incomparable understanding and penetration. On other aspects: "Bismarcks Süddeutschlandpolitik, 1866–1870," Lothar Gall's essay in *EK*, is a skillful survey by an author who is perhaps the most formidable researcher now at work on Bismarckian Germany. *Deutschlands Weg zur Grossmacht: Studien zum Verhältnis von Wirtschaft und Staat während der Reichsgründungszeit, 1848–1871* by Helmut Böhme (Cologne, 1966) achieves the remarkable feat of discovering that Germany could have been unified without Bismarck. Fritz Stern, *Gold and Iron: Bismarck, Bleichröder, and the Building of the German Empire* (New York, 1978) is the work of an artist, written with such competence, such mastery of sources, and such profound detachment that it is likely to be the last word on the subject.

AUSTRIA-HUNGARY. *Österreich-Ungarn und die Gründung des deutschen Reiches* by Heinrich Lutz (Frankfurt am Main, 1979) exhausts the subject. Lutz, "Aussenpolitische Tendenzen der Habsburger Monarchie von 1866 bis 1870" (in *EK*) is also a work of depth, sensitivity, and penetration. *Österreich-Ungarn und der französisch-preussische Krieg 1870–71* by István Diószegi (Budapest, 1974) deals competently with the Austrian liberals and the Hungarians, though more effectively in some places than others. *Die deutsche Politik Beusts von seiner Berufung zum österreichischen Aussenminister, Oktober 1866 bis zum Ausbruch des deutsch-französischen Krieges 1870/71* by

Heinrich Potthoff (Bonn, 1968), though narrow, contains valuable information. "Beusts Kampf gegen Bismarck" by Ernst Grob (Zurich, 1934) is a doctoral dissertation that adds nothing. Hans A. Schmitt, "Count Beust and Germany, 1866–1870," *Central European History* 1 (1968), draws a clear general outline, though with an aggressively anti-French slant. *Autour d'une tentative d'alliance entre la France et l'Autriche, 1867–1870* by Victor-Lucien Tapié (Vienna, 1971) is a slender, subtle essay. *Prime Minister Gyula Andrássy's Influence on Hapsburg Foreign Policy during the Franco-German War of 1870–71* by János Decsy (Boulder, Colo., 1979) is academic writing at its drabbest: plenty of ingredients for a tasty dish, but no cooking.

FRANCE. The *Histoire du Second Empire* by Pierre de La Gorce, 6 vols. (Paris, 1894–1905) is a classic work; the author inclines toward a liberal monarchist point of view, but he appears to have had access to the papers of the more prominent of Napoleon's ministers. *Rome et Napoléon III, 1849–1870* by Émile Bourgeois and Émile Clermont (Rome, 1907) is still the best book on the subject. *Napoleon III and the German Crisis, 1865–1866* by E. Ann Pottinger (Cambridge, Mass., 1962) is not a particularly persuasive defense of French policy, but it is full of new information and compelling theories. *French Opinion on War and Diplomacy during the Second Empire* by L. M. Case (Philadelphia, 1954) is a careful analysis of the attempts of the government to ascertain public opinion, though some of its conclusions have been contested effectively in Jean Stengers, "Aux origines de la guerre de 1870: Gouvernment et opinion publique," *RBPH* 34 (1956); both supersede the earlier work by E. Malcolm Carroll, "French Public Opinion on the War with Prussia in 1870," *AHR* 31 (1926), and his work of larger scope, *French Public Opinion and Foreign Affairs* (New York, 1931), of which the article is a part. *Napoleon III and the Concert of Europe* by William E. Echard (Baton Rouge, 1983) is important for the period after 1863. Gerhard Ritter, "Bismarck und die Rheinpolitik Napoleons III.," *RV* 15/16 (1950/51) is a serious contribution, as is his "Die Politik Napoleons III. und das System der Mainlinie," *KGGAv* 80 (1932), on which the former article is based. *Napoleon III und Bismarck* by Herbert Geuss (Cologne, 1959) offers a sound argument that Bismarck wished to work with, not against, Napoleon III, and a more dubious argument that he used the Hohenzollern candidacy to avert war.

Relations franco-allemandes, 1815–1975 by Ramond Poidevin and Jacques Bariéty (Paris, 1977) provides an exciting view of the entire period from a high-level, imaginative, and sweeping perspective.

GREAT BRITAIN. The major work is *British Foreign Policy and the Coming of the Franco-Prussian War* by Richard Millman (Oxford, 1965), rich in original material but flat in style. It eclipses the earlier, even flatter works by Dora N. Raymond, *British Policy and Opinion during the Franco-Prussian War* (London, 1921) and by Michael Horst, *Bismarck, England und Europa, 1866–1870* (Munich, 1930); the latter gives only a lucky dip from the British archives. *England und der deutsch-französische Krieg, 1870/71* by Kurt Rheindorf (Bonn and Leipzig, 1923) is the account of a historian who was allowed special access to the Prussian archives. For originality, insight, and sheer intellectual firepower, nothing can rival the two brilliant articles by Klaus Hildebrand, "Grossbritannien und die deutsche Reichsgründung," in *ER,* and "Die deutsche Reichsgründung im Urteil der britischen Politik," *F 5* (1977). Hildebrand's work is filled with challenging hypotheses, not the least striking of which is his view that the British would have preferred to see Bismarck annex south Germany to Prussia in 1866, when it would have caused no trouble with France. Hildebrand's thesis is developed further by Helmut Reinalter, "Norddeutscher Kaiser oder Kaiser von Deutschland?" *ZBLG* 39 (1976). One more notable piece should be mentioned in this brief catalogue, trivial in comparison with the Hildebrand articles but admirable in its insight and its focus on matters often forgotten: "Weltmacht auf Distanz: Britische Aussenpolitik, 1860–1870" by Peter Alter, in *EK.* Finally, there is *Gladstone's Foreign Policy* by Paul Knapland (New York, 1935), a book that has long enjoyed a great if exaggerated reputation.

ITALY. All accounts begin with *Storia della politica estera italiana dal 1870 al 1896* by Federico Chabod (Bari, 1951), a truly brilliant book, beautifully balanced, masterly in its control of the sources, and a pleasure to read. Also valuable is the article by Rudolf Lill in *EK,* "Italiens Aussenpolitik, 1866–1871," and two pieces that he produced for the *QuFiAB:* "Beobachtungen zur preussisch-italienischen Allianz, 1866," 44 (1964), and "Aus den italienisch-deutschen Beziehungen 1869–1876," 46 (1966). *Das Ende des Kirchenstaats* by Norbert Miko, 3 vols. (Vienna, 1961–69) is the standard work on the subject. *La situazione europea e la politica estera italiana dal 1867 al 1871* by Carlo di Nola (Rome, 1956) is a thorough examination of the topic. *Diplomat under Stress* by S. William Halperin (Chicago, 1963) deals with the ordeal of Visconti-Venosta; it is accurate and honest within its limits; these limits are narrow. Halperin also produced two articles of value: "Visconti-Venosta and the Diplomatic Crisis of July 1870," *JMH* 31 (December 1959) and "Bismarck and the Italian Envoy in Berlin on the Eve of the Franco-Prussian War," *JMH* 33 (March 1961). Maurice Eddleston, *Italian Neutrality in the Franco-Prussian War* (London, 1935) is a life sentence on a treadmill, and is, in any case, surpassed by the final chapters of *Victor Emanuel, Cavour, and the Risorgimento* by Denis Mack Smith (New York, 1971), a most admirable volume by the preeminent English-speaking historian of the subject; the last two chapters speak to the questions raised in the present work. Federico Curato, "Le origini diplomatiche della guerra franco-prusiana del 1870–1871," *Il risorgimento* 22 (1971) has some points of interest.

RUSSIA. Outstanding here are three works by Dietrich Beyrau: *Russische Orientpolitik und die Entstehung des deutschen Kaiserreiches, 1866–1870/71* (Munich, 1974); "Der deutsche Komplex: Russland zur Zeit der Reichsgründung," in *ER;* and "Russische Interessenzonen und europäisches Gleichgewicht," in *EK.* "Bismarck and the War of 1870," by Chester A. Clark, *JMH* 14 (1942) is out of date.

OTHERS. Some good work has been done on the secondary German states. Heinz W. Schlaich, "Bayern und Deutschland nach dem Prager Frieden," in *Gesellschaft und Herrschaft: Eine Festgabe für Karl Bosl,* ed. Richard van Dülmen (Munich, 1969) is a careful study that contains much valuable information; Wolf D. Gruner, "Bayern, Preussen, und die süddeutschen Staaten, 1866–1870," *ZBLG* 37 (1974) argues in a spirited, convincing fashion that the south Germanies deserved more respect and attention from the Prussians (and from the other Great Powers) than they got. Paul W. Schroeder, "The Lost Intermediaries: The Impact of 1870 on the European States System" *IHR* 6 (1984) is a seminal article, much broader in scope than its title suggests; it makes for good reading as well as for exciting history. *König Lud-*

wig II. und Bismarcks Ringen um Bayern 1870/71 by Hans Rall (Munich, 1973) is a narrative with little-known documents from the anti-Prussian figures in the king's government; it overtakes *Bayern und die Bismarckische Reichsgründung* by Michael Doeberl (Munich, 1925). On Bray-Steinberg's policy there is Eberhard Weis, "Vom Kriegsausbruch zur Reichsgründung. Zur Politik des bayerischen Aussenministers Graf Bray-Steinberg im Jahr 1870," *ZBLG* 33 (1970).

Three articles in *EK* should be included: "Die böhmischen Länder in der Krise von 1870/71" by Jan Křen, not much more than a fly speck; "Zwischen Bismarck und Napoleon: Das Problem der belgischen Neutralität von 1866–1870" by Horst Lademacher is a critical analysis of Napoleon III's policy; and "Die Schweiz und die Wende von 1870/71" by Peter Stadler is an agreeable summary—pugnacious, learned, and plausible.

Márie Corkery, "Ireland and the Franco-Prussian War," *Etudes irlandaises* 7 (1982) casts light on this side issue.

The Origins of the Franco-Prussian War
General

The French produce the most detailed accounts, one of them being magisterial: the *Histoire des relations internationales* by Pierre Renouvin, vol. 5 (Paris, 1954), which covers the years 1815–70 and is much more than a diplomatic history. Another indispensable work is *The Struggle for Mastery in Europe, 1848–1918* by A. J. P. Taylor (Oxford, 1954); it is stamped with the willful personality of its author, but it remains one of the finest studies of its kind, unmatched in its range and power of analysis, to say nothing of its whiplash wit and the dazzling brilliance of its language. There is an extended treatment of the period in Alfred Stern, *Geschichte Europas seit den Verträgen von 1815,* 10 vols. (Berlin, 1894–1924), detailed but dated. A number of good, shorter accounts exist as well. *From Vienna to Versailles* by L. C. B. Seaman (London, 1955), though slight, is a brilliant book; the author, like Taylor, is inclined to hurry events along the way he wants them to go, and I have not escaped his influence. The character of international relations is studied by W. E. Mosse, *The European Powers and the German Question* (Cambridge, 1958), an honest and reliable book. *The Chancelleries of Eu-*

rope by Alan Palmer (London, 1980) is an accomplished literary picture—
though at times overdrawn. *The Diplomatic History of Europe since the Congress of Vienna* by René Albrecht-Carrié (New York, 1958) is a singularly
conventional account; it means no offense and gives none.

Specialized

When it comes to the secondary literature in book form, first mention must
go, unhesitatingly, to the magnificent work published in Paris in two volumes
in 1875 by Albert Sorel entitled *Histoire diplomatique de la guerre franco-
allemande.* Sorel, a professor of history at the Sorbonne and a specialist on
the international history of the French revolution, wrote this book between
1871 and 1874, primarily, one supposes, on the basis of the documents sub-
sequently published as *Les Origines diplomatiques de la guerre 1870–1871,*
but he appears to have supplemented the study by consultation with the
French officials who had personal experience or knowledge of the subject.
The work embraces the period covered by the present volume, plus the ensuing military conflict down to the year 1871. So superior is this treatise in
authority, objectivity, and penetration that I was, strange as it may seem,
repeatedly obliged to ask myself whether an attempt to cover the same
ground 125 years later was really warranted. Several reflections, however,
gave me reassurance. Obviously, a number of materials not available when
Sorel wrote his book are available now. There was no translation of his book
in English, and it would have been a pity to make a translation without use
of the later materials. His account, finally, was a strictly diplomatic one, concerned mainly with the exchanges among governmental chanceries, whereas
the focus of my own curiosity was rather on the motivation of the various
statesmen and actors in the drama. So I chose the path of an entirely new
study. But in presenting this study, I cannot refrain from acknowledging my
deep debt—a debt shared, I am sure, by all those who have interested themselves in this subject—to Sorel for his pioneering work.

Many of the earlier works were written by authors who had some political
or personal ax to grind. Most begin with a general background and then
discuss the crisis of July 1870 in detail. Even the most scholarly tend to have

a propagandist character, the more dangerous when it is concealed by an air of impartiality. A distinguished exception is "The Causes of the Franco-Prussian War" by Lord Acton (J. E. E. Dalberg-Acton) in *Historical Essays and Studies* (London, 1908), a provocative and original effort that has earned its place in the historiography of the subject. There is a superficial analysis of Acton's work in H. W. V. Temperley, "Lord Acton on the Origins of the War of 1870," *Cambridge Historical Journal* 2 (1926), and a much better one in Roberto Vivarelli, "1870 in European History and Historiography," *JMH* 53 (1981).

Of exceptional interest for this study, especially in connection with the activities of the French government and its attempt to throw blame for the war on Bismarck, is the book of Henri Welschinger, *La Guerre de 1870: Causes et responsabilités*, 2 vols. (Paris, 1910). A work reflecting many of the prejudices of the author and of the sentimentalities and exaltations of nationalistic fervor, this account moves uncertainly along the borderline between history and propaganda and represents primarily an attempt to claim for Gramont and Le Boeuf credit for having given the decisive impetus to take up the Prussian challenge. While more significant as a tract for the times than as history, and certainly to be taken with caution (for Welschinger was anything but a dispassionate observer), this book deserves a permanent place among the major early works on the subject. Similar to Welschinger's work in the author's eagerness to cast the Prussians as villains, but far inferior to it in intellectual depth and historical interest, are two skimpy and pretentious little volumes by Arsène Legrelle entitled *La France et la Prusse devant l'histoire* (Paris, 1874–75) and two equally pretentious ones by Richard Cosse, *La France et la Prusse avant la guerre* (Paris, 1907). Both are strongly anti-German *apologia* for the French policy of the period and appear to have been designed to serve a contemporary political purpose: namely, the establishment of the thesis that it was Germany who brought about the war in 1870, with the implication that it was Germany, and only Germany, who would do the same in a later epoch. Viewed as contributions to the history of the period, therefore, these works do not do justice to the erudition of their authors. They do draw, however, on a large and in some respects unusual body of source materials, not all of which are readily available to pres-

231

ent day writers. That of Legrelle, in particular, adds significantly, through detailed attention given to the relations of Gramont and Ollivier on 12 and 13 July 1870, to the available historical record.

Much better, more serious, and more strictly historical is the excellent older work of Hans Delbrück, even though some of its conclusions have been invalidated by later research. This work took the form of a series of articles published in the *PJbb:* "Der Ursprung des Krieges von 1870," 70 (1892); "Zum Ursprung des Krieges von 1870," 79 (1895); "Das Geheimnis der Napoleonischen Politik im Jahr 1870," 82 (1895); and "Ollivier über den Krieg 1870," 137 (1909). Delbrück—at once a historian, an interpreter of military affairs for contemporaries, and a searing critic of the general staff—summarized his arguments in *Erinnerungen, Aufsätze, und Reden,* 3. Aufl. (Berlin, 1905), which perhaps should be included in the section "Other Witnesses."

An excellent work that, though not totally impartial, nevertheless sheds considerable light on the subject is *Les Origines de la guerre de 1870: La Candidature Hohenzollern 1868–1870* by Pierre Lehautcourt [pseudonym for B. E. Palat] (Paris and Nancy, 1912), a book that combines scholarship and accuracy. It is full of fascinating points and contains valuable information even for the expert. The same is true of *L'Incident Hohenzollern: L'Événement, les hommes, les responsabilités* by Henry Salomon (Paris, 1922), a book that, despite its age, provides a splendid analysis of the background of French policy (though it is rather thin on the German side). Some of its themes are repeated and refined in five articles that came out later: Friedrich Frahm, "Frankreich und die Hohenzollernkandidatur bis zum Frühjahr 1869," *HV* 39 (September 1934), lucid and concise, scholarly, and eminently readable; Rudolph von Albertini, "Frankreichs Stellungnahme zur deutschen Einigung während des Zweiten Kaiserreichs," *SZG* 5 (1955), dry diplomatic history based mainly on published documents; Rudolf Morsey, "Die Hohenzollernsche Thronkandidatur in Spanien," *HZ* 186 (1958), a painstaking and accurate chronicle, though perhaps excessively unsympathetic to France; and two articles by Leonhard Muralt, "Bismarcksche Reichsgründung vom Ausland gesehen," *SH* 26 (1947) and "Der Ausbruch des Krieges von 1870/71," *Ostdt. Wissenschaft* 5 (1959), both concise , authoritative summaries of the major decisions on each side.

The events of 12 and 13 July have often been told. *Histoire d'un jour: La Journée du 12 juillet 1870* by Alfred Darimon (Paris, 1888) is one of those rare books that seems to improve with time; it tells of the intrigue in a vivid fashion, much like a detective novel. Pierre Muret, "Émile Ollivier et le duc de Gramont les 12 et 13 juillet," *RHMC* 13 (1909–10) and 14 (1910), is an equally vigorous exposition. Its German counterpart, Hermann Hesselbarth, "König Wilhelm und Bismarck am 12 and 13 Juli 1870," *HZ* 106 (1911), is less successful. William L. Langer, "Bismarck as a Dramatist," in *Studies in Diplomatic History and Historiography,* ed. A. O. Sarkissian (London, 1961) (a festschrift for G. P. Gooch) shoots to pieces Bismarck's myths about the Ems telegram. Langer also destroys the explanations offered by Gramont and Ollivier in a second article, "Red Flag on the Gallic Bull: The French Decision for War in 1870," that he produced for a festschrift for Egmont Zechlin, *Europa und Übersee,* ed. Otto Brunner and Dietrich Gerhard (Hamburg, 1961). *Bismarck, the Hohenzollern Candidacy, and the Origins of the Franco-German War of 1870* by Lawrence D. Steefel (Cambridge, Mass., 1962) is the fullest account of the subject in English if not the most scholarly, for it appears to have borrowed freely and not altogether properly from the older work of Lord discussed above (compare for example pp. 178–82 of the former to 84–87 of the latter). Steefel has also produced a miscellany, "Bismarck, Bucher, and the Letter of Instructions of June 1870," in the Gooch festschrift just noted. Douglas W. Houston, "Émile Ollivier and the Hohenzollern Candidacy," *French Historical Studies* 4 (1965) is a compact, professional job. The most profound and scholarly analysis of the origins of the war remains *Bismarck, Frankreich, und die spanische Thronkandidatur der Hohenzollern* by Jochen Dittrich (Munich, 1962). Its valuable documentary appendices contain the text of ninety-six documents (or excerpts therefrom) found in the holdings of the Hohenzollern archives at Sigmaringen. *Der Kriegsaubruch 1870* by Eberhard Kolb (Göttingen, 1970) is a concise scholarly account of the immediate origins of the war; it downgrades economics and domestic-political factors, defends Bismarck, and criticizes France for provoking the crisis and for demanding a privileged role in the system. The criticism directed against Kolb by S. William Halperin, "The Origins of the Franco-Prussian War Revisited: Bismarck and the Hohenzollern Candidature for the Spanish Throne" *JMH* 65 (1973) is hostile and un-enlightened. A broad but also good book is *The Origins of the Wars of German Unification* by William Carr (New York, 1991).

The most recent and provocative account of the crisis is found in several articles from the skeptical eye and telling pen of Josef Becker. "Zum Problem der Bismarckschen Politik in der spanischen Thronfrage," *HZ* 212 (1971) is well written, provocative, and influential, and it relies on a wide range of sources, though it must be said at once that its views on the origins of the war are far from my own. "Bismarck und die Frage der Aufnahme Badens in den Norddeutschen Bund im Frühjahr 1870," *Zeitschrift für Geschichte des Oberrheins* 119 (1971) is a reconstruction of diplomatic details that contains some surprises. Three other pieces of Becker's merit inclusion: "Der Krieg mit Frankreich als Problem der kleindeutschen Einigungspolitik Bismarcks," in *Das kaiserliche Deutschland, 1870–1918,* ed. Michael Stümer (Düsseldorf, 1970); "Bismarck et l'empire libéral," *F* 2 (1974); and "Bismarck, Prim, die Sigmaringer Hohenzollern und die spanische Thronfrage," *F* 9 (1981)—each of which argues clearly, vigorously, and (I think) wrongly that Bismarck was aiming at preventive war against France. Becker develops this argument further in "Von Bismarcks ‚spanischer Diversion' zur ‚Emser Legende' des Reichsgründers," in *Lange und kurze Wege in den Krieg,* ed. Johannes Burkhardt (Augsburg, 1996), which lacks the force of his previous pieces. Two articles in *EK* redress the balance: "Ansichten eines Krieges. Die ‚Kriegsschuldfrage' von 1870" by Beate Gödde-Baumanns, a first-rate analysis of the problem, and "Mächtepolitik und Kriegsrisiko am Vorabend des Krieges von 1870" by Eberhard Kolb, a work of meticulous scholarship, deep understanding, and easy style leavened with wit.

A final note. Certain of the French newspapers being, for various reasons, particularly revealing, I made such use of them as I could, availing myself for this purpose of the remarkable and unique holdings of journalistic offices in France, poking around for instance among the tattered and crumbling pages both of the *Temps* and of its rival the *Constitutionnel* in the crowded storefront room of its Paris offices. No doubt still others could have been profitably examined, but the sheer bulk of this material, of course, was tremendous. Eye-strain and lack of time placed limitations on what could done. I am sure that whoever could overcome these handicaps would find a good deal to enrich and refine the account presented here, but in many instances the ore is of such low grade, from the standpoint of a study such as this one, that it scarcely pays to attempt to identify and to separate the true metal from the dross. Literally years of effort would be required to examine carefully the files of the leading newspapers of Paris for the period in question. As for the leading Berlin papers—most outstandingly the *Norddeutsche Allgemeine Zeitung* and the *Neue Preussische Zeitung* (*Kreuzzeitung*)—they were useful (like the Italian archival collections) primarily for the clarification of questions left unanswered by other sources. But here again, the bulk of the material was enormous, the type small, and the paper often faded. Scanned in their entirely, they too would no doubt yield numerous items bearing on the subject of this inquiry, but this too would be the work of years.

Military History

On general questions, one must start with *The Politics of the Prussian Army* by Gordon A. Craig (Oxford, 1955), a fascinating book, irresistible for its meticulous learning, magical for its literary charm. An equally indispensable work is *The Franco-Prussian War* by Michael Howard (New York, 1961), a book which is beautifully written and which develops its story with all the brilliance of a symphony conducted by a great master. As to source material, *Bibliographie générale de la guerre de 1870–71* by Barthélemy Edmont Palat (Paris, 1896), which lists over seven thousand titles, must be the starting point for any serious student who wishes to focus on detail. (The author used the pen name Lehautcourt to record the diplomatic history, but chose to use his real name for his work on the military side.) Another excellent work is that by Ferdinand Lecomte, *Relation historique et critique de la guerre franco-allemande en 1870–1871*, 4 vols. (Paris, 1872–74), the lucidity, the eloquence, the passion, and the scholarship of which set standards that few successors can hope to equal.

The secondary literature of a related field was also important for this study: the tangled question of the growth of technology. An excellent work that, while not specifically addressed to the origins of the Franco-Prussian War, sheds considerable light on the subject is *The Rise of Rail Power in War and Conquest* by Edwin A. Pratt (London, 1915); despite its age, this is a most valuable work, which tells its story with elegant detachment. And the same may be said of *Railroads and Rifles: Soldiers, Technology, and the Unification of Germany* by Dennis E. Showalter (Hamden, Conn., 1975).

Let us briefly consider the literature on the armies of the two sides. For the French army under Napoleon III, *Une Loi manquée: La Loi Neil (1866–1868)* by Jean Casevitz (Paris, 1959) is a critical study of the reforms Napoleon attempted. *L'Officier français de 1815 à 1870* by Pierre Chalmin (Paris, 1957) is a first-rate introduction to the subject. Jean Morvan, *Le Soldat impérial* (Paris, 1904) is still of value. *La Société militaire dans la France contemporaine, 1815–1839* by Raoul Girardet (Paris, 1953) is dry, detached, and lacking sparkle. *Les Institutions militaires de la France, 1814–1924* by Joseph Monteilhet (Paris, 1932) is fueled with enthusiasm, passion, and belief and does much to explain the incompetence of the high command.

On the Prussian side: *Moltke* by Eberhard Kessel (Stuttgart, 1957) is the standard life. Gunther Rothenberg, "Moltke, Schlieffen, and the Doctrine of Strategic Development," in *The Makers of Modern Strategy*, ed. Peter Paret et al., 2d ed. (Princeton, 1986), is an important contribution. *Das deutsche Offizierkorps* by Karl Demeter (Berlin, 1930) is clear on the military side, weak on politics. *Die Mobilmachung von 1870/71* by Gustav Lehmann (Berlin, 1905) is out of date. *On the Road to Total War? The American Civil War and the German Wars of Unification,* ed. Stig Förster and Jörg Nadler (New York, 1996) goes competently and devoutly over the subject, but the book is rather dull. *La Guerre de 70* by Françoise Roth (Paris, 1990) is a good popular account.

Index

237